How Different Religions View
Death and Afterlife

How Different Religions View Death and Afterlife

Edited by

Christopher Jay Johnson, PhD
and Marsha G. McGee, PhD

The Charles Press, Publishers
Philadelphia

The Charles Press, Publishers
Post Office Box 15715
Philadelphia, PA 19103

Originally published in hardcover as *Encounters with Eternity: Religious Views of Death and Life After Death.*

ℓoo874 59670

Library of Congress Cataloging-in-Publication Data

How different religions view death and afterlife /
edited by Christopher Jay Johnson and Marsha G. McGee.
      p.   cm.
   Reprint: Originally published: Encounters with eternity.
   New York: Philosophical Library, 1986.
   Includes bibliographical references.
   ISBN 0-914783-55-6
   1. Death—Religious aspects.   2. Future life.
I. Johnson, Christopher Jay.   II. McGee, Marsha G.   III. Title.
[BL504.E53   1991]   91-14236
291.2′3—dc20   CIP

Printed in the United States of America

ISBN 0-914783-55-6 (pbk.)

CONTENTS

5

CONTRIBUTING AUTHORS

Swami Adiswarananda is a monk of the Ramakrishna Order of India who currently serves as the Minister and Spiritual Leader of the Ramakrishna Vivekananda Center of New York. He has edited and authored numerous publications. Swami Adiswarananda is a frequent lecturer at colleges and universities and other religious, educational, and cultural centers throughout the United States and abroad.

Rev. Francis X. Cleary, S.J., is associate professor in the Department of Theological Studies at St. Louis University. He holds a doctorate in Sacred Theology from the Pontifical Gregorian University and a licentiate in Sacred Scripture from the Pontifical Biblical Institute, both in Rome. His service in his profession has included work as editor and author, group and seminar leader, and local and national lecturer.

Richard M. Eyre, a management consultant and writer (Salt Lake City, Utah), holds degrees from Utah State, Brigham Young, and Harvard Universities. He has written seventeen books and lectures frequently on a wide range of topics. He served for two years as a missionary for his church in New York City in the early sixties and for three years as a "Mission President" in London in the late seventies. These were unpaid positions in the Mormon Church's lay ministry. Mr. Eyre is not an official spokesman for his church but has tried to outline its views on death and the hereafter in a clear and accurate way.

John S. Hatcher, Ph.D., is professor of English literature at the University of South Florida in Tampa. He has authored two books on the Baha'i Faith as well as several articles, essays, and reviews in his field. Dr. Hatcher's forte is medieval literature and poetry, and he has published his poetry extensively in professional journals and magazines.

William L. Hendricks, Ph.D., Th.D., teaches at Southern Baptist Theological Seminary in Louisville, Kentucky. A leading Christian educator, he previously taught at Golden Gate Seminary and Southwestern Baptist Seminary. Dr. Hendricks has also pastored churches and authored a number of books and articles. In addition, he has traveled extensively abroad and throughout the United States as a speaker and lecturer.

Stanley M. Horton, Th.D., has pastored churches in several states and has taught in Assemblies of God schools since 1945. He is currently professor of Bible and Theology in the Assemblies of God Theological Seminary, Springfield, Missouri. Dr. Horton has conducted archaeological investigation and research in Palestine and has been guest professor in seven foreign nations. He is the author of a number of books plus several hundred articles and lessons.

Robert M. Johnston, Ph.D., is now Professor of New Testament and Christian Origins at the Seventh-day Adventist

Theological Seminary at Andrews University. He studied at Stanford Seminary and at Hebrew University in Jerusalem. A missionary for twelve years in Korea and the Philippines, he has travelled extensively in the Far East. He is the author of a number of articles for scholarly journals and religious publications.

Anne C. Klein, Ph.D., Lecturer in Religious Studies at Stanford University, has worked with Buddhist scholars and meditation masters in India, Nepal, and the U.S. since 1971. She is an author, translator, and research scholar with particular interest in Buddhist epistemology in sutra and tantra, Buddhist-Christian dialogues, and Buddhism for feminist thought. She is also the author of *Knowledge and Liberation: An Epistemological Analysis in Support of Transformative Religious Experience* (Ithaca: Snow Lion Press, 1985).

Daniel E. Lee, Ph.D., is associate professor of Religion at Augustana College, Rock Island, Illinois. He received his doctorate from Yale; he has been a Fellow of the National Humanities Institute at the University of Chicago. He served as a member of the Lutheran Church in America Task Force on Bioethics and is currently a member of the Lutheran Health Care Foundation Bioethics Committee, Moline, Ill. Dr. Lee is the author of *Death and Dying: Ethical Choices in a Caring Community*.

George N. Marshall, Ph.D., D.D., has served a number of Unitarian-Universalist congregations and has just retired as Minister and Religious Editor at the Church of the Larger Fellowship, Boston, Mass. Dr. Marshall has published numerous books and articles, including *Challenge of a Liberal Faith*, a best-selling story of Unitarian Universalist beliefs, and the recent work *Facing Death and Grief*.

Thomas H. Olbricht, Ph.D., is Chairman of Graduate Studies in the College of Biblical Studies at Abilene Christian University. Dr. Olbricht has served numerous churches and taught at several universities. He is a well-known author and religious leader who has served in positions of leadership in a number of professional associations and with the church.

Rabbi Alan L. Ponn currently serves at Temple Beth Sholom in Danville, Virginia. He is a graduate of Columbia University and Hebrew Union College, and has served congregations in several states. Rabbi Ponn has also worked as both a chaplain and a religious columnist during his career.

Ben Lacy Rose, Th.D., D.D., is an honorably retired minister of the Presbyterian Church, U.S. During his career, Dr. Rose served several pastorates and as an Army chaplain, taught at Union Theological Seminary in Richmond, Virginia, and served in positions of national leadership with the Presbyterian Church. He is an author and seminar leader, and continues to be active in the church in Richmond, Va.

Jane Idleman Smith, Ph.D., is the Associate Dean for Academic Affairs and Lecturer in Comparative Religion at Harvard Divinity School. She is the author of numerous publications and has written and lectured extensively about the role of Muslim women and the Muslim understanding of death and the afterlife.

James Ivey Warren, Jr., Ph.D., studied at Duke University and later completed his doctoral work at Glasgow University. He has served ministerial and chaplaincy roles in Scotland and has worked as both pastor and professor in the United States. Dr. Warren is currently Cadwallader Professor of Global Evangelism and the Mission of the Church at Scarritt Graduate School in Nashville, Tennessee. He is the author of *Workbook on Vital Evangelism.*

INTRODUCTION

Beginning in the 1960s with Elisabeth Kübler-Ross' writings on death and dying, and escalating with the publication of books such as Raymond Moody's *Life After Life* in the 1970s, the number of books on death and dying has grown rapidly. Like so many other topics, it sometimes seems as if death is suffering from overkill. Still, with all this thoughtful analysis, there remains at least one spiritually and sociologically important area that few of these discussions of death have addressed. Previous books have not adequately described different religious perspectives on death. Many of us as individuals have neither examined the beliefs of others nor have we seriously investigated the core of our own religious beliefs about these topics.

As we move into the 21st century, daily news reminds us of a current worldwide move back toward religious fundamentalism and Christian evangelicalism in the United States. Specific groups zealously defend their own doctrines and sometimes condemn others. This trend appears to coexist with a worldwide move toward religious ecumenism, which accelerated in the 1960s and continues to claim many adherents. The pronouncements of Vatican II, the mergers of many Protestant denominations in this century, and the visit of the Archbishop of Canterbury to Pope Paul VI exemplify the growth of this ecumenical spirit. It is our sense that this mixture of religious events and outlooks has left many of us either ignorant of or confused about the beliefs of the different faiths with which we coexist.

Our general goal in this book is to make information available about what a number of key faiths believe about death and what happens after death. In the United States we are offered a supermarket of different beliefs. Where can we even find information about other faiths that will help us evaluate our beliefs? This collection attempts to explore different views about death and what happens afterward as described by theologians and knowledgeable authors from various religious groups. Most of us are curious about death and the beyond. Because many of us are not as knowledgeable as we would like to be, there is a significant need for a book such as this one.

In the hope of helping all of us who are interested in an exploration into religious thought, we solicited chapters from authors who represent three groups: America's most heavily populated organized Christian denominations; smaller but rapidly growing or sociologically and theologically interesting Christian groups; and the largest non-Christian denominations represented in American society. We asked our authors to answer often-asked questions about death, to describe their religions' stance, and to give a brief history outlining the main beliefs of their faiths. Be assured that we fully realize that each of our authors presents his or her personal interpretation of these beliefs. In acknowledgment of this, we took care to insure the acceptability of their views to a broad range of members of their respective faiths. Thus, we tried to select authors who would give a fairly "mid-range" view of what each faith espouses. We certainly consider other beliefs to be of as much interest as those represented here, but obviously we could not include them all. It is our hope that this book will serve as a starting point for religious exploration.

Within Christianity, there are many different beliefs, rituals, and doctrines; it is likewise within Islam, Buddhism, Hinduism, and Judaism, some of the non-Christian faiths we have included. Please bear with us in our necessary over-simplification of these great religions. As we have stated, this book is meant as an introduction to religious points of view, and we cannot begin to cover the richness and diversity of the faiths represented here. By providing information about each of them in small doses, we hope to whet your appetite without overburdening your digestive system.

In deciding which specific denominations to include in this volume, we surveyed the *Statistical Abstracts of the United States* and selected seven of our society's most heavily populated religious groups. These included: the Roman Catholic, the Southern Baptist, the United Methodist, the Lutheran, the Church of Christ, the Presbyterian, and the Jewish (reformed) faiths. As representatives of smaller Christian faiths with varied beliefs about death and the beyond, we selected the Assemblies of God, the Unitarian Universalist, and the Seventh Day Adventist faiths. We also included the Baha'i faith and the Church of Jesus Christ of Latter-day Saints (the Mormons) because we believe they offer an interesting contrast to and comparison with other selected faiths. Finally, we wanted to include denominations representing the presence of other world religions in America. Thus we chose the Tibetan Buddhist tradition, the Hindu faith as viewed by Swami Adiswarananda, and the Sunni sect of the Islamic faith.

In order to display them concisely, we have charted each faith's beliefs about death and the beyond in the same order as chapter presentation (alphabetically). This chart, which is the central focus of our concluding chapter, will prove useful as a source for personal reference, and for use in church groups, study groups, classes, or other organizations.

A final word about our purpose. We believe in the search for knowledge and in the need for religious faith in our lives. If our readers broaden their understanding and empathy or begin to clarify their own religious views, we will have succeeded in our efforts.

Whatever your own beliefs are about death and what happens after death, we encourage you to join us in our search for greater understanding.

ACKNOWLEDGMENTS

Our heartfelt appreciation is extended to the many people who have made it possible for this book to reach your hands. During the months we worked on the manuscript, we sought opinions and advice from too many people to name, but we would like to extend our thanks to each person who expressed an interest in or an opinion about this project. Chris' wife Marsha, son Matt, and daughter Jessica offered their moral support. Sybil O'Neal deserves special thanks for typing and retyping much of the material. Oddessa Allen and Kacee Cobb also assisted with secretarial duties. Bert Roberts offered helpful suggestions about preliminary chapter drafts that were much appreciated.

Many thanks go to our own department head, Dr. G. Dale Welch, who provided us with encouragement and assistance in innumerable ways. Dr. David Boyle gave us good feedback on the Mormon chapter, and John Kelly of J. Kelly Booksellers in Monroe, Louisiana, encouraged us to persevere. Most of all, of course, our thanks go to our contributing authors, who gave so generously of their talents and knowledge in sharing an expression of their faith with you.

Christopher Jay Johnson

Marsha G. McGee

ASSEMBLIES OF GOD

Stanley M. Horton, Th. D.

Background of the Faith

The Assemblies of God, with over eleven million members worldwide, form the largest of the Pentecostal or charismatic churches. The charismatic churches arose from a tremendous Pentecostal revival, which began early in the twentieth century.

The United States in the years between the Civil War and the close of the century was in social and religious ferment.

Moral, political, and economic corruption increased the stresses occasioned by urbanization, industrialization and immigration. The great denominations, successful in Christianizing the frontier, had become complacent and sophisticated, lacking the vision and vitality to meet the changing needs of a distressed populace. Varying degrees of accommodation to popular ideas, newly imported from Europe, which assaulted orthodox Evangelicalism, further weakened the great communions. Against the erosion in the church world arose the Fundamentalist and Holiness movements. It was largely out of the spiritual concern generated in this segment of the church that the yearning for a new Pentecost was born. Prior to 1900 there were charismatic manifestations, but these were isolated and episodic in nature. But the stage was being set for a great outpouring of the Holy Spirit which would quickly encircle the earth, bringing a great refreshing in the Latter Days.[1]

Books such as *The Twofold Life* by the Baptist, A. J. Gordon, (founder of Gordon College, Wenham, Massachusetts), as well as the teaching and writings of men such as Reuben A. Torrey, helped to stimulate interest and stir a sense of need for the power of the Holy Spirit. However, there was little agreement about how to obtain the Holy Spirit's power or baptism in the late 1800's.

New interest arose when a revival began at Bethel Bible College in Topeka, Kansas, on January 1, 1901. From their studies of the Bible, the students came to the conclusion that speaking in tongues, as recorded in Acts 2:4, is evidence that a person has received the baptism in the Holy Spirit as an empowering for Christian service. Miss Agnes Ozman, one of the students, described the experience "as though rivers of living water were proceeding from my innermost being."[2]

From Kansas, the revival spread to Missouri, to Texas, and then to Los Angeles. There, in 1906, a black holiness preacher, W. J. Seymour, found a response among both whites and blacks and secured an old two-story frame building, a former Methodist church, at 312 Azusa Street. Soon the Azusa Street revival caught the attention of the newspapers. People began coming from all over the United States and Canada, even from overseas. Rich and poor, black and white, educated and uneducated joined together as one in worshipping and seeking God. Services ran almost continuously every day from 10 A.M. to midnight. W. J. Seymour, the leader, in simplicity and humility kept a low profile and let the Holy Spirit direct the services. "The meeting did not depend on the human leader. God's presence became more and more wonderful.... All was spontaneous...in testimony, praise, and worship."[3]

The Azusa Street Revival lasted three years. Most of those who received the Pentecostal experience of the baptism in the Holy Spirit took the message and spread it. As a result, a number of Pentecostal groups and denominations soon emerged. Some of these followed a "holiness," a view in which they called for a definite experience of "sanctification" by grace to cleanse the believer from "inbred sin" as a preparation for the baptism in the Holy Spirit. Others taught sanctification as a continuous process involving spiritual growth rather than a crisis experience. These saw faith as the only prerequisite for the baptism in the Holy Spirit. The Assemblies of God eventually became the largest group to hold to the latter position.

> After the Pentecostal outpourings began, numerous publications appeared advocating its teachings and serving as channels for teaching information, and support of missionaries overseas. One of these publications, the *Word and Witness*, edited by Eudorus N. Bell, issued a call in 1913 for a conference of Pentecostal believers to convene in Hot Springs, Arkansas, the following year. This became the founding meeting of the General Council of the Assemblies of God.[4]

Over 300 persons responded. Twelve men were elected to serve as executive presbyters to provide leadership and direct the missionary work of what was termed "a voluntary, cooperative fellowship." E. N. Bell was chosen as chairman (later, superintendent). T. K. Leonard offered his printing plant and school in Findlay, Ohio, as a publishing house and headquarters for the new fellowship. In 1915, this "Gospel Publishing House" was moved to St. Louis and in 1918 to

Springfield, Missouri, "The Queen City of the Ozarks."
Springfield has remained the international headquarters of
the Assemblies of God.

Due to controversy over the nature of the divine Trinity, a
"Statement of Fundamental Truths" as a basis of fellowship
was prepared in 1916.

> "The Statement of Fundamental Truths" was chiefly the
> work of one man, Daniel Warren Kerr, of Cleveland, Ohio.
> Kerr did not fit the popular conception of a powerful defender
> of the faith. A rather shy individual, a man of few words,
> seldom indulging in laughter, but able to light up the whole
> room with his smile. His dry wit was a help, too, in lightening
> the tension of debate and in taking the starch out of his
> opponents.[5]

During the years 1915-1925, John W. Welch, known as
"Daddy" Welch, provided a father image and was a strong,
wise, steadying influence on the growing movement. J.
Roswell Flower, as General Secretary for 27 years, also provided leadership through his organizational ability and
literary skills. A small, alert man with a farsighted view for
the development of the Assemblies of God, he did much to
inspire the fellowship as it continued to grow. By 1927 the
Assemblies of God in the United States had a membership of
72,143. By 1941, this had grown to 209,549, with nearly 400
missionaries in 34 countries.

Growth continued under several leaders. In 1959, Thomas
F. Zimmerman was elected General Superintendent, a post
he retains today (1986). His skill as an administrator and
spiritual leader has consolidated gains made. In 1984 there
were nearly 25,000 ministers of the Assemblies of God in the
United States, with over a million members. Missionaries
minister in more than 90 fields to over 10 million members.

Main Beliefs of the Assemblies of God Faith

Our sole source and authority for our beliefs is the Bible. We believe both the Old and New Testaments are verbally inspired by God and are the unique revelation of God to man, the one authoritative rule of faith and conduct. In the Bible we see that the one true God has revealed Himself as eternally self-existent, the creator of the heavens and earth and the redeemer of mankind. He has further revealed Himself as embodying three distinct persons, which are expressed in specific terms of relationship as Father, Son, and Holy Spirit. Through His Son, our Lord Jesus Christ, He has revealed Himself in a special and supreme way to mankind. Through the Holy Spirit this revelation is made real to us in a vital, personal way.

God created mankind in His image or likeness. Since God is spirit, this means we were created capable of reflecting God's holiness, righteousness, and love; capable also of sharing fellowship with God with understanding and intelligence. In order that this fellowship might be on the highest level, God also gave us freedom of choice. Mankind, however, freely chose to sin. The result was spiritual death (separation from God), physical death, a curse on the natural world, and the inheritance by all mankind of the tendency to sin, so that all are sinners.

God, however, did not give up. He began to carry out a plan to bring salvation and restoration to all who would respond to Him in faith. Central to that plan in the Old Testament times was the promise given to Abraham, that through him and through his descendants all the peoples of the earth would be blessed. The New Testament shows that this blessing comes through Jesus Christ. In Him, God became man, identifying Himself with us from birth to death, taking our place to die on a cruel cross, bearing the guilt and penalty of our sins, then rising from the dead that we might share eternal life with Him and share His glory when He returns to earth again.

Forty days after His resurrection Jesus ascended to the

right hand of God's throne in heaven. There He remains the God-Man, our divine Helper. But He has not left us orphaned here on earth. He and the Father have sent us the Holy Spirit as another Helper to be with us always. He helps us to show our love and faith toward God through faithful, obedient worship and by loving acts to all. He imparts gifts, ministries and graces to help us do the work God wants us to do.

We recognize we are in a world still dominated by sinful men and by the activity of Satan. The devil, or Satan, usurped authority in this world. He was once an angel (messenger) of God, but fell—through rebellion. Evil and sickness are in the world, not only because of man's wrong choices, but because of Satan's activity. Though he is a spirit being, he is a limited being. He cannot be present everywhere, and much of his activity is carried out by evil spirits (demons). He is also limited in that he cannot go beyond what God allows.

We are not helpless against Satan's attacks, however. Our faith in God and Christ shields us. The Holy Spirit uses God's Word to give us victories. Through the baptism in the Holy Spirit, with its initial outward evidence of speaking in tongues, we receive power and gifts to help us against the devil and to help us in our worship and service of God as we build up the Church and serve mankind.

Because for centuries the Holy Spirit was neglected, even ignored by the Christian Church as a whole, we have felt a special calling to proclaim the whole gospel, fully, not just in part. We emphasize Jesus as Savior, Baptizer in the Holy Spirit, Healer, and Coming King. Christ is central in our preaching and teaching. But we endeavor to give the Holy Spirit His proper place as revealed in the New Testament. We encourage believers to enter into the fullness of a new relationship with the Holy Spirit through the baptism in the Holy Spirit and by seeking His gifts and ministries for the blessings they bring to us all.

We find that the Holy Spirit uses God's written Word and spiritual, charismatic gifts to challenge us, encourage us, and comfort us in every situation of life. He gives moral courage in the midst of difficulty and suffering. He provides gracious gifts of healing for minds, souls, and bodies. Many have joined our churches because they have experienced healing, even healing of "incurable" conditions and diseases. The Holy Spirit also gives us comfort and assurance of God's goodness even in the presence of unexplainable death. He makes us know that death is not the end, for God's promise of our resurrection is real.

Our pastors report that, though many Christians have doubts concerning their faith when they face death, this never happens with our Assemblies of God people who have been baptized in the Holy Spirit. Through the experience of this baptism, the Holy Spirit indwells every part of our inner being, including the subconscious. I personally have observed many dying with peace in their hearts and the praises of God on their lips. Instead of the fear of death there is anticipation of blessings on the other side with Christ.

We differ from non-Pentecostal churches in that we emphasize that the baptism in the Holy Spirit with the accompanying evidence of speaking in other tongues (languages) is the normal experience God intends every believer in Christ to enjoy. We expect the Holy Spirit to help us in our prayers. In public worship, we pray aloud all at once, each in his own way, with much praise and thanks to God and to our Lord Jesus Christ. In private prayers we are encouraged to use the gift of speaking in other tongues (Holy Spirit-given languages unknown to the speaker) as a prayer language to pour out our love to Christ and to express feelings beyond the power of human speech to express. The Spirit helps us as we pray in our own language as well. Our desire is to see the spiritual life and love seen in the New Testament restored in our own experience. We invite others to join us who want something more than religious forms and ceremonies, however meaningful these might be. Repentance toward God and faith toward the Lord Jesus Christ are the basic conditions for membership, though local assemblies may ask members to agree to definite standards of Christian living that are biblical.

We do observe two ordinances of the Church: baptism in water by immersion, and the Lord's Supper or Holy Communion. In America the latter is observed using unleavened bread and unfermented wine as solemn emblems or symbols of Christ's broken body and shed blood. We expect our pastors and other ministers to experience God's personal call to their ministry. We ordain them only after they have demonstrated that the Holy Spirit has indeed given them a ministry and blessed it.

Because the Bible is our standard, we try to take the teachings of the Bible as a whole. Thus, we see that premarital sex, homosexuality, and abortion are wrong. Yet we encourage all to seek the forgiveness and restoration that is freely available through the death and resurrection of Christ. We recognize that God hates divorce. Yet Jesus allowed it where one partner had become habitually immoral. The Apostle Paul also allowed it when an unbelieving (non-Christian) partner did not want to live faithfully with the believer. On the other hand, we seek to strengthen marriages in order to prevent divorce.

We have always discouraged the use of alcoholic beverages and tobacco in any form. Our Teen Challenge ministry has a record of about 80 percent of those who go through their program still staying off drugs when contacted after five years. This has been accomplished through the work and power of the Holy Spirit. In general we discourage extremes in clothing, makeup, and deportment. We accept all types of nutritious food as God's good gifts to us. But we put more emphasis on our need of spiritual food (teaching) and on the necessity of doing the will of God joyfully. The Holy Spirit helps us in this by making God's will real through His written Word, the Bible.

Questions about Death and the Afterlife

Though death is in the world because of sin, in the case of believers we do not look at death as punishment. Jesus took all our penalty on the Cross. Death for us is simply transition into the presence of our Lord Jesus where we will share the joys of heaven.

When death comes we normally follow the customs practiced by the majority of the Protestant churches in the community or the part of the country or the world where we live. Our ministers consider the conducting of funeral services as one of their most important opportunities for helping families and serving people. Hymns, often the favorite hymns of the deceased, are sung, usually by a soloist, but sometimes by the congregation. Passages from the Bible are read. A eulogy is given. Always there is a sermon intended to encourage the faith and hope of the family and friends. Tears are common, but a sense of joy in the hope of the resurrection is encouraged. Sometimes the funeral of a godly believer will be triumphant.

At the close of the service, unless the family requests otherwise, those present pass by the open coffin to pay their last respects to the deceased. Then the pastor and the family join to do the same, often with much emotion. Then the coffin is closed and escorts (pallbearers) carry it out. A committal service at the cemetery follows. It is usually brief and includes the reading of a passage from the Bible and a prayer. Then those present line up and go past family members to shake their hands or hug them and offer words of comfort.

Normally, burial takes place about three days after death unless the funeral is delayed to allow family members to come from a distance. Embalming of the body is expected. Most feel there is precedent for this in the Bible. The delay of the decay of the body that embalming brings also fits in with our respect for the body and with our hope of the resurrection. It is also an expression of a love that wishes to do everything that should be done for the deceased. On the other hand, we believe that decay, fire, or destruction of the body by whatever other means will not hinder God from bringing together whatever is necessary for the resurrection of the body. We also believe the body will be swallowed up by a new God-prepared body at the resurrection, a new body that is immortal, not subject to decay or death anymore, a body like Christ's resurrected, glorified body.

With this in mind we feel free to donate body parts for transplant, though the choice is left up to the individual. For this reason also we can allow autopsy if it is deemed necessary. Cremation is discouraged because burial was the normal method used in the Bible. However, since God is the one who resurrects the body and brings it together, we do not forbid cremation, especially in countries where disease or climate calls for it. Normally, the body is displayed at the funeral home for at least a day before funeral services, though some prefer to have it remain in the home of the deceased and others prefer to have it brought to the church sanctuary.

We have no prayer book, for we expect prayer to come spontaneously from the heart. Nor do we have any specified mourning rituals. In some parts of the country the family spends an evening before the funeral at the funeral home with the casket open. Friends are expected to come by and express their condolences. In other parts of the country the family does not gather until the funeral service. Friends and relatives are expected to send flowers to the funeral home, though the family may request that donations be given to a charity, a church organization, or a college instead. In many parts of the country concerned members of the Assembly will plan together and bring food to the home of the deceased to provide a meal for the family after the funeral. Members of the Assembly are expected to give further help and comfort to the family in whatever way they see it is needed.

The services of our pastors are always available whether the deceased is a member of our faith or not. Our pastors consider the conducting of a funeral service as an opportunity to show Christian love, to bring the message of Christ, and to comfort the living by the help of the Holy Spirit. Pastors are willing to assist the family and give them advice concerning the type of service to whatever extent the family wishes. No fee is ever charged for these or any other pastoral services related to the funeral. Most pastors will accept a small honorarium from those outside our faith if it is offered, but most will not accept one from members of their own congregation.

We draw our greatest comfort from the Bible. We have seen its historical truth confirmed again and again by archaeological discoveries. We have had its spiritual truth confirmed to our own hearts and minds by the same Holy Spirit who inspired it. Therefore, we receive its truths and endeavor to apply them in our lives. We recognize that death is inevitable until Jesus returns to earth, for our bodies are all gradually dying. Yet our inner selves are renewed day by day (2 Corinthians 4:16). This gives us courage to keep going no matter what our circumstances or physical condition might be. We have the assurance that God guides us in this life and afterward receives us to glory (Psalm 73:24). The Bible also tells us that to be absent from the body is to be present with the Lord Jesus (2 Corinthians 5:8). Thus, we need not fear death, for it is only an entrance into His presence in the glories of heaven.

When we speak of heaven, we are referring to what the Bible calls the third heaven where the throne of God is and where Paradise is. We understand the first heaven to be the atmospheric heavens, the second heaven to be the starry heavens, and the third heaven to be the place where God (who is everywhere present) manifests His presence in a special way. We take literally the description of the heavenly Jerusalem given in the Book of Revelation. But we see it as the eternal headquarters for Israel and the Church after the final judgment, for it is part of a new creation of the heavens and the earth.

We also recognize that there is much about heaven that cannot be put into our present human language, for our language grows out of our human experience. Even the Apostle Paul was not able to describe in human words what he experienced when he was caught away in vision to the third heaven and Paradise. Isaiah and Paul both let us know that "Eye has not seen, nor ear heard, neither have entered into the heart (including the mind and imagination) of man, the things which God has prepared for them that love Him." But the Bible does not stop there, for "God has revealed them unto us by His Spirit" (1 Corinthians 2:9, 10). That is, the joys, gifts, and blessings we now receive through the Holy Spirit are a foretaste or first installment of what we shall receive in greater fullness in heaven after death as well as in the age to come. Thus we can look forward to wonderful fellowship with Christ in heaven as well as with our loved ones and with the departed men and women of past ages who shared the biblical faith.

We believe that the opportunity to prepare for the joys of heaven is available in this life only. Only in this life are we confronted with God's promises and with the opportunity to accept and follow Christ as Saviour and Lord. The Bible teaches that it is appointed unto mankind once to die, and after death comes God's judgment (Hebrews 9:27). We see that God can make an exception and take prophets like Enoch and Elijah to heaven without dying. But the Bible's main point here is that there is no second chance for salvation after death, nor is there any further opportunity to prepare for the joys of heaven. From this we understand also that there is no reincarnation. The believer who accepts and follows Christ is saved for eternity and retains his same personal identity. The unbeliever who rejects or disregards the Bible's way of salvation through Christ also retains his identity forever, but in a place of punishment.

Since all have sinned through unbelief, disobedience to God, rebellion against God's will, mistreatment of other people, or through exalting ourselves and seeking to please ourselves without regard to others, we all deserve punishment. But the believer who accepts Christ's death on the cross as his substitute and believes God resurrected Jesus from the dead, receives cleansing and forgiveness. Jesus bore all our sins and guilt. He therefore sets us free to walk in newness of life with Christ. Yet the believer is still in this present body and must continue to make choices for the right. Thus, there will be a judgment day for the believer as well as for the unbeliever.

We also understand the Bible to teach that all faithful believers who have maintained a living faith relationship with Christ in this life will be resurrected from the dead and given new immortal bodies when Jesus returns to earth. Those who are still alive at that time will be caught away suddenly to join them for a meeting with Christ in the air (1 Thessalonians 4:17). Their bodies will also be changed, transformed in an instant to new immortal bodies. This resurrection will include only those who have committed their lives to Christ as the divine Son of God and only Savior. It will not include those who in their teachings have reduced Christ to the status of an ordinary human being, even though they, like theological liberals, may consider Him a good man, or like the Moslems may consider Him a prophet.

After the resurrection of these believers they must come before the judgment seat (throne) of Christ. He will judge us all according to our works. But the Bible makes it clear that the judgment of believers will be primarily based on our motives. If we give all our goods to feed the poor but do not have a real, self-giving love for them, it will bring us no reward (1 Corinthians 12:3). If we have done good deeds primarily to win the praise of people, build up our own reputation, or build a little kingdom for ourselves, there will be no reward, even though our faith in Christ will save us and allow us to enter heaven.

The Bible does not tell us where heaven is. We believe it may be beyond the created universe, or perhaps within it, but in a different order of existence. That is, heaven may be all around us, but on a different wave length. All who continue faithful to Christ will attain it, no matter what church they belong to.

God's holiness and justice demand that sin be dealt with. Since all have sinned, we must accept the provision of God's love for the forgiveness of our sins through the blood Jesus shed in His violent, sacrificial death on the cross. If we reject or disregard His love, our sins demand that at death we be transported to the place of punishment the Bible calls Hell or Hades. The Bible does not say where it is. It says only that there is a great, impassible gulf between it and the place where those who died with their faith in our Lord are enjoying His presence. Those in hell are aware that faithful believers in the true God and in His promises are enjoying fellowship with other believers such as Abraham, Moses, the prophets of the Old Testament, and the apostles, prophets, and saints (dedicated believers) of the New Testament.

Hell (Hades) is described both as a place of fire and of

darkness. Its inhabitants are full of remorse and frustration. They are cut off from faith, hope, and love. Human language cannot adequately describe what hell's awful sufferings are really like. But it is not the final state. After the final judgment of the unbelievers, death and hell will be absorbed into an eternal state of punishment outside the new heaven and the new earth, a place called the lake of fire, the second death. It will be the final separation from all the good God has planned for mankind.

The final judgment of unbelievers, including all who have failed to commit themselves by faith to follow Jesus as Lord and Savior, will not take place until after Jesus returns to earth to bring a total end to the present world system and to establish the reign of God over all the earth for a thousand years.

We accept literally the New Testament teaching that at the time of Christ's return believers from all past ages will rise from the dead, clothed with new bodies prepared for them by God. Believers who are still alive will rise with them to meet Jesus and will be transformed instantaneously into their new bodies. These new bodies will be real, tangible, yet immortal, never to be touched again by decay, corruption, or death.[6] They will share in Christ's rule for a thousand years. Christ's return and the work of the Holy Spirit will rid the earth of pollution and restore it to ideal conditions. Before this happens there must be the defeat of a false christ referred to in the Bible as Antichrist and as the man of sin or lawlessness. He and his false prophet will be cast into the lake of fire. The lake of fire will be prepared for the devil and his angels. But men who follow Satan will thus choose to go to Satan's place.

The Bible is concerned about the justice of God. When Jesus administers judgment on the earth, no one can say He deserves judgment too, for He lived totally without sin. Nor can anyone point a finger at Him and say He did not do enough to save them from coming judgment. He gave His life. Some might say that if people knew how wonderful the reign of Christ will be they would all follow Him; yet after the thousand years of Christ's reign Satan will be released for a short time, and many will follow him as soon as they have opportunity, even though they have enjoyed the blessings of the thousand year reign. Thus, the Bible shows they are rebels. God can do nothing with them but separate them off from His new heavens and earth forever in the lake of fire, the "second death." Death here means separation. So the lake of fire will be a final separation from all that is good, righteous, holy, just, and loving.[7]

Before being sent to the lake of fire, the wicked and all unbelievers will be resurrected and brought before God's Great White Throne of Judgment. At the appearance of God's presence and glory in this judgment, the present heavens and earth will go out of existence. Since God the Father has given all judgment to the Son (John 5:22), the one we will see on the throne will be Jesus. He will judge those who are resurrected at this time by their works, and the verdict will be eternal punishment in the lake of fire. After that God will create a brand new heaven and earth. (Some believe the new earth is simply the present earth renovated by fire.)

The New Earth will be of a different order. There will be no more seas or oceans. There will be no need of the sun, for Christ will be its light and His glory will be everywhere present. Thus there will be no night. Many elements will be of a different order. Gold will be as transparent as glass and so common that streets will be paved with it. Christ will mediate His life and energy to us directly, so we shall never be weak or tired. At the outset, the New Jerusalem will come down out of heaven to the new earth. God's throne will be in it. That is, God's "headquarters," the place of His special manifestation will no longer be in heaven but on the new earth. God and mankind will be united in a new degree of fellowship for all eternity. Then, since God is infinite, there will always be new joys, new things to learn about Him, and undoubtedly, more of the new heaven to explore. But the New Jerusalem on the new earth will be our home and headquarters forever.

Our most important responsibility in this present life is to proclaim the New Testament teaching that salvation is by grace through faith in Christ alone. It is necessary to understand also that faith is more than a mental acceptance of a body of belief. It involves personal trust in Jesus as Saviour, receiving His sacrifice on the cross as sufficient penalty for our sins, since He had no sin of His own and thus could bear ours. It means also that we believe God accepted Christ's sacrifice on our behalf and demonstrated His acceptance by raising Jesus from the dead, thus making His resurrection the guarantee of ours, just as Jesus promised.

We also declare our faith by water baptism by immersion. This is our testimony that we, through faith, have died to the old life and have risen to a new life in Christ. We do not believe the water of baptism has any value in itself. Baptism is merely a picture symbolizing what has already happened. Peter compared it in the Bible to the faith of Noah. The fact Noah came through the waters of the great flood was a testimony to the faith he had before the flood, a faith expressed in obedience as he built the ark. So the water of baptism does not cleanse us, nor does it convey salvation. It is simply the testimony of a good conscience that has already been cleansed by Christ.

Our salvation also includes our inheritance, our new bodies and our eternal reign with Christ. Thus we must continue to express our faith through faithfulness in worship and service to God, by obeying His Word, by doing His will, and by showing His love through acts of love to others. This means that like our Heavenly Father we must forgive those who mistreat us and reach out in love to those who do not deserve our love. Thus, we are saved because Christ died and rose again, not because of our good works. But we are saved in order that we might do good works that will bring glory to God.

Then, since Christ's death was accepted by God the Father as a sufficient sacrifice for all our sins, we cannot add to His provision. Because of Christ's sufficient sacrifice also, we do not need to make further sacrifice or pay further penalty for our sins. At death we go directly to heaven. Thus we reject totally the idea of purgatory. Nor do we see any need for limbo. Jesus blessed the little children. He did not ask them to repent. Nor do we see any evidence in the Bible for the baptism of infants. The Bible teaches the baptism of believers. The Book of Acts shows that when the household of the Philippian jailor was baptized, they all first heard the word of God, the gospel, and afterward they all rejoiced. No infants were included. God does not hold accountable children who are too young to understand the gospel. Thus His grace provides salvation for children who die as well as for all who are mentally incapable of understanding the requirements of the gospel. God will mature and perfect them in heaven.

Since faith is the key, we accept all believers of all denominations as children of God and heirs of salvation. We do not believe God holds the members of the Assemblies of God faith in any higher favor than He does other believers in Christ as Lord and only Savior. God's favor is grace, "unmerited favor," and God makes it available to all mankind, to whoever will accept it. We believe that our hope is a sure hope, a hope without any sense of contingency on God's part. Even if we fail, God will find some who will respond, and He will bring the fulfillment of all His promises.

All the Bible has a forward look. Thus, we live enjoying what God has provided us in the present life and at the same time expecting and looking forward to the future life. God's Word is a lamp to guide us here and now. It is also a star to give direction and meaning to our lives. We look ahead to enjoying the presence of Christ in heaven. From the Bible we see also that we will recognize each other there. We shall know our friends and relatives. We shall enjoy fellowship with the saints of old time.

In heaven, however, our primary relationship will always be to Christ and then to all other believers as part of the family of God. Other relationships will still be valued but will be less important. The relationship of a small child in the present life centers around his parents. When the child grows up and marries, the relationship to the marriage partner becomes central. The relationship to the parents is still valued, but it drops somewhat into the background. In heaven our relationship with God through Christ will be central. Other relationships, including the marriage relationship, will drop somewhat into the background. We shall all be in a unity of fellowship with Christ and with one another.

Finally, we understand that the Bible does not tell us about the afterlife simply to satisfy our curiosity. The Bible wants us to see God has a plan. It shows us also that God has the intelligence, power, love, and faithfulness necessary to carry out His plan. As a part of His great overall plan He has a plan for each of us, both in this life and in the afterlife. But He has created us creatures with the responsibility for making choices, and it is up to us to accept His plan for our lives. If we fail, He will not fail. He will find a way to carry out His plan. He tells us of the future in the Bible to encourage us to live for Him and be the kind of person we ought to be now.

The major emphasis of Assemblies of God teaching is on what God does for us now through Christ and through the Holy Spirit and His gifts. At the same time we know the Holy Spirit is preparing us to receive the fullness of our salvation, which includes the inheritance God has for us: our new bodies, our full privileges as heirs of God, and our ruling and reigning with Christ, not only through the thousand years of the Millennium, but also throughout all eternity.

The same Holy Spirit who brings us Christ's salvation, help, and healing now will bring about our resurrection and cause us to rise to meet Jesus in the air when He comes. The same Christ, who is still the God-Man in heaven, is now at the right hand of God the Father. That is, He is at the place of power and authority. There He is interceding for us, waiting for the time when He will come and receive us to Himself.

We are confident that Christ in the afterlife will bring us light and beauty, fullness of knowledge, and freedom from all the weariness, pain, strife, grief, and sorrow of this present life.[8] Above all, the promise is "So shall we ever be with the Lord" (1 Thessalonians 4:17).[9]

Notes

[1] William W. Menzies, *Anointed to Serve: The Story of the Assemblies of God.* (Springfield, MO, Gospel Publishing House, 1971), p. 33.

[2] Stanley H. Frodsham, *With Signs Following* (Springfield, MO, Gospel Publishing House, 1946), p. 20.

[3] Frank Bartleman, *How Pentecost Came to Los Angeles* (Los Angeles, by the author, 1928), p. 58.

[4] Gary B. McGee, "A Brief History of the Modern Pentecostal Outpouring," *Paraclete*, Vol. 18, no. 2, Spring 1984, p. 22.

[5] Carl Brumback, *Like a River* (Springfield, MO, Gospel Publishing House, 1977), p. 55.

[6] Myer Pearlman, *Knowing the Doctrines of the Bible* (Springfield, MO, Gospel Publishing House, 6th ed., 1945), pp. 373-377.

[7] Pearlman, op. cit., pp. 387-394.

[8] Pearlman, op. cit., p. 383.

[9] Bible passages supporting Assemblies of God views can be found in the *Minutes of the 40th Session of the General Council of the Assemblies of God, with Revised Constitution and Bylaws*, pp. 90-95. (Obtainable from the General Secretary, Joseph R. Flower, 1445 Boonville Ave., Springfield, MO 65802). They can also be found in: Nelson, P.C., *Bible Doctrines* (Springfield, MO; Gospel Publishing House, 1948, 174 pages).

BAHA'I FAITH

John S. Hatcher, Ph. D.

Background of the Faith

The word *Baha'i* means "a follower of Baha'u'llah," the prophet-founder of the Baha'i Faith whose title means "the Glory of God." Baha'u'llah (Mirza Husayn-'Ali) was a Persian of noble lineage who was born in Teheran in 1817 and died in Akka, Palestine (now Israel), in 1892 after four successive exiles from His native Persia. The Faith itself dates from May 23, 1844, when the Bab ("the Gate"), a young merchant from Shiraz by the name of Mirza 'Ali Muhammad, announced that He was the Promised Qa'im whose mission it was to prepare the way for the coming of "Him Whom God Shall Make Manifest," a prophet from God whose revelation would usher in world peace and a world civilization as promised in the holy scriptures of *all* world religions.

The Bab and His followers were immediately persecuted by the Islamic clergy in collusion with government officials because they viewed the Bab's religion as heretical and a threat to their authority. Some of the most prominent Islamic scholars became followers of the Bab, but at the height of the persecution of the Babis, over 20,000 followers were cruelly tortured and slaughtered when they refused to recant their beliefs. The Bab Himself was executed by firing squad in the town square of Tabriz under miraculous circumstances. After telling the guards He had not finished dictating His final instructions, He was suspended by ropes from a barracks wall. Thousands of citizens watched in amazement as 750 rifles fired—when the smoke had cleared, the Bab had vanished from sight. He was later found completing his instructions, after which He consented to be taken again before *another* firing squad, and the execution was carried out.

In the bloody persecution that followed, most of the Babi leaders were killed except for Baha'u'llah, whom the Bab had indicated as the very prophet whose coming He had foretold. Baha'u'llah's own revelation began in 1852 when He was imprisoned in the dreaded Siyyah Chal, an underground prison in which were placed the most grievous criminals, their feet in stocks, their necks strung together by a weighty chain. It was in these circumstances that Baha'u'llah received the first intimation of His mission. For a number of years He withheld this information from the other Babis, choosing instead to reorganize the bewildered community.

In 1853 the Shah exiled Baha'u'llah to Baghdad in neighboring Iraq so that the religion would die out in Persia. In Baghdad, however, Baha'u'llah revitalized the disheartened believers, disseminated the teachings of the Bab, as well as the first works of His own revelation, and attracted admirers from various religions far and wide.

Over the next ten years (1853-63) the community rapidly increased in size and acquired renown for its honesty and kindliness. But as the reputation of Baha'u'llah and His followers spread, the jealousy of the Islamic clergy was once more aroused. Through a barrage of petitions to the Shah, some of these mullahs managed to have Baha'u'llah exiled even further from His homeland and, they hoped, from any further influence. Before His departure in 1863, however, Baha'u'llah officially announced to the believers what most had already surmised—that He was "Him Whom God Shall Make Manifest," the prophet alluded to in prophecies of all the world's major religions. Shortly afterwards, the community of believers began to call themselves "Baha' is" as a sign of their recognition of His revelation.

Once again, in 1868, He was exiled, this time to the prison city of Akka, Palestine, where He was expected to die along with the Baha'i Faith itself. For nine years He remained a prisoner within the city walls, though He managed, with the help of His son 'Abdu'l-Baha, to maintain contact with His followers and to write His most important work, The Most Holy Book, the book of Baha'i laws and institutions, what Baha'is view as a blueprint for world civilization. After His release from strict confinement in 1877, He took a residence outside Akka where He continued to write and direct the affairs of the religion. By the end of His ministry He had revealed over one hundred volumes on every subject from kindness to animals to world government.

Upon His death in 1892, 'Abdu'l-Baha assumed authority over the Baha'i Faith, in compliance with the explicit dictates of Baha'u'llah's will, and He began to organize the religion worldwide according to the plan set forth in His father's writings. In 1912 He visited the West, traveling across the United States to meet with the members of the various Baha'i communities. Upon His death in 1921, Shoghi Effendi, 'Abdu'l-Baha's grandson, assumed guardianship of the Baha'i Faith, in accordance with the will and testament of 'Abdu'l-Baha. Gradually He guided construction of the worldwide administrative institutions of the Baha'i Faith as designed by Baha'u'llah. After His death in 1957 the final part of that design was completed with the election in 1963 of the Universal House of Justice, a nine-membered body elected every five years to guide the affairs of the Baha'i Faith. The House of Justice resides in Haifa, Israel, the world center for the religion. As of 1985, the Baha'i faith had over four million adherents in some 207 countries and dependencies. In the United States, there are over 100,000 Baha'is who reside in over 7,300 localities and comprise 1,750 organized communities.

Major Beliefs of the Baha'i Faith

The Baha'i Faith is not a cult, a sect, not an offshoot of Islam, but an independent world religion. Neither is it man-made (eclectic or syncretic), but a revealed religion following in a progression of revelation derived from the eternal or ancient covenant between God and man—that God will never leave man without guidance and that man will strive both to recognize the divine Manifestations when they appear and to follow their teachings. This is the pivotal teaching of Baha'u'llah, that God's purpose for man, collectively and individually, is spiritual education and transformation and that to assist man in this endeavor, God has periodically sent exemplary beings to advance further mankind's understanding of His spiritual nature and to incorporate more completely that knowledge in action. In short, the Baha'i Faith affirms the oneness of God, the oneness of religion and the oneness of mankind.

From the Baha'i perspective, these successive Manifestations or Prophets are like perfect mirrors, each reflecting in his life and teachings the reality of God. Each is endowed by God with a capacity far beyond that of human beings, but each reveals only what is appropriate to the capacities of mankind for the historical period in which he appears. In this sense all the world religions are one religion revealed in successive stages, inasmuch as all the Manifestations are equal in capacity, fully coordinated in their efforts, and willing agents in this eternal plan of spiritual evolution.

At the center of this divinely ordained education system is the student, mankind, because only the human being is endowed with a soul and is, therefore, uniquely capable of recognizing and acquiring spiritual attributes. According to the Baha'i teachings, the soul takes its beginning at conception, develops according to man's free will during its association with the physical body, and continues its development in the next life. From this view, there is no source of evil in creation, no Satanic force except the willful rejection of spiritual growth. The purpose of mankind in this life is a two-fold process of coming to understand the spiritual perfections of God through these Manifestations and of reflecting that knowledge in every aspect of daily life (prayer, vocation, good works, etc.).

In general, therefore, the Baha'i writings portray the physical experience as the first stage in an eternal process whereby each individual soul is exhorted and assisted to strive toward perfection. Clearly not every soul encounters the same experience, the same opportunities, but the Baha'i writings explain that because this is only a beginning and because God is just and merciful, all that seems unjust or inequitable from our limited terrestrial perspective (unjust suffering, infant mortality, natural disasters, etc.) is taken care of in the successive stages of our existence in the afterlife.

Such a belief does not imply a passive acceptance of injustice or the status quo. At the heart of the Baha'i life is the daily striving to put into physical and social form the spiritual principles that Baha'u'llah has revealed for this stage in the spiritual advancement of the planet. Among the most significant principles are the recognition of the essential unity of mankind and the abolition of all forms of prejudice—whether racial, national or religious—the recognition of the harmony of science and religion, of the equality of men and women, and of the necessity for each individual to investigate truth independently. Some of the measures which Baha'u'llah elucidates for bringing about these conditions are the establishment of a universal auxiliary language, a universal system of weights and measures, universal compulsory education, the abolition of the extremes of poverty and wealth, and the founding of a world federation of governments to ensure a universal and lasting peace. In short, the "Revelation proclaimed by Baha'u'llah, His followers believe, is divine in origin, all-embracing in scope, broad in its outlook, scientific in its method, humanitarian in its principles and dynamic in the influence it exerts on the hearts and minds of men."[1]

Death Questions

1. The Baha'i Funeral
   The Baha'i writings state, "I have made death a messenger of joy to thee. Wherefore dost thou grieve?"[2] Since the Baha'i teachings affirm the continuation of the individual soul after its association with the body, the focus of a Baha'i funeral or memorial service is on commemorating the spiritual contributions the deceased has rendered. In grieving, the family and fellow believers lament the loss of that association, not the condition of the departed. And even this separation is viewed as temporary. In consoling a bereaved widow, 'Abdu'l-Baha stated, "This separation is temporal; this remoteness and sorrow is counted only by days. Thou shalt find him in the Kingdom of God and thou wilt attain to the everlasting union."[3]
   The Baha'i funeral or memorial service itself is largely devoid of ritual. It consists primarily of prayers and other appropriate readings from the Baha'i sacred scriptures. There may be music, a eulogy, whatever the family desires. Likewise, the casket may be open or closed. Finally, since there is no clergy in the Baha'i Faith, the service may be conducted by the family itself or by whomever the family chooses. The only required part of the funeral service is the *Prayer for the Dead* revealed by Baha'u'llah, which is to be "recited by one believer while all present stand."[4]

2. Treatment and Interment of the Body

While there are relatively few regulations regarding the service, there are important Baha'i laws concerning the treatment and interment of the body. First, embalming is prohibited unless it is required by law. Secondly, the body must not be transported more than an hour's journey from the place of death not even for purposes of interment. Thirdly, the body must not be cremated. The Baha'i is free to donate his body to science, provided that the body is treated with respect and the laws prohibiting cremation and removal of the body more than one hour's journey from the place of death are observed.[5] According to Shoghi Effendi, guardian of the Baha'i Faith, "The spirit has no more connection with the body after it departs, but as the body was once the temple of the spirit, we Baha'is are taught that it must be treated with respect."[6]

The appropriate symbols for the grave marker are the nine-pointed star, the word *Baha'i*, or a nine-pointed star or rosette with the word *Baha'i* in the center, the number nine being associated in the Arabic language with the name of Baha'u'llah:

The wording on the gravestone is "left to the discretion of the relatives of the deceased"[7]; for example, any appropriate quote from Baha'i writings may be used.

3. Responding to the Bereaved

The Baha'i Faith has no mourning rituals nor is there any recommended response to the bereaved, though there are myriad passages in the Baha'i writings that deal pointedly and poignantly with this subject. Most generally, the Baha'i writings make it quite clear that the physical life is but the initial portion of an eternal existence that begins with the soul's association with the body at conception. From the Baha'i perspective, the soul continues its development after this life and retains its awareness of identity—"thou wilt not forget (there) the life that thou hast had in the material world."[8] Furthermore, Baha'u'llah states that "the soul, after its separation from the body, will continue to progress until it attaineth the presence of God, in a state and condition which neither the revolution of ages and centuries, nor the changes and chances of this world, can alter."[9]

But in addition to these assurances that the soul continues and that the separation is temporary, since souls will recognize each other in the spiritual world,[10] 'Abdu'l-Baha offers several comforting analogies that explain the relationship between the body and the soul. In one, for example, he compares the soul to a bird and the body to a cage:

> To consider that after the death of the body the spirit perishes is like imagining that a bird in a cage will be destroyed if the cage is broken, though the bird has nothing to fear from the destruction of the cage. Our body is like the cage, and the spirit is like the bird....if the cage becomes broken, the bird will continue and exist. Its feelings will be even more powerful, its perceptions greater, and its happiness increased.[11]

From the Baha'i view, death marks the beginning of another and greater stage in the spiritual education of the soul. Since the soul does not enter the body, but temporarily associates with it, it will not be hampered in its development when that relationship terminates. 'Abdu'l-Baha explains this in another analogy when he compares the soul to a light and the body to a mirror:

> The spirit never entered this body, so in quitting it, it will not be in need of an abiding-place: no, the spirit is connected with the body, as this light is with this mirror. When the mirror is clear and perfect, the light of the lamp will be apparent in it, and when the mirror becomes covered with dust or breaks, the light will disappear.[12]

The grief we feel, then, results from the fact that we are for a time prevented from seeing that light because the mirror has been shattered. But if earthly companionship is ultimately destined for separation, the "heavenly association is eternal."[13] 'Abdu'l-Baha states, "Whenever thou rememberest the eternal and never ending union, thou wilt be comforted and blissful."[14]

4.   Burial of Non-Believers

While Baha'is or Baha'i institutions may conduct services for non-Baha'is, the laws incumbent on a Baha'i would not be binding (i.e., that there be no cremation or removal of the body over an hour's journey from the place of death, no embalming unless required by law, etc.). In this sense, the burial would not be, strictly speaking, a Baha'i funeral. But inasmuch as the Baha'i service itself has no ritual, certainly the prayers and readings that comprise such a service can be used for anyone.

Life After Death Questions

1.   General Baha'i Beliefs about Life After Death

On the one hand, it is clear in the Baha'i writings that we can only hazily understand the nature of the soul and its progress in the afterlife. Baha'u'llah states, for example, that the "nature of the soul after death can never be described, nor is it meet and permissible to reveal its whole character to the eyes of men."[15] In like manner, Baha'u'llah states, "The world beyond is as different from this world as this world is different from that of the child while still in the womb of its mother."[16] On the other hand, the essential reality and purpose of this life, as it relates to our progress in the next life, is delineated with clarity in the Baha'i writings.

First of all, the Baha'i writings teach that the awareness, identity and reality of all human beings is the soul, a spiritual entity which, unique in creation, has a beginning but no end. Baha'is believe that the soul begins with its association with the body at conception, develops by means of education and noble effort in the physical reality, and continues its progress after its association with the corporeal world. Thus, as the period of gestation is a preparation of the physical man for its entrance into a reality where senses and all the bodily capacities are essential to human advancement and learning, so the earthly life is a period of preparation for the new life wherein spiritual faculties and perceptions are essential.

Viewed from this perspective, the physical life is not detrimental to the soul's continuation; used properly, the physical reality is a divinely ordained training for life after death, which is but another stage in a process begun in this reality, not a separate existence:

> The Prophets and Messengers of God have been sent down for the sole purpose of guiding mankind to the straight Path of Truth. The purpose underlying their revelation hath been to educate all men, that they may, at the hour of death, ascend, in the utmost purity and sanctity and with absolute detachment, to the throne of the Most High.[17]

More specifically, the Baha'i writings teach that each person retains his identity, recalls his past life in the physical realm, and will recognize his deceased companions. As here, the purpose in the next life is the spiritual progress of the soul. 'Abdu'l-Baha notes, "as the perfections of humanity are endless, man can also make progress in perfections after leaving this world."[18]

2.   Baha'i Beliefs about Reincarnation

Baha'u'llah states that "the worlds of God are countless in their number, and infinite in their range."[19] Likewise, it is clear that the stages in the spiritual evolution of a single human soul are quite beyond our temporal comprehension. At the same time, it is abundantly clear that there is, from a

Baha'i view, but one physical experience for each soul—
Baha'is believe in neither transmigration nor reincarnation.
The physical experience is not viewed as unimportant—the
Baha'i perceives physical reality as a unique beginning to
an endless spiritual journey, a reality in which we are challenged to perceive the essential spiritual reality underlying
the physical metaphors and symbols that comprise this life:
"Know thou that every created thing is a sign of the revelation of God."[20] However, it is also clear that the physical
world is only a beginning, that progress of the soul after this
life is not finally conditioned by one's earthly experience,
and that divine justice for the individual is not contingent
solely on its expression in the physical world.

3.   Baha'i Beliefs Regarding Heaven and Hell
   The Baha'i Faith recognizes the importance of the relationship between one's efforts at spiritual development in
the physical world and one's experience after death. However, Baha'is do not believe in heaven and hell as physical
places nor as eternally fixed conditions of the soul. In most
general terms, Baha'u'llah describes the use of these terms
by previous Manifestations as the attempt to explain an
abstract or spiritual condition in symbolic or metaphorical
terms—thus, proximity to God is portrayed as Heaven,
remoteness as Hell, and Baha'u'llah employs these terms
Himself.[21] Likewise, the figure of Satan is not a literal being
or demi-god, but a personification of the sort of selfishness
and willfulness that deters spiritual growth.
   This does not mean that the Baha'i does not believe in
reward and punishment in the afterlife. In a number of
places Baha'u'llah emphatically delineates the relationship
between one's earthly life and the experience after death:

> They that are the followers of the one true God shall, the
> moment they depart out of this life, experience such joy and
> gladness as would be impossible to describe, while they that
> live in error shall be seized with such fear and trembling, and
> shall be filled with such consternation, as nothing can
> exceed.[22]

But since the next stages in our development also involve change and growth, the initial experience after death may become altered so that the understanding and faith of the righteous may become heightened and "the condition of those who have died in sin and unbelief may become changed...."[23]

This principle of spiritual development after death is, in the Baha'i writings, not a vague notion. It is clear, for example, that understanding and learning are achieved through such means as conversing with "the Prophet and His chosen ones."[24] "The mysteries of which man is heedless in this earthly world, those he will discover in the heavenly world, and there will he be informed of the secret of truth...."[25] Some of the other means by which the soul progresses are "through the intercession and the sincere prayers of other human souls, or through the charities and important good works which are performed in its name," and "through the bounty and grace of the Lord alone,"[26] a grace that includes the opportunity to pray for forgiveness: "Through their own prayers and supplications they can also progress, more especially when they are the object of the intercession of the holy manifestations."[27]

From such a view it is possible to conceive of a soul becoming so willfully perverted that it could be devoid of the capacity for progress, but whether or not a soul in the next life is ever beyond hope we cannot know from the limited perspective of this life. However, it is clear that our actions have consequence in both this life and in the next and that no formulaic act can alter that process. Thus, while Baha'u'llah exhorts all mankind to recognize the truth of this revelation, He does not describe the rewards in the next life as confined to those who call themselves Baha'is. Instead, Baha'u'llah uses such terms as "Every pure, every refined and sanctified soul,"[28] and "Every soul that walketh humbly with its God, in this Day, and cleaveth unto Him."[29]

What is clear from the Baha'i point of view, is that the next world is quite beyond our comprehension except in these broad terms. Part of our inability to understand is the result of our not having a frame of reference. Also, the concealment of that reality from us is part of divinely ordained training for understanding and growth. Still another reason the next life is concealed is that if we were fully aware of it, we would not be able to restrain ourselves from attaining it:

> If any man be told that which hath been ordained for such a soul in the worlds of God, the Lord of the throne on high and of earth below, his whole being will instantly blaze out in his great longing to attain that most exalted, that sanctified and resplendent station....[30]

4. The Time of the End

Just as Baha'is believe that the literalistic Pharasaic Jews failed to understand the symbolic and metaphoric nature of the prophesies regarding the Messiah (that He would come from an unknown place, would rule with a rod of iron, and would sit upon the throne of David, etc.), so Baha'is believe that the signs regarding the "Day of Judgment" and the "Time of the End" are likewise figurative.[31] More specifically, Baha'is believe that the time of the end is alluding to the process of progressive revelation by which man is evolving on this planet, a process that is cyclical in nature and marked by certain leaps forward in mankind's understanding of his spiritual nature. According to the Baha'i writings, mankind is currently in an immense transition, not simply from the Islamic dispensation to the Baha'i dispensation, but from one era of development to another, a transition, in effect, from adolescence to adulthood. From this perspective, Muhammad was the "Seal of the Prophets" because He was the last Manifestation in the Adamic or prophetic cycle; and the Bab was the first Manifestation in the new era of man's development, the Baha'i Era, which is destined to endure for not less than five hundred thousand years. As Baha'u'llah Himself states, this "Day," this period in the history of mankind, has been longingly awaited by every previous Manifestation:

> "It is evident," He in another passage explains, "that every age in which a Manifestation of God hath lived is divinely-

ordained, and may, in a sense, be characterized as God's
appointed Day. This Day, however, is unique, and is to be
distinguished from those that have preceded it. The designation 'Seal of the Prophets' fully revealeth its high station. The
Prophetic Cycle hath verily ended. The Eternal Truth is now
come...." "In this most mighty Revelation," He, in categorical
language, declares, "all the Dispensations of the past have
attained their highest, their final consummation."[32]

Thus, the "Time of the End," Baha'is believe, refers not to
the end of the earth, but the end of one era and the beginning
of another, an era of mankind's fulfillment. But as with the
coming of any new Manifestation, the followers of the previous Prophets are tested, are judged, as were the Jews with
the coming of Christ. One of these tests is the challenge to
discern in prophesies the hidden or inner significance
regarding this period. One of Baha'u'llah's most weighty
tablets, *The Book of Certitude*, is, among other things, virtually a casebook study of such signs as the trumpet call, the
day of judgment, coming "in the clouds," the sun becoming
darkened, and the stars falling from heaven.[33] In one sense,
then, the events prophesied have already occurred. However, inasmuch as mankind is yet unaware of these events
and their significance and since the transition to a new
awareness is still taking place, we are still living in that
period and some of the prophesies are yet to be fulfilled.

5.   Bodily Resurrection at the Time of the End
    In keeping with the Baha'i belief regarding the essentially
spiritual nature of man, the Baha'i writings view the "resurrection" as a symbol of a spiritual condition, a state of revitalized spirituality. 'Abdu'l-Baha explains that the Resurrection of Christ was significant as a spiritual analogue, not
as a physical fact:

    It is clear, then, that when it is said that the Son of man is
    come from heaven, this has not an outward but an inward
    signification; it is a spiritual, not a material, fact.... And as it
    has become evident that Christ came from the spiritual

heaven of the Divine Kingdom, therefore His disappearance under the earth for three days has an inner signification and is not an outward fact. In the same way, His resurrection from the interior of the earth is also symbolical; it is a spiritual and divine fact, and not material; and likewise His ascension to heaven is a spiritual and not material ascension.[34]

Christ himself did not mention the bodily resurrection of the believers as a characteristic of the coming of the Son of man, and when Paul discusses the subject in the first letter to the Corinthians, chapter 15, he speaks of an imperishable "spiritual body" to replace the physical one. As Baha'u'llah explains in *The Book of Certitude*, the term "resurrection" is often used as figurative expression of spiritual revivification, just as the condition of sleep or death is a common symbol in the scriptures for spiritual obliviousness.[35] Thus the resurrection of mankind alluded to by both Christians and Moslems alike as a sign of this period is understood by Baha'is to refer to the spiritual transformation of the planet, which is about to occur and which will result in the eventual establishment of world peace, a world commonwealth, and an advancement in learning and civilization as has not occurred before in the history of this planet.

6. Baha'i Beliefs about Purgatory or Limbo

As already mentioned, the Baha'i writings reject the idea of physical places or conditions in an existence that is by nature a spiritual reality, although physical descriptions may sometimes be used to portray figuratively a metaphysical experience. Baha'u'llah indicates that the worlds of God, and presumably the experiences of the soul within those worlds, are infinite in variety: "Know thou of a truth that the worlds of God are countless in their number, and infinite in their range."[36] It is no doubt possible that there is a spiritual condition in the next world which the figurative concept of Purgatory or Limbo attempts to depict, a state in which the soul accomplishes a purgation or transition to a higher condition. But clearly the details of such a process, as have been portrayed often by artists and theologians alike, are something we can only guess at from our limited understanding of the next life.

7.   The Baha'i Concept of Salvation

While the concept of "salvation" varies greatly among the world religions, the term as used by many Western religions has come to signify a dramatic turning point in one's spiritual life. This transformation, or doctrinally based belief that one is secure, most generally involves a profession of faith, an inductive leap of some sort, which is largely independent of deeds or merit; one is "saved" by grace, by theological technicalities that conform to the structures of particular religious belief.

For the most part, the Baha'i concept of salvation is quite different. First of all, in the Baha'i Faith there is no particular point in one's spiritual progress where growth and development is finalized or eternally secure; the most abysmal failure can suddenly ascend, and the most elite of men is capable of rejecting his belief. Clearly, however, the Baha'i does not believe that faith and salvation are capricious or whimsical—the Baha'i writings carefully delineate the means by which one can daily ensure spiritual progress so that gradually doubt is replaced by certitude, and one's daily life becomes a clear reflection of one's spiritual conviction. The point is that this is an ongoing process, whether in this life or the next, and that the exertion of free will in seeking salvation, from a Baha'i point of view, involves not merely a single act of determination but daily assessment and effort.

Underlying this general concept of salvation as a continuous evolution of the soul are several significant ingredients. First, the Baha'i writings teach that each human soul is capable of infinite growth or perfectability; therefore at no point is that evolution finalized:

> Know that nothing which exists remains in a state of repose—
> that is to say, all things are in motion. Everything is either
> growing or declining....[37]

* * *

> There is no other being higher than a perfect man. But man when he has reached this state can still make progress in perfections but not in state because there is no state higher than that of a perfect man to which he can transfer himself....

> Hence, as the perfections of humanity are endless, man can also make progress in perfections after leaving this world.[38]

Secondly, faith or belief, from a Baha'i view, is not a matter of blind affirmation or acceptance, but independent investigation of truth, a belief grounded in the confirmation and corroboration of evidence:

> If religious beliefs and opinions are found contrary to the standards of science they are mere superstitions and imaginations; for the antithesis of knowledge is ignorance, and the child of ignorance is superstition.... If a question be found contrary to reason, faith and belief in it are impossible and there is no outcome but wavering and vacillation.[39]

Thirdly, religious conviction or faith is not the mere statement of belief; salvation or spiritual evolution must be achieved by putting that belief in action. 'Abdu'l-Baha states, "By faith is meant, first, conscious knowledge, and second, the practice of good deeds."[40] While this does not imply that one precisely earns salvation, it does indicate that belief without action is hollow and worthless.

But while the spiritual progress of the soul is a continuum, the Baha'i writings do describe stages of development in which one is relatively secure. For example, Baha'u'llah frequently uses the metaphor "the City of Certitude" to represent a condition wherein one is confirmed in his belief:

> When the channel of the human soul is cleansed of all worldly and impeding attachments, it will unfailingly perceive the breath of the Beloved across immeasurable distances, and will, led by its perfume, attain and enter the City of Certitude.[41]

Nevertheless, Baha'u'llah exhorts all people regardless of how meritorious their deeds or firm their faith to "bring thyself to account each day ere thou art summoned to a reckoning; for death, unheralded, shall come upon thee and thou shalt be called to give account for thy deeds."[42]

There is no distinction, then, between the salvation of a Baha'i and a non-Baha'i in the sense that a just and loving God no doubt takes into account how each soul responds to his opportunities and capacities. In effect, one is not saved by the name he bears. Many people who call themselves Baha'is may not follow the guidance revealed by Baha'u'llah, and many who have never heard of the Baha'i Faith may live spiritual lives. But it is clear that, from a Baha'i view, it is the plan of God that mankind as a whole recognize this most recent Manifestation, Baha'u'llah, and follow His teachings for this period in the spiritual evolution of mankind. This concept of the eternal covenant as the source of salvation of mankind is expressed throughout the Baha'i writings. It is expressed in religious history in terms of the literal ark of Noah, which was a source of salvation for the faithful, and by the Ark of the Covenant, which was the chest containing the Ten Commandments which, as God's revealed law, were a source of salvation for the Jews. Thus, from a Baha'i view, the surest source of salvation for mankind in this day, the "ark of salvation," as 'Abdu'l-Baha describes it,[43] is in the teachings of Baha'u'llah and in the institutions He established as the most recent expression of this ancient covenant.

By becoming a Baha'i, one is not necessarily assured of salvation or of becoming more spiritual than someone who is not a Baha'i. But Baha'is believe that God has designated Baha'u'llah's teachings as the source of salvation of mankind for this dispensation, a period which shall endure for at least a thousand years. Therefore Baha'is also believe that the best means for the transformation and ascent of the human soul can presently be found in recognizing the station of Baha'u'llah and in following the guidance He has revealed.

8. Recognition of Friends and Family in the Next World

'Abdu'l-Baha states: "As to thy question whether the souls will recognize each other in the spiritual world: This fact is certain; for the Kingdom is the world of vision where all the concealed realities will become disclosed. How much more the well-known souls will become manifest. The mysteries of which man is heedless in the earthly world, those he will discover in the heavenly world, and there will he be informed of the secret of truth; how much more will he recognize or discover persons with whom he hath been associated."[44] On another occasion, 'Abdu'l-Baha wrote to a bereaved widow, "a love that one may have entertained for any one will not be forgotten in the world of the Kingdom. Likewise, thou wilt not forget [there] the life that thou hast had in the material world."[45] This association is not confined to friends and family, however; Baha'u'llah states that the soul will "freely converse" with the prophets and the "chosen ones" and will "recount unto them that which it hath been made to endure in the path of God, the Lord of all worlds."[46]

9. The Sequence of Events at the Moment of Death

On the one hand, considerations of time are obviously irrelevant in the next life, which is eternal. Yet, Baha'u'llah indicates that the sense of reward or punishment occurs even before death itself. For example, Baha'u'llah states that those who have rejected spiritual development "shall... when breathing their last be made aware of the good things that have escaped them, and shall bemoan their plight, and shall humble themselves before God. They shall continue doing so after the separation of their souls from their bodies."[47]

We can understand in only a limited way the nature of this experience, but it is common to all souls that "all men shall, after their physical death, estimate the worth of their deeds, and realize all that their hands have wrought."[48] Obviously those who have lived good lives will be immediately "rewarded" by a feeling of "joy and gladness as would be impossible to describe."[49] Whereas those who have lived "in error" shall "be seized with such fear and trembling, and shall be filled with such consternation, as nothing can exceed."[50] How long these conditions last, or what sequence of events or what spiritual process succeeds them, we can only imagine. But the sense of reward and punishment represented by the scriptural symbols of "Heaven" and "Hell" is experienced immediately.

Related to this question is the matter of whether or not "every soul without exception" will "achieve life everlasting."[51] In a response to this, 'Abdu'l-Baha has stated:

> Know thou that immortality belongeth to those souls in whom hath been breathed the spirit of life from God. All save these are lifeless—they are the dead, even as Christ hath explained in the Gospel text. He whose eyes the Lord hath opened will see the souls of men in the stations they will occupy after their release from the body. He will find the living ones thriving within the precincts of their Lord, and the dead sunk down in the lowest abyss of perdition.[52]

10. Baha'i Beliefs about The Second Coming of Christ

Since Baha'is believe in the continuous succession of prophets throughout history, each Manifestation is the return of the same spirit that the previous Manifestation reflected, and each Manifestation affirms this by alluding to the previous prophets and prophesying the future prophets. Thus, Christ stated:

> Therefore I send you prophets and wise men and scribes, some of whom you will kill and crucify, and some you will scourge in your synagogues and persecute from town to town.... O Jerusalem, Jerusalem, killing the prophets and stoning those who are sent to you![53]

Likewise in the Qur'an, Muhammad stated:

> Moreover, to Moses gave we "the Book," and we raised up apostles after him; and to Jesus, son of Mary, gave we clear proofs of his mission, and strengthened him by the Holy Spirit. So oft then as an apostle cometh to you with that which

your souls desire not, swell ye with pride, and treat some as imposters, and slay others?[54]

When Christ alluded to the Manifestations who would succeed Him, He used various appelations—the Counsellor, the Holy Spirit, the Son of Man. Likewise, on several occasions, Christ described various conditions that would accompany the advent of this figure. What is generally referred to as "The Second Coming," then, is the appearance that Christ described in such passages as Matthew, chapter 24; Mark, chapter 13; Luke, chapters 17 and 21; and John, chapter 16. These all seem to allude to a particularly significant return that would be accompanied by historically momentous circumstances. Likewise, various passages in the Old Testament allude to the appearance of Christ, but others, like the description of the "Desolation" in the book of Daniel, seem to prophesy a later point in history.

From the Baha'i view, Muhammad was the return of Christ, since He was the next Manifestation in history, and Christ was sometimes alluding to that appearance. The particular return that will usher in a universal transformation of mankind, however, the return commonly referred to as "The Second Coming," this Baha'is believe to be the appearance of Baha'u'llah. Likewise the historical events that are prefigured in the veiled metaphors and symbols of the scriptures have taken place, are currently taking place, or will shortly occur in the future.

There are numerous passages in the writings of Baha'u'-llah and 'Abdu'l-Baha that discuss this matter in detail, [55] and William Sears has written a most readable analysis of these prophesies regarding the Second Coming in his book *Thief in the Night: The Case of the Missing Millennium.*[56] A major theme in all of these is that while all the prophets have come to educate mankind "to carry forward an ever-advancing civilization"[57] this particular point in the spiritual evolution of mankind signals the fruition of all the previous stages of development:

Great indeed is this Day! The allusions made to it in all the

sacred Scriptures as the Day of God attest its greatness. The
soul of every Prophet of God, of every Divine Messenger, hath
thirsted for this wondrous Day. All the divers kindreds of the
earth have, likewise, yearned to attain it.[58]

Notes

[1] Shoghi Effendi, *The World Order of Baha'u'llah.* (Wilmette,
Ill.: Baha'i Publishing Trust, 1955), p. xi.

[2] Baha'u'llah, *The Hidden Worlds of Baha'u'llah*, trans. Shoghi
Effendi, rev. ed. (Wilmette, Ill.: Baha'i Publishing Trust, 1939), p.
11.

[3] Quoted in "The Open Door." (Wilmette, Ill.: Baha'i Publishing
Trust), pp. 6-7.

[4] *A Synopsis and Codification of "The Kitab-i-Aqdas."* (Haifa,
Israel: Baha'i World Centre, 1973), p. 58.

[5] *National Baha'i Review,* No. 121 (1983), p. 6.

[6] Ibid.

[7] The Universal House of Justice, Letter 23, April 1969.

[8] Quoted in "The Open Door," pp. 8-9.

[9] *Gleanings from the Writings of Baha'u'llah*, trans. Shoghi
Effendi, 2nd rev. ed. (Wilmette, Ill.: Baha'i Publishing Trust, 1976),
p. 155.

[10] "The Open Door," p. 7.

[11] *Some Answered Questions*, comp. and trans. Laura Clifford
Barney, rev. ed. (Wilmette, Ill.: Baha'i Publishing Trust, 1981), p.
228.

[12] Ibid., p. 239.

[13] "The Open Door," p. 7.

[14] Ibid.

[15] *Gleanings*, p. 156.

[16] Ibid., p. 157.

[17] Ibid., pp. 156-7.

[18] *Some Answered Questions*, p. 237.

[19] *Gleanings*, pp. 151-2.

[20] Ibid., p. 184.

[21] Ibid., p. 158.

22 Ibid., p. 171.

23 *Some Answered Questions*, p. 232.

24 "The Open Door," p. 9.

25 Ibid., pp. 7-8.

26 *Some Answered Questions*, p. 240.

27 Ibid., p. 232.

28 *Gleanings*, p. 154.

29 Ibid., p. 159.

30 *Gleanings*, p. 156.

31 See *Some Answered Questions*, pp. 110-112; J. E. Esslemont, *Baha'u'llah and the New Era* (Wilmette, Ill., 1980), pp. 6-7; Baha'-u'llah, *The Book of Certitude* (Wilmette, Ill.: Baha'i Publishing Trust, 1950), p. 143 ff; William Sears, *Thief in the Night* (Oxford: George Ronald, 1977), pp. 74-75.

32 Quoted by Shoghi Effendi in *World Order of Baha'u'llah*, p. 167.

33 The whole of Part One of *The Book of Certitude* focuses importantly on explaining the prophesies of Christianity and Islam.

34 *Some Answered Questions*, pp. 103-104.

35 *The Book of Certitude*, p. 117 ff.

36 *Gleanings*, pp. 151-2.

37 *Some Answered Questions*, p. 233.

38 Ibid., p. 237.

39 'Abdu'l-Baha in *Baha'i World Faith: Selected Writings of Baha'u'llah and 'Abdu'l-Baha*, rev. ed. (Wilmette, Ill.: Baha'i Publishing Trust, 1976), p. 240.

40 Ibid., p. 383.

41 *Gleanings*, p. 268.

42 *The Hidden Worlds of Baha'u'llah*, p. 11.

43 *Selections from the Writings of 'Abdu'l-Baha* (Haifa: Baha'i World Centre, 1978), p. 187.

44 "The Open Door," pp. 7-8.

45 Ibid., pp. 8-9.

46 Ibid., p. 9.

47 *Gleanings*, pp. 170-1.

48 Ibid., p. 171.

49 Ibid.

50 Ibid.

51 Selections from the *Writings of 'Abdu'l-Baha*, p. 189.

52 Ibid., pp. 189-190.

53 Matthew 23:34-7.

54 Muhammad, The Koran, trans. J. M. Rodwell (London: J. M. Dent, 1953), p. 346. (Sura "The Cow," verse 81.)

[55] See note 31.
[56] See note 31.
[57] *Gleanings*, p. 215.
[58] Ibid., p. 11.

A BAPTIST PERSPECTIVE

William L. Hendricks, Ph.D., Th.D.

Background of the Faith

This chapter must be *a* Baptist perspective, for there is no *the* Baptist perspective on anything. There are at least fifty-two kinds of Baptists in the United States ranging from the small (less than 200) two-seed-in-the-Spirit predestinarian Baptists to the large (nearly 15 million) Southern Baptist Convention. One of the general characteristics of Baptists is their fierce independence of viewpoint. Never trust a Baptist who says "All Baptists believe. . . ."

Most Baptists are born again. All Baptists die. They don't die because they are born again. They die because they are born. For death is a universal phenomenon and obviously religious preference doesn't change the biological inevitability of death. Yet religious beliefs can and do shape how one looks at death. In the first portion of the chapter, I will articulate a Baptist belief system which is drawn from Baptist sources. The theory of death I will articulate is extrapolated from experiences of thirty-five years in Baptist ministry, twenty-five of which have been spent teaching Baptist ministers in Southern Baptist seminaries. In the second part of the discussion, we must ask how theory fits practice, how Baptists relate to the reality of death, what positions they prefer in matters of life and death, and how they face the "technocracy of death" medically available in contemporary society.

The problem of sources is acute. As previously indicated, there is no Baptist dogma, i.e., an officially accepted doctrine that must be believed by all adherents of a religious community. There are generally accepted beliefs among Baptists, chief of which is the authority and integrity of Scripture.[1] Baptists are often called a people of the Book. And it was generally the case in the frontier life of our country that a second book completed the library of every farm house, namely a hymn book. Baptists began and continue both as biblicists (despite the scholars' aversion to the term) and as a singing people. The primary sources for this chapter are the Bible and Baptist hymnody. Baptists have drawn up formal, but no binding, statements about what they believe. These are called confessions of faith rather than creeds.[2] Baptists have, contrary to popular opinion, an honorable intellectual and academic heritage, and there are Baptist scholars who have written theologies from a Baptist perspective. These theologies have somewhat influenced Baptist ministers who were taught these sources, and these ministers have, in turn, molded the thinking of Baptist congregations. It must be acknowledged (to my regret) that the formal theological instruction plays only a minor part in shaping the beliefs of the Baptist in the pew.[3] All of these sources—Scripture, hymnody, confessions of faith and Baptist systematic theologies will be used, in that order and in a line of descending importance, as they have affected popular beliefs about death among some Baptists.

The Theory of Death

Aristotle is not the only one who used his powers of perception to see that death is an inevitable part of life (see his *Generation and Corruption*). Generations of Baptists, rural farming folk, have also observed and given rudimentary philosophical explanations of the cycles of birth and death in the world around us. Crops are planted so they may be harvested. Animals are raised to be used for food. These truisms were naturally adopted by rural people. Death as a phenomenon in nature and of the subhuman species required no explanation beyond the obvious; and the agrarian saying of Jesus "Truly, truly I say to you, unless a grain of wheat falls into the earth and dies, it remains by itself alone; but if it dies it bears much fruit" Jo. 12:24* embodies a self-evident, natural principle.

But the question of human death with its emotional entailments and its existential Angst is quite another matter. Most Baptists, aware of Aristotle or not, would accept his naturalist assumptions about death in nature. Few Baptists would emulate Aristotle's pupil, Alexander the Great, and be awakened each morning with the less than cheerful news "Alexander, someday you must die." But when it becomes apparent that one must die and that one's loved ones must die, then it is time to think theologically. The question arises, why must we die?

---

*All biblical quotations are from the New American Standard Version unless otherwise noted.

The Double View of Death

When the question of death as a human phenomenon arises and becomes, in fact, the boundary question that calls life and meaning into question, then one must have recourse to the sources of faith.[4]

The first place a Baptist would look for a theological rationale for death would be the Bible. And the first place in the Bible a Baptist would look for his theology would be the New Testament. And, within the New Testament, the first source of things theological would be Paul. And, within the writings of Paul, a universally known and frequently quoted passage is Rom. 6:23 "For the wages of sin is death, but the free gift of God is eternal life in Christ Jesus our Lord." Most Baptists would take this terse expression as the basis for their double view about death. That double view is on the one hand that death is evil and a punishment for sin, and on the other hand, that because of the death of Jesus Christ, death may be the gate to another, better life.

Whereas other groups of classical Christians tend to come to a theological focus for death sequentially through the Old Testament to the New, most Baptists would come at death consequentially and work back to Adam from the New Testament focus. This is especially true among those Baptists who have not been so greatly influenced by Calvinism and who do not have a formal doctrine of original sin. Most Baptists would say death came because of sin. All persons sin. Therefore, all die. Adam was the first of the line and just as he sinned we also will sin, therefore we must die (see Rom. 3, 5, I Cor. 15). The average Baptist is oblivious to, and unconcerned with, theories of transmission of original sin (see A. H. Strong's elaborate chart, Systematic Theology, p. 628). Most Baptists are certain that Adam was a historical figure, the first human. But most are certain that it is personal guilt and not any inherited guilt that brings about individual death. Corporate and covenantal ideas, so prominent in Reformed theology, have carried the day with some Baptists, but not many. For most Baptists, there are no ready academic answers as to why all people do sin, but there is solid biblical evidence (Rom. 3:23, 6:23, I Cor. 15:1-3); and any additional corroboration required may be found on the evening news, in the uneasy conscience of modern man, or by a long look in the mirror. This does not mean mankind is worthless, just ornery. Beyond the inevitable fact of sin and its ineluctable consequence of death, there is an inherent worth in mankind and a resolution of the dilemma posed by death. About the nature of mankind and the murky relationship to Adam, the "Baptist Faith and Message" says:

> Man was created by the special act of God, in His own image, and is the crowning work of His creation. In the beginning man was innocent of sin and was endowed by His Creator with freedom of choice. By his free choice man sinned against God and brought sin into the human race. Through the temptation of Satan man transgressed the command of God, and fell from his original innocence; whereby his posterity inherit a nature and an environment inclined toward sin, and as soon as they are capable of moral action become transgressors and are under condemnation. Only the grace of God can bring man into His holy fellowship and enable man to fulfill the creative purpose of God. The sacredness of human personality is evident in that God created man in His own image, and in that Christ died for man; therefore every man possesses dignity and is worthy of respect and Christian love.[5]

The unambiguous if unexplained first affirmation of Baptists as to death's cause is that death is a result of sin. Therefore, death is evil and is a woe that sinful mankind must face.

If death is the last enemy (I Cor. 15:26), what possible good can come from it? Must not we lose loved ones and grieve? Do we not all go down into the pit, gathered to our fathers echoing David's logical sentence "The child cannot come to me, but I can go to him" (referring to his dead son by Bathsheba). Grief is intense enough by virtue of the loss of those loved; it is intensified when death is viewed as related to sin. If sorrow joined with evil is Baptists' first expression about death, the negative aspect, what is the second?

The second way Baptists view death is as a cure and a release. Of course this insight of faith is maintained Christologically. Because of Christ's death, death has been overcome. By assuming the curse of death, Christ removes death's curses for us. And by virtue of Christ's resurrection we who believe in Him may have a resurrected life with Him in the world to come. "Truly, truly I say to you, he who hears my word, and believes Him who sent Me, has eternal life, and does not come into judgment but has passed out of death into life" (Jo. 5:24). "Truly, truly, I say to you, if anyone keeps my word he shall never see death" (Jo. 8:51). Baptists, with other Christians, affirm that the purpose of God has been revealed in Christ "who abolished death, and brought life and immortality to light through the Gospel" (II Tim. 1:10).

Obviously this abolition of death and the affirmation that Christ has overcome death are forensic declarations of faith. Baptists do not believe they will not have to die biologically. The reality of biological death is an incontrovertible reality. What the positive focus of faith assures is that God is with us in death, through it and beyond it. I Cor. 15 is the great Christian manifesto that death, the enemy of mankind, has been defeated by Christ in his resurrection. The double determination about death is that it is connected with sin and with salvation. It is obvious that theological value judgments and faith affirmation have heightened biological death by relating it to both the source of man's weakness and the possibility of his ultimate destiny. This double determination is a quasi-metaphorical use of the term death—a use that is related to other more strictly metaphorical uses of death.

Death as Metaphor

Baptists know (no less than Alexander the Great) that some day they must die biologically. Furthermore the dread of death is compounded because death is theologically related to sin, "the sting of death is sin" (I Cor. 15:56a). But death has been overcome "swallowed up in victory" (I Cor.

15:54c). For the Christian, these theological additions add grandeur, awe, and resolution to the dilemma. When one has faith that the ultimate dimension of life involves more than the physical and psychological expressions of human reality, then the resources of this faith dimension become the "real" or motivational springs of human existence. It may be metaphorical from a biological or psychological viewpoint that death is a result of sin and is overcome by Christ's death and resurrection, but from the believer's perspective these affirmations are just as "real" as the pragmatic fact of death.

What the believer means when he says death is overcome is that he is "not alone" in death and that through and beyond death there is a resolution to what otherwise seems a definitive closure to his existence. Rhapsodic singing expresses this metaphorical overcoming of death in the spiritual, "I Won't Have to Cross Jordan Alone," and in the old gospel song, "My Savior First of All." The first verse of the latter says:

> When life on earth is ended
> And I cross the swelling tide
> And the glory of His resurrection share,
> I shall know my Redeemer
> Over on the other side,
> And His face will be
> The first to greet me there
>
> *Refrain*
> I shall know Him, I shall know Him
> As redeemed by His side I shall stand.
> I shall know Him, I shall know Him
> By the prints of the nails in His hand.

In addition to the affirmations about faith, which speak of death as result of sin and death as overcome, there is a metaphorical use of death that Baptists often use in relation to the ethical and devotional expressions of their lives here and now.

This present-focused use of death as metaphor begins with

conversion. Baptists espouse a conversionist theology. This view, which speaks with the birth metaphor of being born again (Jo. 3), also speaks of a death metaphor of "dying to the old self." "For the mind set on the flesh is death, but the mind set on the Spirit is life and peace. And if Christ is in you, though the body is dead because of sin, yet the spirit is alive because of righteousness. But if the Spirit of Him who raised Jesus from the dead dwells in you, He who raised Christ Jesus from the dead will also give life to your mortal bodies through His Spirit who indwells you" (Rom. 8:6, 10-11). Baptists believe all were once dead in "sins and trespasses" (Eph. 2:1). There is therefore, theologically a spiritual death from which one enters into new life at conversion. The symbol of this is baptism, "we have been buried with Him through the baptism into death, in order that as Christ was raised from the dead through the glory of the Father, so we too might walk in newness of life" (Rom. 6:4). Furthermore the characteristics of a baptized convert are that "our old self was crucified with Him, that our body of sin might be done away with, that we should no longer be slaves to sin; for he who has died is freed from sin" (Rom. 6:6-7). Baptists usually understand this "dying to the old self" and "dying to sin" as a dynamic process rather than a forensic announcement or an instantaneous achievement. Gospel songs such as "Must Jesus Bear the Cross Alone," "More Like the Master," and "Higher Ground" are typical expressions of this process of dying to one way of life or a lower nature while struggling to attain new life. Defining the Christian life as a type of dying—and the ethical struggle as the "overcoming" of death is a metaphorical usage that gives a more sustained and experiential flavor to the idea of death. Without these metaphorical uses death would remain an unresolved absolute. These metaphorical uses of death are of great value to Baptists in relativizing and relating to biological death.

By metaphorical extension, death is not merely biological termination. It is also: (1) a spiritual state of unbelief, (2) that is overcome by a new life, being born again, (3) and this overcoming of death is symbolized by being buried in the waters of baptism, (4) these experiences lead to a new way of life which is daily overcoming and "putting to death" the old person by desirable ethical actions. This rich metaphorical use of death makes the term a part of the ongoing process of life and tends to relativize, for the believer, the idea of death as only a final, punctiliar act.

One final metaphorical use of death is important in a Baptist perspective of death, namely, the "second death." The biblical funding for the concept of "second death" is in the Book of Revelation (Rev. 2:11, 20:14, 21:8). "Second death" is a theological term for the undesirable and irrevocable state of the wicked in the world to come. Baptists feel they have escaped this second death and are obliged to help others do likewise. The idea of a "second death" as a final state of the wicked is an impetus to Baptist evangelism. The "second death" is not death in the sense of ceasing to be or a passing into non-existence. It is a final confirmation of spiritual death, the "first death" of unbelievers. Second death is the negative pole of the two-fold inevitability that mankind faces.

The Two-Fold Inevitability

Baptists would add a third sure thing to the two-fold inevitabilities of life and death. The third element is judgment. "And inasmuch as it is appointed for men to die once, and after this comes judgment" (Heb. 9:27). The inevitability of judgment is, for Baptists, as certain as the inevitability of death. In an annotated edition of the Bible published by Broadman Press the section on judgment includes the following biblical references: I. Chron. 16:33, Job 21:30, Ps. 9:7, Ps. 50:3, Ps. 96:13, Eccl. 12:14, Matt. 3:12, 11:22, 12:36, 16:27 (and parallels), II Cor. 5:10, II Tim. 4:1, and Heb. 9:27.

All world religions have concepts of the afterlife. Most world religions have a perspective of judgment with a resultant system of rewards and punishments. Classical Christianity is no exception. In some areas of contemporary Christian theology the idea of a judgment in the world to come has diminished, and in even more circles, the reality of punishment and/or a place for it has declined in belief systems. Among a majority of Baptists these doctrines are still firmly held.

The theological, two-fold inevitability for mankind is death and judgment, and the two-fold, inevitable results of judgment are heaven or hell. Heaven and hell are conceived of as places where the redeemed and the damned either receive their rewards and undergo eternal felicity or are alienated from God. In one there is the fellowship with God, in the other the possibility of fellowship does not exist. The one is characterized by mansions, golden streets, home, and reunion with loved ones. The other by outer darkness, fire, torment, isolation. Scriptures that corroborate these pictures of heaven are: Matt. 6:20, 25:34; Lk. 15:7; 16; Jo. 5:28-29; 14; II Peter 3:13; Rev. 2:7, 20-22. Scriptures concering hell are: Matt. 3:12; 5:29; 7:13-14; 8:11; 10:28; 13:49-50; 18:9; 23:15; Mk. 9:43; Jas. 3:6; II Pet. 2:4; Rev. 9:1; 20:10; 21:8. Whereas formerly both the concepts of heaven and hell were believed with equal intensity, in contemporary practical church life, heaven is stressed more than hell. The accent is on the positive rather than the negative. The older Baptist theologies of Strong[2] and Mullins[3] give equal space to hell and to heaven; in fact, Strong gives considerably more space to hell. Conner[4] has more about heaven than hell. Moody,[5] the most recent author of a major Baptist systematic theology, has no discussion of hell. The American Baptist, Langdon Gilkey, affirms that the redemptive love of God will overcome all opposition.[6]

Baptist hymnody demonstrates this preference for the positive in such hymns and gospel songs as "O Love, That Will Not Let Me Go," "In the Sweet By and By," "Ring the Bells of Heaven" and, in some circles, the still much-used funeral song, "I'll Fly Away, O Glory." The "Baptist Faith and Message" has two brief sentences about the fate of the dead. "The unrighteous will be consigned to Hell, the place of everlasting punishment. The righteous in their resurrected and glorified bodies will dwell forever in Heaven with the Lord."[7]

Given the inevitability of death and the inescapability of

judgment with its indubitable results of heaven or hell, Baptists have a theology that places significant weight on death as a final door to destiny. This heightened status of death as gate to eternal felicity or damnation has pastoral and psychological consequences. What happens in death and after death? Since the inevitable comes upon us, curiosity about the particulars of what happens at death and beyond is natural.

The Way It Happens

What happens when you die? That's a question asked by eight- and eighty-year-olds and by people of all ages in between. Understandably, Baptists are not too specific about these matters. The reason they are not is because the biblical sources do not provide details. The old Reformation dictum "where the Bible speaks we speak" and its concommitant principle "where it is silent, so are we" is invoked.

The outline of a personal eschatology (doctrine of last things) would involve the following elements: At the "appointed time" one dies. There is a strong Calvinist undercurrent of providence in setting the boundaries of individual existence. The dead go immediately into the presence of God in a conscious state. The parable of Dives and Lazarus (Lk. 16) is often used as a proof-text for this assertion. The dead are in heaven or hell in some intermediate form (II Cor. 5:1-5). Baptists do not, on the one hand, espouse the doctrine of soul sleep until the general resurrection of the dead; nor, on the other hand, do they affirm that the final, general resurrection of all persons takes place at death. Consequently, some type of conscious intermediate form is required. The dead are "souls" waiting the resurrection of the body. (No amount of Baptist scholarly wholism about the totality of the person seems able to shake the Platonic notion of the flight of a soul from a body—an idea held by most Baptists.) At the end of the age, Christ comes, ushers in the new age, confirms by final judgment what is already *de facto*, namely the reward of the righteous and the punishment of the wicked. Judgment is preceded by the resurrection of the body. Judgment is followed by, or simultaneous with, the formation of a new heaven and a new earth with all wickedness shut away so that corruption and destruction cannot continue. This outline of things to come is pieced together from various portions of the New Testament (Matt. 16:27; 18:8-9; 19:28; 24:27, 30, 36, 44; 24:31-46; 26:64; Mark 8:38; 9:43-48; Luke 12:40, 48; 16:19-26; 17:22-37; 21:27-28; John 14:1-3; Acts 1:11; 17:31; Rom. 14:10; 1 Cor. 4:5; 15:24-28, 35-58; 2 Cor. 5:10; Phil. 3:20-21; Col. 1:5; 3:4; 1 Thess. 4:14-18; 5:1 ff.; 2 Thess. 1:7 ff.; 2; 1 Tim. 6:14; 2 Tim. 4:1, 8; Titus 2:13; Heb. 9:27-28; James 5:8; 2 Peter 3:7 ff.; 1 John 2:28; 3:2; Jude 14; Rev. 1:18; 3:11; 20:1 to 22:13). An overview is drawn especially from Rev. 21:1-5:·

> Then I saw a new heaven and a new earth; for the first heaven and the first earth had passed away, and the sea was no more. And I saw the holy city, new Jerusalem, coming down out of heaven from God, prepared as a bride adorned for her husband; and I heard a great voice from the throne saying, "Behold, the dwelling of God is with men. He will dwell with them, and they shall be his people, and God himself will be with them; he will wipe away every tear from their eyes, and death shall be no more, neither shall there be mourning nor crying nor pain any more, for the former things have passed away."
>
> And he who sat upon the throne said, "Behold I make all things new." Also he said, "Write this, for these words are trustworthy and true."

Songs expressing the joy and blessings of the final condition of mankind abound. "There's A New Name Written Down In Glory," "When They Ring Those Golden Bells for You and Me," "Victory in Jesus," and, of recent vintage and much in vogue, the choral work "The King Is Coming." I recall only one gospel song used to any extent in Baptist congregations that regales the terrors of hell, and that description is found in the middle verses of the Appalachian Gospel Song, "Brethren We Have Met to Worship" in which one sees his father, mother, brothers, and sisters "sinking down," "trembling on the brink of woe." He is advised that "death is coming, hell is moving" and is asked "can you bear to see them go?"

The features of the afterlife are, for the most part, sketchy. What is certain is that one is in God's presence, one is conscious, one is resurrected. Death is overcome. Life goes on. The last enemy has been defeated. Absent loved ones are "with the Lord." And that same Lord who came to earth at Bethlehem will come at the end of the age to judge, reward and punish. The destiny of those who trust in Christ is secure, for the "friend we have in Jesus" is the guarantor of these promises.

When one accents the positive all seems to the good, but there are two grim realities that persist: the fact of physical death and the biblical teaching that evil intensifies "in the last days," which means that there will be increased suffering and trials even for, and perhaps especially for, Christians. All could be corrected if there were some possibilities of escaping either death and/or suffering and crisis at the end of the age. Some Baptists hold to such a possibility.

An Escapist Possibility

In some of Paul's earliest correspondence there is comfort given about believers who have "fallen asleep." Then he says " then [at Christ's coming] we who are alive and remain shall be caught up together with them in the clouds to meet the Lord in the air, and thus we shall always be with the Lord. Therefore comfort one another with these words" (I Thess. 4:17-18).

What a comfort it would be if we could escape physical death! And it is with this intent that modern interpreters read the passage. The original intention of the passage was to give some word of well-being about those who had died before Christ came back. And that is still, in my opinion, the basic intention of the biblical writer.

Yet the question intrudes, does the Bible say some people will not have to face physical death? If so, wouldn't this be the ultimate panacea and a splendid "selling point" for Christianity? The answer is yes, but it is a highly qualified yes, which must be accompanied by the full expression of Paul's teaching. The full expression is that only those alive when Christ does terminate the age will be "translated," for want of a better term, and will not undergo physical death.

A more recent, less documentable, view is held by some Baptists, via dispensational theology, that Christians will be taken away from any suffering and trauma that precedes the final days.[8] This refinement provides a double protection against suffering and death.

The two things are not of equal certainty on the basis of biblical teaching. The first possibility of escape from death is a possibility only if one is living at the end of the age. The second possibility is also dependent upon being in the last days. But it seems contrary to the New Testament pattern of suffering as a necessary part of the Christian pilgrimage.

Certainly ours is an age that is apocalyptic in outlook. Furthermore, those individuals and groups, and there are many Baptists among them, who see signs of the end of the times are certainly making a large appeal and a good "selling point" out of a theological system that promises actual escape from death and probable escape from suffering. The dilemma of these escapist possibilities is time. The more of it that passes and the greater the number of people who die and suffer, the more diminishing are the returns of a system that capitalizes on these special escape clauses.

The above section has dealt with theory and belief systems of Baptists. How are these theological beliefs related to life and death in the actual *Sitz im Leben* of Baptists today? How does theology affect life and, in particular, how does a theology of death affect the life of one who takes it seriously?

Forging Theory to Fact

These boundary situations of life and death are lonely and momentous occasions. This is especially true of death, for the birthing is a cooperative, participatory process ordinarily accompanied by joy and sustained caring of an individual whose thought processes are, as yet, unformed. Whereas death is individual, possibly surrounded by pain and Angst and amid grieving persons, or worse, without them in sterile medical facilities. It is very difficult to know how one relates a faith theory to dying for several reasons: 1) Until recently, more specifically the 1950's and the early Kübler-Ross research, people did not speak of death. 2) The ministers, priests, and rabbis who were charged with "comforting the dying" and/or the grieving interpreted what the theological theory of death was supposed to mean to persons *in extremis* rather than listened for how those undergoing the experience were relating faith and fact. 3) Properly speaking one does not experience death, only dying. 4) Modern medical science has attenuated "life" to such a degree that the boundaries between life and death are controversial medically and legally.

Despite these factors, and in part because of them, "death" has become a significant topic in the last half of the twentieth century. Religious communities, due to technological possibilities and the shifting of social mores, have been obliged to make formal statements about matters of life and death. *In nuce*, the sources for this second section, for want of adequate research based on appropriate questionnaires, will have to be based on those pronouncements of Baptists about matters of life and death, my experiences of teaching Baptist ministers for twenty-five years, and my experiences with laypersons in dozens of churches I have served as interim minister. The following conclusions are purely my own and I will take responsibility for them even while insisting that they are broadly based in experience, if not scientifically verifiable by the research instruments of the social sciences.

The Double View of Death

Baptists have a theoretical bifocal view of death, death as curse due to sin, and death as redemptive possibility because of Christ's vicarious death. In my opinion, they raise one focus of this bifocal view much more than the other. The less-used focus is death-as-curse-of-sin view. This is partic- ularly true in instances of infant mortality. In this century one never hears about why, theologically, infants die. The death is attributed, when possible, to social or biological reasons if appropriate. If not, generally mystery and other principles of the theodicy are invoked. But in all instances the mercy of God and the loving redemption of Christ are held forth as resolutions to the grieving as the simple focus of theological counsel. And, in my opinion, this is all to the good.[9]

The doctrine of the priesthood of all believers teaches Bap- tists that they are individually competent and responsible before God for their own spiritual well-being. The logical extension of this doctrine is that God cares for those who are, for whatever reason, incompetent to exercise that responsi- bility. Applying this to infants creates the one-focus view of death. Further, the priesthood of all believers declares that we are to exercise a priestly concern for the incompetent, the uninformed and the impuissant. When this aspect of the priesthood of all believers is applied, the roots of Baptist evangelistic impulses are seen. One further step grows from this caring concern of the priesthood on behalf of the hap- less. It is the affirmation that life is the gift of God and must be nurtured, particularly for those who cannot help them- selves. This is the positive basis for Baptists' objection to abortions in most instances.[10] When extended to the disad- vantaged this regard for the life of others and the guardian- ship under God for the disabled has provided the impetus for the enviable record Baptists have had in work with the handicapped, the homeless, and others in need of Christian social ministries.[11]

This affirmation of life as God's gift and the acceptance of the guardian, priestly concern for the hapless are also the basis for a denial of euthanasia.

Returning from the social concerns to the responsible individual I suspect that most Baptists would not intrinsic- ally relate their own individual biological death to any form of guilt or ancestral sin. Inveterate individualism would tend to see death more as a mark of finitude than a sign of culpability. Whatever Scripture says about the corporate involvements of the individual or the relationships between all men and Adam is left to be worked out by the theologians and the clergy. Baptist lay persons tend toward responsible individualism, even in matters of their own deaths.

The practical stress of Baptists about death is largely, if not exclusively, the positive expression that Christ's death has made our death more bearable, for by His death and resurrection He has overcome eternal death. Likewise, in His death He has identified with mankind in such a way that He is with us in our death. The music Baptists sing is almost entirely on this positive focus. Whether it be the spirited chorus, taught to children, "I've Got a Home In Gloryland that Outshines the Sun" or the more sonorous "O Love That Will Not Let Me Go," the emphasis is on deliverance from death. What is in theory a double view of death becomes, in practice, more of a single focus. The "as in Adam all die, even so in Christ shall all be made alive" is taken seriously by Baptists. But they assume that the individual has a responsibility in both parts of that dictum.

Death as Metaphor

It is my opinion that by an extensive metaphorical use of death Baptists find it easier and more comforting to face biological death. The autonomy and hegemony of biological death has created an absolute with attendant fear and dread. If death is more than biology, if in a variety of guises and on a number of levels, one has already experienced death or met it and survived, then the grim reaper is not so grim. Albeit unconscious and unreflective, and I feel it is both, this flattening of death into process serves a good purpose and may actually assist believers in the process of dying.

By the belief that all persons actively rebel against God, place themselves as aliens to him, and actualize the destructive possibilities of existence and by calling this condition spiritual death, Baptists add a dimension to the concept of death. This dimension of being lost, unsaved, "dead in sins and trespasses" is overcome by being born again, by exercising the gift of faith, by an experience that transforms by its promise of hope and by its promise of a restored wholeness with God, the ground of one's being. Conversion is an emergence from spiritual death. Therefore death, in some of its expanded dimensions, can be overcome. The liturgical experience of baptism is a visible sign of this renewal. Baptism is a rite of passage, which among Baptists (who adhere to believer's baptism) is performed upon those who are surrounded by relatives and an affirming community who see one "buried with Christ in baptism and rise to walk in newness of life." This transformation, renewal and harbinger of ultimate resurrection is a powerful spiritual and psychological assurance of the overcoming of death.

Furthermore, the Christian pilgrimage is a constant struggle to overcome the lesser self. This "putting to death the old man" is a way of defeating death in life. The ethical actions of Christian conduct should be, in my opinion and often are according to my observation, placed against ultimate values. Why should one give up "enjoyable" habits and actions here and now even if they contradict Christian mores? Because ultimately they shape one who is an essential person, and if one's way of life and tastes are contrary to the exclusively life-affirming and positive conditions of the eternal order, there will be a radical adjustment necessary to enter God's world. This daily dying is conducive to ethical and life-affirming actions now. It is also preparatory for the eternal dimension. Among Baptists a common way of expressing this notion is "don't be so worldly that you won't enjoy God's world."

Thus, by way of extension, Baptists have met and fought death many times. To geriatric persons who have used these metaphors, there is bound to be some surplus of comfort when they apply this same principle to biological death, which by relativization has become one form, but not the only form, of death.

The Two Options

A theological, metaphorical use of death provides a broadening of the idea of death. The rigorous and rigid notion of two options following death—heaven or hell—promotes the narrowing of death as the passage to ultimate destiny, felicitous or fatal.

It is obvious how the doctrine of heaven would comfort and sustain believers. It is no less obvious that the doctrine of hell would pose many difficulties for its adherents. The first dilemma for one who believes in hell is the obvious pain of eternal separation from loved ones who are not believers. This is handled in the following ways. Funeral services for unbelievers, those who have consciously rejected Christ, are usually as comforting as possible for those who attend. The funeral service is, after all, for the living. The goodness and mercy of God are spoken of as well as any and all humanly desirable characteristics of the deceased. The general attitude is one of emphasizing the positive, and providing bases for future ministry to the mourners. Ministers, when queried, will add some extenuating theological affirmations. These are: 1) God only is judge of all persons, 2) people are judged according "to the light" (awareness, or opportunities they have) (cf. Rom. 1), and 3) there are degrees of rewards and punishments, (cf. Jesus' parables Lk: 7:41-43; 12:47-48; 19: 12-27). There may be those who mourn morbidly or in a sustained traumatic fashion for dead loved ones who were not believers, but I have not known of any personally. I have "heard the confession" of a few older Baptists who acknowledged (despite the formal theology and the general Baptist view of biblical teachings on the subject) beliefs in universalism (all mankind will be saved), annihilationism (the unbelieving do not go into eternal life but pass out of existence), that there is no life after this life, and even one hesitant affirmation of reincarnation. Whereas these individual expressions are not numerous, they are an outgrowth of the individualism of Baptists who sometimes extend the "priesthood of the believers" to mean that they may tailor doctrine and biblical teachings to suit their preferences.

The positive use made of the doctrine of hell is a rationale for a militant evangelism. In other words, the best way to avoid the consequences of hell is to accept the offer of heaven and consequently to "seek the salvation of our kindred and acquaintances"[12] so that they too will share the comfort of the promise of being with God in fellowship eternally. It is this positive provision that will be explored in the following section.

What Actually Happens

People ask more questions and desire more specific details than the biblical materials answer. Based on the sources above, a brief resumé of what happens to the believer at death and beyond would be: individuals undergo the transition of death, i.e. a loss of consciousness; one "wakes up," to use an extension of the New Testament analogy of death as sleep, in the presence of God; one remains with God in a conscious state and in an intermediate form until the final, general resurrection, at which point one is given a final resurrection form and dwells eternally as a recognizable being embodying essential continuity with one's historical identity. Loved ones are known and reunited. Whereas, marriage in heaven is not a physical exercise of sexuality (cf. Matt. 22:30), there is no reason to exclude sexual identity as male or female or partnerships from the eternal dimension. The above is based on a logical extension of the biblical theophanies (resurrection appearances) of Jesus and the return to the historical dimension of dead persons, e.g. Moses and Elijah at the transfiguration.

Unanswered or more tenuous are the specific questions people want to know. Will infants grow? Will we live as families? Are physical abnormalities corrected? Presumably so since it is a perfect world. Can a suicide go to heaven? Yes, if one has established a relationship of forgiveness with God in this life, it may be assumed one can ask forgiveness of a final sin in the world to come.[13] What age will we be in heaven? Some incautious ministers have suggested 21, others 33, Jesus' historical age. By and large pastors and professors acknowledge that such specific information is beyond our resources and leave matters in the hands of God.

The phrase the "Baptist Faith and Message" uses about the state of the dead would be the phrase most repeated and held by Baptists. The dead are "with the Lord."

The Escapist Possibility

What of the escape clause? Will those who are living at Christ's return die? No. But two observations should be noted: 1) It is not known whether "translation," the going into the eternal dimension directly without undergoing physical death (e.g. Elijah), is intrinsically any different from death; the transition is analogous to sleep with its next moment of conscious waking. 2) One must reckon that, according to biblical materials (Matt. 25:13; Mk. 13:32), one cannot know the specific time of the end of the age. Many people and their elaborate systems of the end times have lived and died. The only specific apocalyptist one should take seriously is the sign-carrying recluse who has left all to proclaim the end. And what one should take seriously about such an apocalyptist is his zeal, not his knowledge.

It is my experience that geriatric persons do not take too seriously the apocalyptic escape clause. Aging persons, by and large, are not planning on getting out of life alive. Many, via the routes of pain and problems, have come with firm faith to look upon death as a friend and even a welcome relief. It is often the young, the over-achieving middle-aged, who in the blush of vigor and strength and in the period of acquisition of things (all of which are heavily insured) desire the insurance of getting out without death. And one suspects that if it were put to a vote, most people who are agitating academically for an immediate closure of the age would vote for a delay. Most senior citizens have lived long enough to take life and death as it comes. The promise of grace, the prospect of heaven, these are the mainstays of our faith. As to our fate and that of those we love, we are able to say—and most often do reply—that they and we through Jesus Christ are "with the Lord."

Notes

[1]   William Richardson White, *Baptist Distinctives* (Nashville: Sunday School Board of the Southern Baptist Convention, 1946) pp. 12-20. Harold L. Fickett, *Baptist Beliefs—A Series of Seven Studies in Distinctive Doctrines* (Nashville: Broadman Press, 1945), pp. 2-8. Herschel H. Hobbs, *The Baptist Faith and Message* (Nashville: Convention Press, 1971), pp. 18-30.

[2]   William Latane Lumpkin, *Baptist Confessions of Faith*, rev. ed. (Valley Forge: Judson Press, 1969). W. J. McGlothlin, *Baptist Confessions of Faith* (Philadelphia: American Baptist Publication Society, 1911), pp. ix-xii.

[3]   James Petigru Boyce, *Abstracts of Systematic Theology* (Baltimore: H. M. Wharton, 1887). Walter Thomas Conner, *Christian Doctrine* (Nashville: Broadman Press, 1937). Langdon Brown Gilkey, *Message and Existence* (New York: Seabury Press, 1979). William L. Hendricks, *A Theology for Children* (Nashville: Broadman Press, 1980). Dale Moody, *The World of Truth* (Grand Rapids: W. B. Eerdmans Pub., 1981). Edgar Young Mullins, *The Christian Religion in its Doctrinal Expression* (Nashville: Sunday School Board of the Southern Baptist Convention). Augustus Hopkins Strong, *Systematic Theology* (Philadelphia: Judson Press, 1907).

[4]   Many Baptists are oblivious to Heidegger's definition that "life is unto death," and many Baptist ministers have railed against what they hear of existentialism. Nevertheless, the strong experiential and implicit common sense realism of Baptists would bear a parallel translation of theological pietism to many existentialist insights.

[5]   "The Baptist Faith and Message" Nashville: The Sunday School Board of the Southern Baptist Convention, 1963, p. 10.

[6]   See above in note 3.

[7] "Baptist Faith and Message," p. 15.

[8] For an explanation of this view see Ray Summers, *The Life Beyond* (Nashville: Broadman Press, 1959). For an explanation of this exclusion of Christians from suffering see Dwight Pentecost's *Things to Come: A Study in Biblical Eschatology* (Grand Rapids: Zondervan Pub. House, 1972).

[9] See my *Theology for Children* (Nashville: Broadman Press, 1980).

[10] It is my opinion that it is a stronger position to stress this positive aspect than it is to belabor exclusively the prescriptions of the divine commands against killing, which serve as the necessary negative base for these positions.

[11] Marv Know and Dan Martin, *Challenge of the Cities* (Atlanta: Home Mission Board of the Southern Baptist Convention, 1981). Arthur B. Rutledge, *Mission to America: A Century and a Quarter of Southern Baptist Home Missions, rev. ed.* (Nashville: Broadman Press, 1976), pp. 172-183. "Program Report of the Home Mission Board" in *Annual of the Southern Baptist Convention* (Nashville, Executive Committee, Southern Baptist Convention).

[12] A phrase taken from a church covenant widely used in Southern Baptist Churches found in Walter Hines Sims, *Baptist Hymnal* (Nashville: Convention Press, 1956), p. 476.

[13] See a sermon on suicide available from the author.

BUDDHISM

Anne C. Klein, Ph.D.

Background of the Faith

Discussions of impermanence and death are at the heart of Buddhism's understanding of the human situation and recommendations for its transformation. These views derive from the historical Buddha, known as Gautama or Shakyamuni. He is revered as an extraordinary teacher who, in the 5th century B.C., demonstrated how enlightenment is attained. He is neither the first nor the only enlightened Buddha to appear, but what sets Gautama apart is that he revealed his attainment when the teachings of the previous Buddha, Kashyapa, who lived prior to historical time, had disappeared. Having manifested enlightenment at age 35, he spent the remaining forty-five years of his life teaching others how to attain it.[1] All the many schools of Buddhism throughout Asia trace their origins to the discourses known as *sutras*, regarded as spoken by Gautama during this period. Moreover, it is commonly understood that Gautama's observation of human disease and death provided a major impetus force for his spiritual quest.

According to Buddhist legends, Gautama was born a prince in the Shakya clan of northern India. At his birth a seer predicted he would excel either as a worldly monarch or spiritual leader. His father, wishing to ensure the former, ordered all persons whose ugly, decrepit, or unwholesome appearance might inspire other-worldly interests, to be barred from the royal compound, and did not allow the young prince beyond its confines. In time, Gautama married and became a father; he reached the age of twenty-nine having known only the luxurious life of his father's contrivance. Certain Hindu gods intervened at this juncture to alter the young man's goals forever.[2] On three different occasions they caused to appear along the prince's chariot route a sick man, a very old man, and finally, a corpse. Stunned at what he had never seen before, the sheltered prince demanded an explanation. Each incident was more disturbing than the previous one. After the third experience, the encounter with death,

> Courageous though he was, the king's son was suddenly filled with dismay. Leaning his shoulder against the top of the chariot rail, he spoke these words in a forceful voice: This is the end which has been fixed for all, and yet the world forgets its fears and takes no heed!... Turn back the chariot! This is not time...for pleasure excursions. How could an intelligent person pay no heed at a time of disaster, when he was aware of his impending destruction?[3]

Returning home, the prince began to meditate on birth and

death. Soon his mind was concentrated and blissful. At this juncture a religious mendicant approached and revealed that "...terrified by birth and death, [I] have adopted a homeless life to win salvation. Since all that lives is doomed to extinction... I search for that most blessed state in which extinction is unknown."[4] His sense of urgency aroused by this confrontation with death, Gautama left home to seek the "blessed state of freedom."[5] Specifically he sought liberation from the endless round of birth and death known by Hindus and Buddhists alike as *saṃsāra*. He began seven years of severe ascetic practices, according to the custom of his day. When these practices brought him to the brink of death rather than to liberation, he became determined to forge his own path.

The culmination of this endeavor occurred under a pipal tree in Bodhgaya, in northeast India about 531 B.C. Buddhist tradition holds that Gautama took his seat there in the evening, vowing not to arise until he achieved enlightenment. He meditated throughout the night and attained his goal at dawn. In doing so, he became the fourth Buddha of the present aeon, during which one thousand persons will openly reveal themselves as Buddhas in our world. This world, most Buddhists believe, is one of the billion worlds that make up a world system. The billion such world systems in the cosmos all go through cyclical periods of production, abiding, destruction, and disappearance.[6] There is no time envisioned when all billion world systems—which include heavens and hells into which one can be reborn for long periods of time—will be destroyed simultaneously so that continued rebirth is impossible.

According to the older traditions of Buddhism, especially Theravada, "the way of the Elders," Gautama is the only person in the present aeon who will attain Buddhahood.[7] Thus, practitioners in this tradition do not seek Buddhahood but liberation from cyclic existence as an *Arhat*. This term is variously etymologized as "Worthy One" or "Foe Destroyer," one's own afflictions and limitations being the foe that prevents liberation. After an Arhat attains liberation, he spends the remainder of his life in beneficial activities, especially teaching. At his death, his continuum is extinguished in a state known as parinirvana, and he never again takes rebirth.

Mahayana Buddhists, whose traditions emerged in force in India 400 years after Buddha's death, consider the nature of the mind to be such that its utter cessation is impossible. Thus, they find Hinayana mistaken regarding the final destiny of its Arhats.[8] According to Mahayana, Arhats eventually encounter compassionate Buddhas who teach them to attain full enlightenment. In the Indo-Tibetan Mahayana tradition, both male and female practitioners are exhorted to seek the complete enlightenment of Buddhahood in order to fulfill their ultimate religious goal of offering maximum help to humanity. As a Buddha one does not disappear at death but has full control over the process of death and rebirth, conjoined with an omniscient understanding of where and how one can be of most help. Buddhas continuously take birth or manifest in ways and places that provide greatest help to others. Virtually all Mahayana schools believe that every living being can attain Buddhahood.[9] Moreover, countless persons have already attained this station, though they do not necessarily reveal themselves as enlightened but take on any appropriate or useful role.

Buddhism flourished in India until the 11th century B.C. when a combination of internal political and economic changes, especially repeated Muslim invasions from the northwest, virtually destroyed it, leaving only small pockets in the northeasternmost regions of India to continue. By that time, Buddhism had spread to much of Asia. Buddhist emissaries became established in Central Asia by the first century B.C.; from there Buddhism made its entry into the Han Dynasty of China.[10] Monks sent by the Indian King Ashoka in the third century B.C. brought Buddhism to Sri Lanka and Burma. In the 7th century A.D., Indian Buddhist scholars and adepts visiting Tibet initiated an extensive period of contact with Indian Buddhist thought. From these three areas—Sri Lanka and Burma, China, and Tibet, Buddhism gradually spread yet further abroad.

China, where Mahayana Buddhism predominated, was a

major force in the first millennium of Buddhist history.
From there, Buddhism travelled via Korea to Japan in the
sixth century. Chan or Zen first surfaced in seventh-century
China, later taking hold in Korea and Japan. Since the
1950's Soto and Rinzai Zen have been popular in the United
States; these date back to 13th-century Japanese developments in the Zen tradition.

The Theravada Buddhism initially fostered by Ashoka's
emissaries in Sri Lanka and Burma took hold in the 12th
century in Cambodia, and later in the 13th century in Thai-
land.[11] Since the mid-1970's Theravada insight meditation
teachers have established centers and conducted meditation
retreats in the United States and other Western countries.

Another major sphere of Buddhist influence developed
north of India. In the 7th century teams of Indian and Tibetan translators began a four-hundred-year-long collabora-
tion for the purpose of translating Indian sutras and com-
mentaries into Tibetan. Mahayana held sway in Tibet and
in the countries that identified with its religious traditions:
Sikkhim, Ladakh (both now part of India), Bhutan, Mongo-
lia, and the Sherpa peoples of Nepal.[12] In the last 15 years,
teachers from all four orders of Tibetan Buddhism—
Nyingma, Geluk, Kagyu, and Sakya—have established centers in the West. Thus, the present century has been paradox-
ically significant for Buddhist history. Ravages of war and
revolution have virtually destroyed it along with other great
cultural achievements of Cambodia, China, Laos, Tibet, and
Vietnam. At the same time, and to a significant degree aided
by the dispersal of Asian refugees, Buddhist influence has
been increasingly felt in the U.S., Canada, Western Europe,
and areas of Australia, New Zealand, and South America.

Major Principles of Buddhist Practice

On the eve of his enlightenment, Gautama saw the cyclical birth, death and rebirth of all living beings everywhere.
He recalled innumerable past lives, others' and his own,

linking this knowledge with a direct understanding of the
process of *karma*, the cause and effect of actions.

> With the purified divine eye surpassing that of (ordinary)
> human beings, I see people as they move on or come to be; I
> comprehend that beings are mean, excellent, comely, ugly,
> proceeding well or proceeding badly according to the conse-
> quences of their actions...[13]

Buddhas are considered the most exalted type of beings that
exist. However, they neither created the world nor arbitrate
rewards and punishments after death. This is governed by
the process known as the cause and effect of actions, or
karma, according to which, just as fire heats and ice chills,
good actions lead to happiness and bad ones to suffering.
This process has been at work beginninglessly. Unlike the
West where, as classically stated by Aquinas, an infinite
regress of cause and effect is widely considered unworkable,
Buddhists find this less problematic than explaining how a
first cause such as a creator deity could arise. Buddhists thus
find it more logical to propose that the universe has no
creator-god and no first moment.[14] Buddhas and other special god-like beings can help one to cultivate the virtues that
yield happiness in future lives, but it is one's own behavior
that brings this about. Circumstances of life and death thus
result from one's own actions, not from judgment by a super-
ior being. Because even the best rebirth leads to suffering
and death, and because as long as one lives, one inevitably
creates causes for future rebirths, the only way to eliminate
suffering is to escape this process entirely. One does this by
changing the mind in specified ways. The training involved,
and the type of mind cultivated, all bear on Buddhism's
discussion of death.

Thus, death and its sister subject, impermanence, are significant in the mythic origins of Buddhism as well as the
meditative and philosophical traditions that are an important part of its religious life. Following several strands of
Buddhist discourse, we will discuss the fact and nature of
death in several contexts. Briefly stated, these have to do
with (1) the importance and method of facing one's own

mortality, (2) the relevance of this understanding for a classic presentation of the path to enlightenment, (3) the stages of dying and their significance for practitioners of meditation and, (4) descriptions of the period after death and of rebirth. Because Buddhist traditions are far too diverse to accommodate with brevity, and because specifics are more informative than generalities, we will focus on the Tibetan Mahayana's particularly rich treatment of these four issues.

Facing Mortality: Death as Incentive

For Buddhists, the conviction that birth follows death heightens the imperative to make best use of the present life. Although rebirth is guaranteed, the type of rebirth is not. Because a human life is the result of powerful virtue, it is difficult to attain. Even more difficult is a human life in which one has the physical and mental leisure to give some attention to spiritual development.

The difficulty of gaining a human life in which religious practice is possible is likened to the plight of a blind turtle in a turbulent ocean. At the surface drifts a golden hoop, just large enough for a turtle's head. The likelihood that this blind turtle, who comes up for air once in a hundred years, will put his head through the hoop, exemplifies our chances for another leisurely human life. Thus, one who now has such a circumstance must not waste it. To overcome the universal tendency to do so, Tibetan Mahayana Buddhists, incorporating several elements common to Theravada, use a detailed meditative strategy for dealing with issues such as death's inevitability. This is so simple intellectually, and so difficult psychologically, that it takes practice to slow the mind down sufficiently for its import to be internalized. Thus, Buddhism developed ways of deconstructing this simple point into topics for reflection. Paul Ricoeur once said that deconstruction means getting to the questions behind the answers in a text or tradition, and emphasized that this is really a religious issue.[15] In the Tibetan tradition, one probes fundamental questions such as "How can I know that my death is definite, its time indefinite, and what will be most helpful to me in that circumstance?" Specific patterns of reflection, grouped into three main segments, are suggested.[16]

First, to internalize the certainty of one's own death, one can reflect that all great persons of the past—saints, heroes, or geniuses—have died; that even planets, suns, and galaxies are subject to destruction. How then could I escape it?[17] Also, the time remaining to us continually decreases and cannot be extended. Tsong-ka-pa, a 14th-century major religious figure in Tibet, writes:

> When animals such as sheep are led to the slaughter, they move closer to death with every step they take. The water carried by the current of a strong river or the water in a waterfall on a steep mountain quickly disappears. Just so, one's life is quickly spent and gone.[18]

Second, death is inescapable. It cannot be avoided through any of the techniques familiar to us: there is no place we can go to escape it, no amount of money that can ransom or bribe it, and no weapons that might counter it. Our own death is definite. Not only this, but the exigencies of life allow very little time for spiritual development. Tsong-ka-pa states that if we subtract time spent in gaining maturity, sleeping, taking care of necessities, illness, and old age, a life-span of sixty years allows five years for religious endeavor. But there is no certainty that we will be allowed sixty years, or any definite period. This compounds the issue. Though we might accept death as inevitable, if we know it will not come round for, say, twenty years, we can plan accordingly. But we do not know when death will visit us. Our life-spans are of uncertain length and our bodies vulnerable. Although causes of life are relatively few, causes of death are many. If misused or polluted, even life-sustaining elements like food and water become causes of death.

Having incorporated the view that one's death is definite and imminent, the third phase is to ask what can help in the face of death. Friends and relatives can neither alter one's fate nor accompany one through death. One must die alone. Possessions too will be useless; they give no enjoyment as one lies dying. One cannot carry even a needle and thread through this transition. Nor is one's body of use; it will not accompany us. The mind however, *does* continue, so that wholesome capacities developed internally—especially love and compassion, as well as insight into the dependently arisen yet empty nature of things—will help at death.

Each of these points is the focus for one or several sessions of meditation. In reflecting thus, one alternates between analytical and stabilizing meditation.[19] To contemplate reasons and examples of death's inevitability and unpredictability is a form of analytical meditation. When some degree of internal experience arises, one leaves aside words and concentrates or stabilizes on that effect.

In this way, Buddhists seek to internalize the reality and unpredictability of death, and to engender a sense of urgency regarding spiritual development. This is not meant to exclude other responsibilities but is a call to organize time and choose activities with real concern for their ultimate value. That value derives more from the spirit in which "religious" or "worldly" actions are done than their surface nature. In general, any activity done with good motivation, especially if conjoined with an understanding of the nature of reality or the emptiness to be discussed below, is seen as a Mahayana practice.

What is the net result of such reflection? Tsong-ka-pa says it relieves our fear of death, which he describes as derived from the implicit hope that it can somehow be escaped. Presumption of immortality breeds excessive attachment to one's own physical identity and material possessions, the result of which is that the menace of death looms even larger. In short, these reflections are intended not only to direct increased energy toward goals chosen in recognition of death's inevitability but also to make death itself less fearful.[20] Near-death experiences in our culture typically result in a heightened sense of life's joys, renewed energy and a willingness to overlook lesser annoyances. The purpose of

facing death through systematic reflection is to reap the
benefits of such an encounter early in life and without the
risks of an actual brush with death. For Tsong-ka-pa, con-
templating death not only revivifies one's energies but also
turns them toward goals that have ultimate value for Buddhist practitioners.

Given the conclusion of these reflections that only religious practice is beneficial at death, the next questions naturally have to do with the nature of religious motivation and
practice. Here, too, impermanence and death figure significantly.

Impermanence and the Religious Path

Non-religious and religious motivation are distinguished
in the Indo-Tibetan Mahayana tradition. Persons who use
worldly or religious activities to pursue happiness in this life
with no concern for future lives are not seen as religiously
motivated. At the very least, religious motivation is concerned that future lives take place in fortunate circumstances. This however is inferior to either non-Mahayana or
Mahayana concerns. Non-Mahayanists seek liberation from
cyclic existence because they consider that to wander in
cyclic existence is to be like a fly trapped inside a jar—one
can go higher or lower but, always remains trapped. Six
realms of rebirth are enumerated; the lowest and most painful being the hot and cold hells. Rebirth as a hungry ghost or
animal also involves extreme suffering; relatively happy are
births as humans, demi-gods, or gods.[21]

Even the best rebirth—that of a god in a heavenly realm—
involves suffering when, like a rocket running out of fuel, the
virtuous activity that propelled one there is consumed and
one must leave that blissful realm for a far inferior rebirth.
To seek liberation is thus a more suitable, and hence higher
goal than merely to seek a good rebirth. The Mahayanist,
who shares this perspective, has an additional concern that
he or she be able to help others achieve their own highest
welfare, and for this reason seeks not merely liberation but

the full enlightenment of a Buddha so as to be able to lead other beings to their enlightenment.[22] The Indo-Tibetan tradition sees one with such motivation as a person of greatest capacity.

In this way, all levels of religious motivation—to achieve good rebirth, liberation, or a Buddha's capacity for helping others—derive from a recognition of the present situation as impermanent. The Mahayanist specifically connects this understanding with a concern for others' welfare. Initially, compassion merely sees beings as suffering and in need of solace; as insight progresses, beings are understood also as impermanent, not only because they are mortal but because they are "evanescent or momentarily disintegrating, like (a reflected) moon in water stirred by a breeze."[23] Building on this, Mahayana compassion becomes akin to wisdom as it becomes a concern for persons seen as characterized by coarse and subtle impermanence. The *most* insightful compassion is that directed at persons seen not only as impermanent but as empty of inherently existing.[24]

Understanding the instability of life is thus a necessary component of the wish to leave cyclic existence; knowing living beings as impermanent is a necessary aspect of the more profound forms of Mahayana compassion. These, the determination to leave cyclic existence and the compassionate aspiration to enlightenment, are two of the three principal features of the path to enlightenment described in the Indo-Tibetan tradition.[25] The third feature—cultivation of wisdom—is discussed below. In brief, it involves reversal of ordinary assumptions regarding apparently static or solid objects. Such reorientation itself presumes the momentary change and disintegration of all produced things. Thus, whereas reflection on one's own death can provide sustained impetus toward religious practice, the chief elements of that practice—the decision to leave cyclic existence, the gaining of mature compassion, and wisdom—come to completion in large measure through reflection on death and other forms of impermanence. In this way, impermanence, whose hallmark is death, has a central role in this form of Buddhist practice.

The motivating potential, compassionate insight and wisdom that deep recognition of impermanence and death can instill is not the only significance this issue has for Buddhist thought. For a fuller perspective we turn now to the Tantric branch of Mahayana, which, originating in India, dominated Tibetan understanding of the process of dying, death, and rebirth. Much of what follows is unique to that perspective, being altogether absent in Theravada and differently elaborated in other Mahayana traditions.

Death as Religious Opportunity

Wisdom and skillful methods are both essential for enlightenment. Compassion is the chief skillful method of Mahayana and, at its most profound, wishes others to be free from suffering while seeing them as insubstantial and evanescent. In short, it understands that beings lack or are empty of the type of solid, substantial, inherently independent status that one ordinarily presumes them—and oneself—to possess. Such overly reified or solidified status is the "self" negated in Buddhist theories of selflessness.

Selflessness, in both sutra and tantra, does *not* mean persons do not exist at all. "Self" here does not signify the "you" or "me" of ordinary language but refers to an overly concrete and otherwise misconstrued existential status. Nothing— neither persons, places, Buddhas, nor enlightenment itself— exists *inherently*. But they *do* exist. Only the inherently independent existence attributed to them does not. If, as some have misunderstood Buddhism to mean, persons did not exist at all, then the essential Buddhist doctrines of the cause and effect of actions, the process of rebirth and death, would be impossible. The compatibility of cause and effect, of the world of objects, with the principle of emptiness is an essential feature of Indo-Tibetan Mahayana. It means that neither emptiness nor realization of it undermines successful functioning in the world. Rather, when things and, especially, one's own mind are understood as empty, their full potential becomes apparent. It may *seem* easier to live with the concept of a permanent, autonomous self, but this is deceptive.[26] Through holding onto a mistaken concept of self, good and bad actions, causes of future birth and suffering, are undertaken; moreover, to the extent that the present self is over-concretized, one foregoes transformative growth.

Still, if what we ordinarily consider self does not exist, what takes rebirth? Clearly, the body does not. In Buddhist countries this is usually burned or, as in Tibet, dismembered and left to feed wild animals. There is no expectation of bodily resurrection. Thus, only some form of mentality or consciousness can take rebirth. This is what is not stopped by death.

In the process of dying, the senses and energies that worked in concert with consciousness deteriorate and so become incapable of supporting the workings of consciousness. Consciousness itself, described as an entity of clarity and knowing, retreats from the sense organs, finally gathering at the center of the heart before departing the body. During this process, the dying person has eight distinct visions, corresponding to the withdrawal of consciousness from specific areas of the body. Meditators study these stages as a traveler might pore over maps of a foreign country. Knowing them serves as a guide. A person familiar with this process is less likely to be frightened by it. Most important, advanced meditators are able to simulate this experience at will, thereby gaining control over this process. Full control is tantamount to Buddhahood and even partial control means one can choose the next rebirth instead of being, as all ordinary persons are, simply blown about by uncontrolled forces unleashed by one's previous activities.

Prior to this, while the dying person can still relate to others, family members and friends are advised to bid the person farewell. Ideally this is done without tears or drama, so as not to cause excessive regret or longing in the dying person. Such states of mind could, in conjunction with tendencies established by non-virtuous activities of this or an earlier life, precipitate an unfortunate rebirth. The state of mind in which one dies is a powerful determinant of the next rebirth. Suicides, therefore, who generally die amid powerful feelings of depression, anger, or desperation, are considered at great risk.

These eight stages occur in all living things; in humans they ordinarily span from twelve hours to three days.[27] In more subtle form, the eight transpire each time one goes in or out of sleep or dream, sneezes, faints, or has an orgasm.[28] This is considered a process ingrained in our being, yet we have no awareness or control of it except through considerable training.

The eye organ is the first to be affected; one's eyesight dims and there occurs a mirage-like vision, marking the first of the eight stages. Second, the ear loses its capacity to hear; its humming sound disappears; at this time there is an internal appearance of smoke. Next, the nasal sense is incapacitated; at this third stage one is no longer mindful of the affairs of persons with whom one has been closely involved, and one has an internal vision likened to fireflies in smoke.

During the fourth stage, tongue and body lose their sensory capacities and one ceases to be mindful even of one's own concerns. The internal vision now is of a sputtering candle flame. *Inhalation and exhalation cease.* Nonetheless, four stages remain before the person is considered dead. Usually Buddhists do not disturb the body while the consciousness remains there. To do so makes it even more difficult for the person to accomplish any spiritual purpose during the latter stages. Most accomplished teachers maintain that since ordinary persons cannot remain aware at this time, handling of the body or other disturbances do no harm. Still, out of a sense of respect and, perhaps, an acknowledgment that one cannot know with certainty the capacity of another, peaceful surroundings are preserved.

For skilled meditators, an important feature of the fourth stage is that all thought ceases. Because the mind operates without its usual sense of subject and object as distinct, it spontaneously comes to approximate wisdom, the third element of the path. Moreover, being non-dual, clear and steady, it is a powerful consciousness with which to realize emptiness. If one can use this mind to know or merge with emptiness, full enlightenment is at hand.

In the fifth through the eighth stages, one has successive visions likened to the suffusing light of (5) white moonlight, (6) red sunlight, (7) black darkness, and (8) white dawn pervading a clear, expansive sky. It is as if one's mind is wholly fused with the clear sky pervaded by such light. During the period of darkness, the seventh stage, one swoons as in a faint, and then awakens into what is called the *clear light of death*, the eighth stage. At this time consciousness exists as a very subtle mind sustained by a subtle form of energy that, having withdrawn from the extremities, abides at the heart center. The more one can remain aware during these eight stages, the more likely it is one will remember this life after rebirth. For, according to the present Dalai Lama,

> This is like the fact that if at night before going to sleep we strongly determine with clear awareness what time we want to rise in the morning and what we are going to do after rising, then even if while asleep we are not remembering this, due to the previous intentionality we rise right at that time and immediately remember what we are to do.[29]

Witnesses report some persons have remained in the clear light as if asleep for weeks without any odor coming from the body, even in the heat of India.[30] The consciousness has not yet left the body; it is radiantly non-dualistic, thus enhancing one's possibility of deepening realization of selflessness such that one can complete the causes of enlightenment. If successful, the consciousness can proceed at will to its next manifestation.

During these stages the dying person's religious teacher, a knowledgeable friend or relative, may recite instructions, reminding one to remain calm and aware of the clear light of death. Prayers, mantra recitation, incense, or other offerings may also be made for the person's benefit. The subtle consciousness has innumerable predispositions for happy and unhappy rebirth; dying with a virtuous mind such as a wish for others' happiness, in a peaceful meditative state, or in reflection on impermanence or emptiness, can cause virtuous predispositions to take precedence over non-virtuous ones, thus sending one to a good situation. The prayers and blessings of friends and teachers may also have this effect. The essential presumption is that one's existence continues; thus, there is a saying in Tibetan that although there are persons who have died, there are no dead persons.[31]

Once the consciousness leaves the body, an occurrence augured by excretions from nose, genitals, or both, relatives may dispose of the corpse. The body of a highly regarded meditator is often displayed for a time so that disciples and others may pay respects by circumambulating and bowing down to it. In any case, disposal of the body, though usually presided over by a religious figure who leads recitation of appropriate prayers, is not the central concern of Buddhist ritual at this time. Focus is on the consciousness that is now in a particularly precarious situation.

For an indeterminate time, the mind of clear light remains utterly still. Then the merest quiver of movement occurs within it, and the eight visions commence in reverse order, beginning with the all-pervasive blackness. From this moment one is in the intermediate state. The all-pervasive red and white appearances then arise in sequence, through to the mirage-like vision. Having departed the body, the unit of subtle energy and consciousness that had gathered at the heart is in a state between death and rebirth. One may not realize immediately that one has died, but try to converse with friends and relatives. Their lack of response is puzzling until one understands what has happened. During this period one can travel anywhere instantaneously; although without a material physical body, one has the capacities of all five senses. One's mental body is indestructible; also, it is not obstructed by walls, mountains, or anything except its future place of rebirth. The intermediate state is traditionally said to last no more than forty-nine days. Like tumbling into a dream, delightful and terrifying images can occur. An extensive literature, of which the *Tibetan Book of the Dead* is but one example, describes experiences that may occur at this time. If while alive one trained in visualization and other meditative techniques to become familiar with them,

peaceful and wrathful deities famous in Tantric icono-
graphy can appear. If one is deluded as to their nature, one
cannot avoid being plunged into rebirth at the mercy of one's
own past actions. However, if on the basis of previous practice one recognizes the nature of these and moves toward
them, instead of toward less frightening apparitions of light,
which treacherously lead to rebirth and suffering, one can
gain the enlightenment one failed to achieve during the clear
light of death.[32] Persons able to recognize when they are
dreaming and who can control dream events are in a good
position to remain aware in the intermediate state. By realizing the true status of intermediate state visions, one can be
freed from uncontrolled rebirth.

Prayers for the well-being of a person in the intermediate
state are recited daily or weekly for forty-nine days. These
prayers, conducted by monks or teachers and usually
attended by the family can involve considerable ritual, but
the purpose is simple: to remind the departed that she or he is
in the intermediate state, that the manifold appearances
cannot harm unless one is deceived by them, and that one
has an opportunity for liberation. Prayers are also made to
increase the potency of the person's good actions or karma,
so that these, rather than any unwholesome ones, propel the
next rebirth.

Until rebirth occurs, one whirls unimpeded over vast dis-
tances, until finally, impelled by one's own previous actions,
one is driven to the womb, egg, or other environment from
where one will be reborn. In the case of humans, the consciousness is attracted by its vision of a copulating couple
and enters into the midst of the drop of sperm and blood in
the mother's womb. If one is to be born as a female, one
rushes there due to an overwhelming attraction to the father,
and if as a male, out of attraction to the mother.[33]

This drop containing the subtle consciousness is the core
around which the body forms and the receptacle into which
the consciousness later dissolves at death. Thus, everything
included in the name "person" folds and unfolds from the
mind of clear light. The sequential visions culminating with
clear light mark one's death from the intermediate state; a

continuation of such clear light enters the center of the semen and blood of father and mother, making the connection to the new life. Then the other visions arise and with them associated factors such as dualistic thought and the capacity to function in concert with sense and mental consciousness.[34] This emergence from and dissolution into the mind of clear light can be likened to the workings of a kaleidoscope. Rich designs spiral out of its empty white space, then dissolve back again, only to emerge in an altogether different configuration. Complexity and brilliance of design in no way undermines the essential clarity that is the design's source and foundation. However, whereas everything arises from within the kaleidoscope, Buddhists believe that the new individual's consciousness, unlike the body, does not result from the union of father and mother.

Why presume that the consciousness originates elsewhere than in the new mother's womb? Buddhists in general agree that although form and consciousness function in close alignment, one cannot cause the other. Only form can act as a cause of material form, and only a consciousness as a cause of consciousness. For, all impermanent things must have a cause similar in substance to themselves. The substantial cause of a clay pot, for example, is clay; of a table, wood, and so forth. Consciousness cannot arise solely from material causes. Thus, the mind—like cyclic existence—is beginningless. It always arises as the effect of a former moment of mind. Mother and father provide the physical bases in connection with which a mind can function, but the material substances of sperm and egg cannot themselves produce consciousness.

Just as issues associated with impermanence and death are woven throughout the fabric of the Buddhist path, so it is with rebirth. We have seen that the prospect of endless rebirths is an incentive to leave cyclic existence, and that this motivation is the first of three classic elements of religious practice in the Indo-Tibetan tradition. Moreover, given that everyone has experienced countless rebirths, we have all been in every possible relationship to one another—most importantly, mother, father, and best friend. In short, we have a long and intimate history with others during which we have received much kindness for which we can be grateful, and which it is appropriate to repay. On this basis, and recognizing that, like oneself, everyone must face death and uncertain rebirth, one cultivates concern for others' well-being.[35] Thus, discussion of rebirth reinforces the second element required for highest enlightenment—the chief Mahayana method of compassion.

Perception of life as a kaleidoscopic continuum of change can counter an overly solidified identification of oneself and others as limited to the present condition. It denies an inherent identification with one's present mind and body and in this way loosens the misconceived sense of self. Indeed, the premise of rebirth is used to aid development of the third essential element of religious practice, wisdom. Such wisdom transforms the mind, vanquishing the misunderstanding that is an essential component of the cyclic existence. When the mistaken conception of inherent existence is overcome, the otherwise intractable cycle of actions and their effects—the workings of karma—is broken. Thus, although no beginning can be assigned to the process of wandering among the regions of rebirth, enlightenment brings one's own wandering to an end. Anyone who achieves the compassion and insight necessary for this state attains it, whether Buddhist or not; the advantage Buddhism sees for itself is its rich textual and oral traditions that detail the theoretical principles and methods most efficacious for accomplishing this goal.

Finally, descriptions of dying, death, the intermediate state and rebirth bespeaks a profound optimism regarding human potential. The mind is deeper than its ordinary uses lead us to suspect; it is capable of sustained, conscious activity even when dualistic conceptions like subject and object, on which all ordinary experience is based, vanish. When its capacity is realized, mind is transformed. In this way, descriptions of death and rebirth are meant to reveal the processes by which ordinary persons achieve full enlightenment. Analysis of these processes provides a basis for understanding the enlightened state, with its capacity for consciously choosing future births, as a style of endless activity on behalf of all other, closely related, living beings. Underscoring this is the possibility that one can entirely overcome rigid, obscuring conceptions while still retaining vibrance and clarity of mind. Finally, for Buddhists, the profound harmony of variegated appearances with such clarity points to the possibility of enlightened, compassionate engagement with the world.

Notes

[1]   Chronology here follows A.K. Warder, *Indian Buddhism*, (Motilal Banarsidass: Delhi, 1970) p. 44.

[2]   Hindu Gods were occasionally appropriated into Buddhist stories, probably to impress their Hindu audiences. The deities here are the Shuddhādhivāsa—pure-dwelling or perfumed gods—mentioned by Ashvagosha in the *Deeds of the Buddhas* (Buddhacarita). See deBary, ed., *The Buddhist Tradition* (NY: Modern Library Books, 1969), p. 61.

[3]   "Deeds of the Buddha" tr. Edward Conze in *Buddhist Scriptures* (Middlesex, England: Penguin Books, 1968) p. 40; see also *The Buddhist Tradition* p. 64.

[4]   *Buddhist Scriptures* p. 43; see also *The Buddhist Tradition*, p. 65.

[5]   This is how the future Buddha justifies leaving home when urged by his father to remain a householder: "Oh King, if I were given a guarantee on four matters...That my life would not be committed to death; that my health would not be overcome by disease; that my youth would not be marred by old age; and that prosperity would not be taken away by disaster" (*The Buddhist Tradition*, p. 66).

[6]   A traditional Tibetan interpretation. See Jeffrey Hopkins, *Meditation on Emptiness* (London: Wisdom Publications, 1983) pp. 353-55; see also Khetsun Sangpo, *Tantric Practice in Nyingma* (Ithaca: Snow Lion, 1982), pp. 57-58.

[7]   *Meditation on Emptiness* p. 392.

[8]   See *Compassion in Tibetan Buddhism* (Ithaca: Snow Lion, 1980), pp. 170-171 for Tsong-ka-pa's views on the meaning of cessation; this is a translation of *dbU ma dgongs ba rab gsal* (*Illumina-*

tion of the Thought) (Dharamsala: Tibetan Cultural Printing Press, n.d.), p. 34.22.

⁹ The Cittamātra (Mind-Only) school of Asaṅga is the major exception.

¹⁰ Kenneth Ch'en, *Buddhism in China* (Princeton: Princeton University Press, 1964), p. 20-21.

¹¹ Major sources for historical overview here, in addition to Ch'en, are: Richard Robinson and Willard Johnson, assisted by Kathryn Tsai and Shinzen Young, *The Buddhist Religion* (Belmont, CA: Wadsworth Publishing Co., Third Edition, 1982) and H. Byron Earhart, *Japanese Religion* (Belmont, CA: Wadsworth Publishing Co., Third Edition, 1982).

¹² Two excellent sources for the history of Tibet are: Snellgrove and Richardson, *A Cultural History of Tibet* (reprinted in Boulder: Prajna Press, 1980) and R.A. Stein, *Tibetan Civilization* (Stanford: Stanford University Press, 1983).

¹³ *Bhayabherasutta* (*Discourse on Fear and Trembling*) from *Majjhima-Nikāya* (London: Pali Text Society) I 22, translated by I.B. Horner, *Middle Length Sayings* Vol. I (London: Pali Text Society, 1976), p. 29.

¹⁴ For a discussion of theological and philosophical implications of a creatorless religious paradigm, see A. Klein "Non-Dualism and the Great Bliss Queen" in the *Journal of Feminist Studies in Religion* (Scholars Press), Vol. I, Spring 1985.

¹⁵ In a faculty colloquium at Harvard Divinity School, Spring 1983.

¹⁶ This discussion is largely from Tsong-ka-pa, *Great Exposition of the Stages of the Path* (*Lam rim chen mo*), (Dharamsala: Shes rig par khang), 1964, 65b. 1ff. My presentation is also based on lectures delivered by Ven, Lati Rinboche, abbot emeritus of Ganden Shardzay Monastic College in Mundgod, India, while Visiting Professor at the University of Virginia in 1977. He synopsized the three main headings into nine segments:

I. Death is definite
   a. Death will come and we will not be able to escape it.
   b. Life diminishes uninterruptedly; we cannot augment it.
   c. A normal life leaves little time for religious practice—one is too young, too busy with family, or too old.
II. Death's coming is unpredictable
   a. Life in general is short; moreover, the young and

    healthy may die before the old and infirm.
   b. There are many causes of life, few of death, and the
    former can easily turn into the latter.
   c. The body is weak and susceptible.
  III. Only religious practice is of help at death
   a. Wealth is no help.
   b. Friends and relatives cannot help.
   c. The body cannot help at that time.

Similar themes are discussed by Gam-po-pa in *The Jewel Ornament of Liberation* tr. by Herbert Guenther (Boulder: Prajna Press, 1981), pp. 41-54. For a Theravada meditation on death, see Buddhaghosa, *The Path of Purification (Visuddhimagga)* tr. by Bhikhu Nyānamoli, (Berkeley & London: Shambala, 1976) V.I., VII. 8ff (pp. 248-259).

[17] A strikingly similar theme appears in the *Path of Purification*, V.I., VIII. 18ff (p. 251) where, as part of the meditation on death, one compares oneself to a famous person of great merit, strength or power.

[18] Tr. by Prof. Donald S. Lopez, Jr., unpublished ms. 1984. Tsong-ka-pa here appears to echo a motif of the Samyutta Nikāya i. 109, quoted in the *Path of Purification*, p. 249:

  The nights and days go slipping by
  As life keeps dwindling steadily
  Till mortals' spans, like water pools
  In failing rills, is all used up.

[19] *dpyad sgom* and *'jog sgom*. These Tibetan terms appear to have no Sanskrit equivalents. They are analogues, but not equivalents, of the more well known terms "insight" (Skt. *vipaśyanā*, Tib. *hlag mthong*) and "calm abiding" (Skt. *śamatha*, Tib. *gzhi gnas*).

[20] A similar perspective emerges in, for example, existential psychotherapy. Irvin D. Yalom, a major proponent, finds failure to come to terms with death to be an eminent source of psychological dysfunction. An unrecognized fear of annihilation can vent itself in symptoms such as fear of becoming a true adult, reluctance to complete relationships or projects lest one be "finished," or an exaggerated sense of specialness. See Irvin D. Yalom, *Existential Psychotherapy* (New York: Basic Books, Inc., 1980) especially pp. 27-49 and 117ff.

[21] Sufferings of the six realms of rebirth are detailed in numerous texts; see, for example, *Tantric Practice in Nyingma*, pp. 64-72.

²² Classification of motivation is from *Compassion in Tibetan Buddhism*, pp. 17-21. The first section of this book is an excellent introduction to Tibetan Buddhism, especially the conjunction of its ethical perspective—exemplified by the altruistic intention to attain enlightenment—with the transcendent wisdom which such empowers.

²³ See *Compassion in Tibetan Buddhism*, 120ff for a translation of p. 65. 22ff in Tsong-ka-pa's *Illumination of the Thought* commenting on v. 4abc of Chandrakīrti's *Entry to the Middle Way* (*Mādhyamakāvatāra*).

²⁴ Ibid.

²⁵ See Tsong-ka-pa's *Three Principle Aspects of the Path* (*Lam gyi 'dzo bo 'rnam gsum*) tr. by Geshe Sopa and Jeffrey Hopkins in *Practice and Theory in Tibetan Buddhism* (London: Rider 1976) and by Geshe Wangyal, in *The Door of Liberation* (NY: Girodias, 1973).

²⁶ See Yalom's discussion of this, p. 117 ff.

²⁷ For full description of these, see Rinbochay and Hopkins, *Death, the Intermediate State and Rebirth* (Ithaca: Snow Lion, 1979). The present discussion of these stages is taken from the text, a translation of the 18th century scholar-yogi Yang-chen-ga-way-lo-dro's (dbYangs-can-dga'ba'i-blo-gros also known as A-skya Yongs'dzin) *Lamp Thoroughly Illuminating the Three Basic Bodies* (*gZhi'i sku gsum gyi rnam gzhag rab gsal sgron me*) in *The Collected Works of A-skya Yongs'dzin*, Vol. I (New Delhi, Lama Guru Deva, 1971).

²⁸ Ibid., p. 20

²⁹ His Holiness Tenzin Gyatso, XIV Dalai Lama in *Kindness, Clarity, and Insight* (Ithaca, Snow Lion Publications), 1984 p. 177.

³⁰ Ibid., p. 178. The Dalai Lama states that since 1959, when Tibetan refugees began arriving in India, approximately ten instances of this have occurred. The scholar-meditator Denma Lochö Rinboche reports that Para Rinboche, a high-ranking monk of Ganden Monastic University, remained for seven days in Buxador, India: "His body did not decay despite the fact that it was subjected to the heat of many butter lamps left as offerings in addition to the great heat of the area itself." (Unpublished University of Virginia transcript, p. 71.)

³¹ Ven Denma Lochö Rinbochay, U. Va. seminar, 1979.

³² *Kindness, Clarity and Insight*, p. 180. Texts such as the one by Yang-chen-ga-way-lo-drö, our main source here on stages of death,

describe the intermediate state solely in terms of the powers one possesses there, and how one enters and leaves it. There is no reference to the appearance of deities, something that is so stressed in works such as *The Tibetan Book of the Dead* which have dominated western understanding of Tibetan views of the intermediate state. The latter text is not explicit about whether such appearances are "automatic" or not; the implication seems to be that they are. For a clear description of the series of intermediate state visions see Freemantle and Trungpa, *The Tibetan Book of the Dead* (Boulder, Shambala Publications, 1975).

[33] *Jewel Ornament of Liberation* Boulder, Col.: Prajna Press, 1981) p. 63.

[34] See *Death, the Intermediate State and Rebirth*, pp. 58ff.

[35] For a seven-fold meditation developing love and compassion based on this principle, see *Compassion in Tibetan Buddhism*, pp. 1-50.

THE CHURCHES OF CHRIST

Thomas H. Olbricht, Ph.D.

Background of the Faith

The Churches of Christ in America result from an indige-
nous American movement seeking to restore the church of
the New Testament. For this reason the term "Restoration
Movement" has been employed as a self-designation, though
this particular phraseology is not widely employed to identify these churches by outsiders. Three sizable constituencies jelled from the early beginnings. The names of these
groups are more widely recognized: (1) The Disciples of

Christ, (2) The Christian Churches, and (3) The Churches of Christ.[1] The Churches of Christ tend to be the most theologically conservative of the three. They are the conservative wing of the first major split in the movement identified independently by the Federal Census Bureau in 1906. The Churches of Christ have approximately 2,000,000 members throughout the world, most of whom are in the United States.[2] The majority in the United States are located in the region running from Pittsburgh to El Paso, with the north border extending from Pittsburgh through Indianapolis, St. Louis, Wichita, and Albuquerque, and the southern through Atlanta, Montgomery, Baton Rouge, Houston, and San Antonio.

Historical Roots

The roots of the Restoration Movement extend backward to the period after the Revolutionary War in which several Americans with religious interests grew restless over autocratic structure, confessional boundaries, and European control and theology. These pressures revamped the mainline churches, but also resulted in independent constituencies springing up in various regions. Four such groups of independent churches played a role in the crystallization of the Restoration Movement in the 1830's.

Two of these groups were in New England and Virginia. Their roles were contributory rather than direct. In Virginia in the 1780's, a group of Methodist ministers led by James O'Kelley sought freedom from supervision so that Methodist circuit riders could determine their own itineraries. For a time it seemed they would win out, but the result was that preaching assignments were placed in the hands of the Bishop. Those who favored self-determination broke away, founding the Republican Methodist Church. In 1794 they changed the name of the body to the Christian Church.[3] In New England, especially in the newly developing regions, persons of Baptist heritage, chiefly Abner Jones and Elias Smith, formed new believing bodies. They went by the name Christian Church, or Christian Connexion. They championed defeat of tax support for establishment ministers, and rejected the Calvinistic features of Puritan theology. In both cases the Bible was heralded, especially the New Testament, as the only source of authority and faith. In their opinion, Christians should cut adrift from the historical encrustations so as to create the New Testament church in its first century purity.[4]

The two most important tributaries for the larger movement resulted from the work of Barton W. Stone and the two Campbells—father and son. At the turn of the century the second great awakening titillated the Kentucky and Ohio frontiers. Camp meetings sprang up throughout the region, the largest being the 1801 extravaganza at Cane Ridge, Kentucky, northeast of Lexington. Denominational barriers crumbled away and the call to struggle and conversion diluted traditional election theology. As the months wore on, some of the preachers, especially among the Presbyterians, favored the ecumenical flavor of the awakening. They therefore formed a presbytery the members of which held these sentiments. Not too long after, carrying their interests to their logical conclusions, they dissolved the Springfield Presbytery in order to "sink into union with the body of Christ at large."[5] These leaders found many frontiersmen ready to embrace these sentiments, and rapid growth ensued. Barton W. Stone eventually emerged as the chief spokesman.

In 1807 Thomas Campbell (of Scottish descent) arrived in Pennsylvania from North Ireland, settling in Washington. Long a Presbyterian minister, he exerted considerable energy in the land of his nativity struggling to bring together dissident Presbyterian groups. His efforts at similar rapprochement in Pennsylvania resulted in litigation to oust him from the presbytery in which he was licensed. Seeing the handwriting on the wall he resigned, and with others of like mind, formed the Christian Association of Washington. In 1809, his gifted son Alexander arrived from a stint at the University of Glasgow in Scotland. Out of these men's efforts, and those allied with them, churches were formed in the region around Pittsburgh. After 1816, the Campbells associated with Baptist ministers, winning several Ohio and Kentucky Baptist churches to their views.[6] The Campbells envisioned a mass exodus of believers from sectarian protestantism who would become one body, one New Testament church as set forth in the pages of the New Testament. Early in the 1830's the churches from the Stone and Campbell groups commenced merging. By 1850 Alexander Campbell, because of his journal editing, book publishing, debating, and lecturing, became the best known leader of the movement. His ideas left a permanent stamp on all his descendants, regardless of location, on the theological spectrum. His views definitely influenced the Churches of Christ even though the leadership of David Lipscomb in the latter part of the nineteenth century modified some of them.[7]

By the 1830's immigration patterns brought persons from these four groups together in the border states east of the Mississippi. What occurred was the emergence of a mainstream with all four groups contributing. The Campbell and Stone forces provided the core for the growing constituency. Some churches, however, from the three groups other than the Campbell movement, remained independent even in Ohio and Indiana and in the 1890's formed a coalition of their own.[8]

Central Affirmations

Because of these concerns in their early history, the Churches of Christ have grounded their theology and world views in Biblical perspectives as they have ascertained them. Because they placed their emphasis on restoring the New Testament church, they focused on practical aspects of church order and worship. Beliefs about life after death developed out of traditional protestant conservative views, but always in the light of the scriptures, especially the New Testament.[9]

The Meaning of Life and Death

By consensus, persons in the Churches of Christ see life on earth as a period in which an individual, living in the face of God's call and command, makes decisions that determine where he will spend eternity. The basic decisions he faces are 1) whether to obey God, and thereby become a Christian, and 2) having made that decision, whether to live as a Christian in a style of life consistent with the commands of God.[10]

The sequence of these decisions is as follows: The basic first step should be made when a child reaches a level of maturation at which he can understand commitments and their ramifications. This crucial step is called the age of accountability and is normally thought to be about 12 years old.[11] Children who seem mature and understand that Christ died for their sins may, on occasion, be baptized as young as 8 or 9. In this period when the child learns of God's action in Christ he is expected to make a decision to accept God's gracious gift of salvation. If he decides to respond to the call, he believes that Jesus is the Christ, the Son of God, repents of his sins, confesses his faith "with his lips," and is "buried with his Lord in baptism."[12] He is not considered a Christian until all these stages have been completed, including baptism. Once the decision has been made and acted upon the crucial matter of where one will spend eternity, that is, heaven, has been settled.

The act of becoming a Christian does not alone, however, settle the matter of eternal destiny. Even a Christian can disobey God and be rejected on the day of judgment. To live eternally with God one must be scrupulous in keeping his commands as found in the New Testament.[13] The one who is faithful until death is permitted beyond the grave to live with God forever in eternal peace and rest. The person who fails to measure up is doomed to eternal punishment, along with all those who failed to become a Christian for whatever reason.

In the conviction of most members of the Churches of Christ, God is one, Jesus is his son but a different person; and the Holy Spirit is a person and, in the opinion of some,

only acts in the twentieth century through the influence of
the scripture when it is read.[14] In any case, the Holy Spirit
does not now convert or teach the ways of God. The scripture
and its proclamation is the channel through which God now
does his work among men. God is obviously different from
man. Not much more can be said except that he is spirit and
for that reason other than flesh and blood.

The universe was made by God *ex nihilo*, that is, from
nothing through words spoken by God. "And God said, 'Let
there be lights in the expanse of the sky to separate the day
from the night, and let them serve as signs to mark seasons
and days and years, and let them be lights in the expanse of
the sky to give light on the earth' " (Genesis 1:14, 15). Once
created, the universe functions through the natural laws
which God set in place. Since the days of creation, any time
God has acted in the world it has been necessary that even
He suspend the natural laws. Any time God does so a miracle
occurs. It is the majority conviction among the members of
the Churches of Christ that while God pushed the button to
stop the laws several times from Adam to John the Apostle,
since the first century he has left the universe to pursue its
own course consonant with the natural laws. Miracles therefore ceased when the New Testament was completed.[15] Man
was created by God in the same manner as the universe. In
the case of the first man, Adam, God provided a biological
body but a non-organic soul. God creates the soul of each
human sometime in or after human conception. The typical
view is that God creates the soul at the time of conception
and, if not then, at least before birth. A consensus position
has not as yet emerged. The soul, once created, is indestructible.[16]

Death is the separation of the soul from the body. The body
of flesh and blood remains in the visible human universe.
The indissoluble aspect of man, the soul, goes to the place of
the dead awaiting the end of history. The soul retains consciousness even after death and is transported to Hades, the
place of the dead. Hades is divided into Paradise, where the
righteous are settled in, and Tartarus, the location for the
wicked.[17] At the end of history Jesus will return and the dead

will be raised for judgment. Those who have accepted Christ and have lived faithfully according to God's way will enter the heavenly realm of God. Those who have not accepted Christ along with those who failed to live according to their Christian commitment will be punished in Gehenna (Hell) forever. Many church members may not be able to reiterate accurately these details and Bible scholars who work in the Churches of Christ may question whether the New Testament use of these words warrant the traditional delineation, nevertheless these divisions of the place where the dead reside until judgment are perpetuated.[18]

Among members of the Churches of Christ the long-held rule of thumb for interpreting the scripture is that all statements are literal unless the context makes explicit a figurative interpretation. It is therefore the universal conclusion that the devil is a literal person in scripture and must be so construed in conviction.[19] The devil is believed to influence human behavior through working on the emotions and especially during the excitement of extreme passions. Exactly how he accomplishes this feat is not spelled out. It is commonly held that the devil no longer appears to people, talks with them, or inhabits their innermost being through demonic possession, though he did so in Biblical times.[20] Satan is always at work distracting and luring the unwary away from the safe fold of God. He rules and controls the lives of those who spurn the salvation offered by God through his Son. One ramification of salvation is that through appropriating it by obedience to Jesus Christ one is saved from the wiles of the devil.

Life is a testing ground. It is a boot camp for soul-making. God is the friend and champion of those who seek what is good. Satan is the great enemy, tempting, distracting, and deceiving. The believer is ultimately victorious only if he accepts God's salvific offer and responds openly to the continual presence and assistance of the Son and the Holy Spirit. Death is a traumatic prospect since the merits of the life of most believers is touch and go. The unknown is always a cause for fear and anxiety. The experience of death brings much anxiety, because it is the great unknown. The parameters of the experience of death are unexplored, and the prospect that one will have to face up to life's miscues are unnerving. One is continually confronted by the possibility that, even as a believer, at any point he may be weighed in the balance and found wanting.[21] An increasing conviction, however, affirms that if one truly believes in the glorious hope held out by God, fear of death and judgment will abate. With such deep trust one can face death in peace, anticipation and hope.[22]

The prevailing view among members of the Churches of Christ is that suffering and death is caused by sin in certain obvious situations, for example, when a person becomes intoxicated, hits a bridge abutment and dies. It is agreed, however, that on occasion some persons suffer without obvious cause, and that death may be inopportune because of both age and situation. In the first six decades of this century, most people held that God in his wisdom has reasons for these inexplicable turns of events.[23] Man, however, has no channel for inside information and cannot ascertain most of the reasons, nor is it proper for him to speculate on them. What we cannot learn now, God will disclose in the end time. The words of an old hymn express well the common sentiment, "We'll understand it better by and by."[24]

The last few years have brought increasing conviction that, in fact, man is not without powers of discernment. If he puts his mind to it and seeks understanding through prayer he may well be able to ascertain why hardships and catastrophies occur. Suffering may be for the purpose of strengthening faith and conviction, for enabling onlookers to share empathy and goods, and for disturbing the complacency of friends and relatives who are unbelievers.[25] If one is open to the ways of God it may be possible to discern what he is out to accomplish in a series of events. To do so, however, requires a person who is into the Word and prayer.

The common belief among members of the Churches of Christ is that life is a time of sifting and weighing to determine whether, in the life beyond, one will reside in heaven or hell. One is assisted by God or detracted by the devil, but, in the final analysis, the decision about whom to follow belongs to the individual. Death is cataclysmic for the unbeliever and the believer who doesn't have his house in order. For the person who has been faithful to the demands of God, however, death is a welcome relief and the passageway to eternal rest in the presence of God and his Son. If one is obedient and follows the path of servanthood, death is not a threat. It is not improper, however, for friends and relatives to mourn and express sorrow. Sorrow on the part of believers is not for the fate of the loved one, but rather for themselves since they can no longer share moments of rejoicing over favorable developments or ponder ominous ones.

Funerals

Funeral practices in Churches of Christ vary according to local customs. Most funerals were held in church buildings prior to World War II. Since that time, with the advent of chapels in mortuaries, the majority of funerals are arranged there and not in church buildings. Respected public figures and church leaders, as well as persons known and loved throughout the community, often warrant services in church buildings since mortuary chapels are too small to seat all those who wish to attend. To some extent this development represents a secularizing of the funeral.[26]

The funeral attains only a quasi-religious status as far as most members of the Churches of Christ are concerned. In that regard, it belongs in the same category as the marriage ceremony. That which has official status in the church is identical with that which has scriptural warrant. Scriptural authority prevails for gatherings in which the central focus is the teaching of God's word. That which has the highest priority is the Sunday service or services, normally held in the morning and the evening. These services attain their status by the fact that the five acts of worship authorized by God take place there: singing, praying, preaching, giving, and the celebrating of the Lord's supper.[27] A meeting of believers on another day of the week, for example, Wednesday night, contains all these acts, especially teaching (preaching), except for the Lord's supper and the contribution. The funeral, as well as the wedding, however, are not settings in which these worship acts occur. Rather they are extraordinary. Since they do not fall into the regular routine they are at best quasi-religious. It is proper, however, for the focus to be religious even though the religious overtones are optional. Most members of Churches of Christ would not object to a funeral or a wedding conducted by military regulations, if appropriate, therefore mostly civil in orientation. Therefore funerals probably have become more secular in the last fifty years while weddings have become more religious. Weddings are much more likely to be held in church buildings these days than in former times. While a non-member civic figure or churchman from another religious group would be prohibited from conducting a worship service, it is acceptable for such persons to conduct or assist with a funeral.[28]

Ministers achieve their status in Churches of Christ as the result of an individual congregation permitting them to function as a minister. For that reason ministers are not ordained as a religious action; such, it is argued, is not in keeping with the scriptures. Any person is qualified to render service to God. In states, however, in which ordination is required for performing marriage ceremonies, the eldership of a church will attest to a minister's ordination without holding a formal ordination ceremony. Because of these convictions any male member is considered qualified to conduct or participate in a funeral. Normally, however, funerals are conducted by the minister or one of the ministers in a multi-staff church, or by an elder who may have served as a minister previously.[29]

Fifty years ago most funerals were held in church buildings. The family itself made most of the arrangements except for the service itself. The preacher was approached about a funeral sermon and that was the extent of his involvement. The service consisted of singing without accompaniment (since musical instruments are prohibited in church buildings), reading the obituary, prayer, and extended remarks, usually designated a funeral sermon.[30] The singing was typically congregational, though on occasion a small group or mixed quartet was employed. Comments were made for the benefit of the auditors. They were the ones to contemplate the seriousness and consequences of death and the call of God to a righteous life. It was also considered improper to judge the whereabouts of the deceased—whether in paradise or torment, unless their life and works clearly indicated their destination, and even then perilous, since the final decision is up to God. The appropriate course of action in the sermon was to bring the audience to serious confrontation with their own eternal destiny. The occasion of the funeral was thought to be particularly appropriate for observations of this sort since a person's status beyond death is foremost in his mind as he faces the death of an acquaintance, friend, or relative. It was therefore the duty of the preacher to set forth the precise ways of God for his church, the plan of salvation, and the call for sinners to repent.[31] For believers who had become negligent or dropped out, the sermon was a call to take up former ways and live for God. The sermons therefore tended to be judgmental and were so construed by those directly affected. The service throughout was a strong demand to get one's life in order so as to be prepared to meet God.

Funeral services have changed over the years even though the basic structure remains much the same. These days the minister, especially if well-known by the family, is looked to for all sorts of advice and comfort, and the normal expectation is that the one called upon to do the service will spend considerable time with the family during these trying days. He also visits regularly during the illness if it lasts for an extended period. One reason for these new expectations is that in the 1930's most preachers were evangelists traveling about the country. It was thought they should be out preaching the gospel rather than taking care of individual needs. The singing at the service is now much more likely to be a mixed group of six to twenty. In mortuary chapels, organ music is permissible before and after the service, but is rarely employed in the service proper. The sermon normally focuses on the personal qualities of the deceased, and then words of comfort and hope pertaining to the resurrection.[32]

Most of the activities at the time of the death of the church member are situated on the day of burial, except that frequently a viewing of the body is arranged the night before at the mortuary. The visiting time extends from one to three hours. Usually several of the relatives are present to greet the visitors.[33] No refreshments are served. If the funeral is in the afternoon, the family gathers at the residence of a relative to eat a light lunch. The food is normally supplied by women from the congregation. When the funeral is over the family will likely eat together again, sometimes in facilities of the church if the group is large. These meals exhibit a serious mood, but not often mourning. They are convenient occasions for members of the family to catch up on what the children and grandchildren are doing since at least some are likely to live a considerable distance away.[34] During conversations on this occasion, family members are likely to remember some kindness or anecdote about the deceased. A second meal will involve more friendly banter, but also the sadness of saying goodbye to persons with whom little future time together is possible.

A funeral service is always projected as the norm whether in a church building or in a chapel, and that is followed by a graveside service. If it is anticipated that only a few persons will be present, graveside rites alone are acceptable. Since worship patterns are never written in books of prayer, no standard liturgy exists for funerals in regard to songs, prayers, or sermonic materials.[35] In fact, in recent years, the preferences of the family are consulted and most ministers tailor the prayers, remarks and songs to take into account the deceased, the situation, and the preferences of the relatives. Reading scriptures that offer assurance and hope for life beyond the grave is characteristic of most services. Funeral times follow local customs, sometimes in the morning, more frequently in the afternoons in small towns, and usually not on Sunday since it is the day of worship. A Sunday afternoon funeral may occur, however, infrequently, and is acceptable if it is the most convenient time for everyone involved.

The approaches to burial essentially follow the local customs. Normally a funeral plot and casket is purchased and arrangements are made for embalming. The grave is later marked by a standard granite marker, though some cemetaries now prohibit markers. No theological reasons influence the decision whether or not to embalm, whether an autopsy should be performed, or whether it is acceptable to donate organs or the body to science.[36] The first two occur according to the laws of the state, local customs, and secular needs. The donation of organs and the body now occurs more frequently. Fifty years ago most members of the Churches of Christ lived in rural areas. In that setting the donating of a body to science would be unusual and therefore questionable. Religious scruples might be raised, but no consensus resulted. Cremation is viewed from the same perspective. Those in the churches who argue for a resurrection of the physical body either see cremation as exceedingly objectionable or feel extremely uneasy about it. An age old Christian tradition prohibits cremation because it destroys the physical body which is later to be raised.[37] The matter is little discussed in the churches, but may be more in the future as the incidence of cremation increases.

It is the standard practice for the casket to remain closed during the funeral but opened for viewing following the service. Funeral directors arrange for persons to walk one at a time past the open casket. In case of accidents and disfiguration, the casket remains closed. The family may exercise its preferences, for example, keeping the casket closed only to be viewed by the immediate family, or only open before the service to be viewed by those who wish to walk by at their own discretion.[38]

The manner in which church members assist the bereaved is not well defined. There are no mourning rituals. Standard approaches are to call at the house where the family gathers or at the mortuary. There friends and fellow church members visit, express sympathy, and pay their respects. In addition, fellow believers often send sympathy cards and attend the funeral. Following the funeral, arrangements are often made to supply food for the immediate family for three or four days. It is commonly assumed that what is needed most is support and friendship, not so much the right set of words. It is always appropriate to recall kind deeds and favorite expressions of the deceased, but inappropriate to bring up the matter of the eternal destiny of the one who has passed on. A century ago much conversation may have ensued on the future prospects of the deceased.[39]

The Afterlife

Although details about the afterlife have been set out, it may serve a useful purpose to reiterate them in schematic fashion. Members of the Churches of Christ believe that we only have one lifetime and that the decisions made in that lifetime determine our future. Life beyond the grave will not be upon the earth since the earth will be destroyed. Immediately upon death the soul resides in an intermediate place awaiting final judgment. When Christ returns to earth (the second coming) all the dead will be resurrected, both good and evil. The judgment will then occur after which each individual will dwell in hell or heaven forever.[40]

Because of these convictions, reincarnation is rejected as entirely foreign to the Biblical faith. Reincarnation suggests that more than one chance to prepare for heaven is possible, and since the scripture tells of only one life, reincarnation must be rejected. For the same reason purgatory is unacceptable since the doctrine implies that souls may be rescued from this realm with certain actions on earth.[41] Limbo is rejected on the ground that it is not mentioned in scripture; furthermore, there can be no future place for those who are neither good or bad, that is, in limbo, since there is only a place for the good, at first paradise, then heaven, or the bad, Tartarus, then hell.

In these closing days of the twentieth century no precise

information is advanced about the location of the dead in the
in-between time. A hundred years ago most members probably believed that the intermediate place of the dead is somewhere in the interior of the earth, and hell is located deep in
the center. Heaven then was located somewhere up in the
sky.[42] But now most members accept modern cosmology.
Where souls exist in the in-between time is not clear. The
souls of the dead are neither in the earth nor anywhere in
space in an identifiable location. Perhaps sophisticated
minds will conclude that they are in another dimension; but
few members of the Churches of Christ would suggest that
they depart through black holes.[43]

The person who makes it to heaven must hear the gospel,
believe that Jesus is the Christ the son of God, repent of his
sins, confess faith in Christ and be immersed. Everyone who
does this is a member of the Church of Christ whether or not
he worships in a building with a sign proclaiming Church of
Christ above the door. The early proponents of the restoration movement saw it as their task to encourage Christians
to exit from the denominations in order to be just Christians.
They claimed not to be the only Christians, but Christians
only. At the time when the division formed two wings—the
Disciples of Christ and the Churches of Christ—the members
of the Churches of Christ thought in exclusive terms, consid-
ering themselves to be the only Christians. Even now the
majority of members identify the church of Christ with the
Churches of Christ, but such exclusivism has recently attenuated in some quarters.[44]

Most members of the Churches of Christ now believe that,
since we will have a spiritual body in heaven, we will know
each other there because the spiritual body has continuity
with the physical body. Fifty years ago the view prevailed
that we will not know each other in heaven, for if we were to
know each other, once in heaven we could ascertain whether
our mother, father, sister, brother, wife, or husband made
it.[45] If our loved ones fail to make it, we can only be miserable
for eternity, so heaven will not be heaven after all—that is, a
place of peace and contentment. Heaven is best realized if we
are without that information and resultant misery.

Conclusion

The message for life and death proclaimed in the Churches of Christ is that life is the singular opportunity to declare for God through believing in his son Jesus Christ. The person who accepts Christ lives a full, fruitful, rewarding life here and now, and at death goes to be with God for eternity. This is a message of great hope, comfort and joy. The person who refuses to accept Christ, or who never hears the gospel proclaimed, or who accepts but is unfaithful, lives a shallow, confused and troubled life here and now, and on the other side of death is punished for eternity. Even though the joys and rewards of eternal life are known, the majority succumb to the temptations of Satan, and in the end are consigned to eternal punishment. Death therefore is an anxious moment because in it one faces the unknown. For the one who believes he has been faithful to his trust, it is a time of peace, a passageway to the joys of eternal life. The one, however, who rejects the gracious salvation offered by God should of necessity greatly fear death. For him it is a passageway to separation, torture, and eternal destruction.

Notes

[1]   The standard histories are: about the Disciples of Christ, William E. Tucker and Lester G. McAllister, *Journey in Faith* (St. Louis: Bethany Press, 1975); the Christian Churches (NACC), James DeForest Murch, *Christians Only* (Cincinnati: Standard Publishing Co., 1962); Churches of Christ, Earl West, *Search for the Ancient Order* (Vol. I, Nashville: The Gospel Advocate Co., 1949, Vol. II, Indianapolis: Religious Book Service, 1950, and Vol. III, Indianapolis: Religious Book Service, 1979) and Leroy Garrett, *The Stone-Campbell Movement: An Anecdotal History of Three Churches* (Joplin, MO.: College Press Publishing Co., 1981). For a survey of recent studies see: Richard T. Hughes, "Twenty-Five Years of Restoration Scholarship: The Churches of Christ," *Restoration Quarterly* (Part I, 25:4, 1982, pp. 233-256, Part II, 26:1, 1983), pp. 39-64.

² For a judicious, but perhaps conservative estimate of members of the Churches of Christ, see Mac Lynn, ed., *Where the Saints Meet* (Austin, TX: Firm Foundation Publishing House, 1983), pp. v-ix.

³ Winfred Ernest Garrison and Alfred T. DeGroot, *The Disciples of Christ: A History* (St. Louis: The Bethany Press, 1948), pp. 82-87.

⁴ Thomas H. Olbricht, "Christian Connexion and Unitarian Relations: 1800-1844," *Restoration Quarterly* 9:3, 1966, pp. 160-186.

⁵ "The Last Will and Testament of the Springfield Presbytery," in Charles Alexander Young, *Historical Documents Advocating Christian Union* (Chicago: The Century Company, 1904), pp. 19-26.

⁶ Garrison and DeGroot, pp. 123-179.

⁷ Robert Hooper, *Crying in the Wilderness: A Biography of David Lipscomb* (Nashville: David Lipscomb College, 1979).

⁸ Milo True Morrill, *A History of the Christian Denomination in America* (Dayton: The Christian Publishing Association, 1912).

⁹ Though sometimes spelled out more specifically the views stated in The Westminster Confession of Faith (1646), chapters XXXII and XXXIII are acceptable to most persons in the Churches of Christ. See *Creeds of the Churches*, John H. Leith, ed. (Atlanta: John Knox Press, 1977), pp. 228-234.

¹⁰ These views, though not always explicitly stated, are nevertheless implicit from Alexander Campbell on. See *Compend of Alexander Campbell's Theology*, Royal Humbert, ed. (St. Louis: The Bethany Press, 1961), pp. 202-234. See also J. J. Turner, *Life, Death, and Beyond* (Shreveport: Lambert Book House, 1975), pp. 20-22.

¹¹ This is expressed in a book of sermons mined by preachers in the 1940's and 1950's as a treasury of model discourses. Leroy Brownlow, *Why I Am A Member of the Church of Christ* (Fort Worth: Leroy Brownlow Publisher, 1945), pp. 154-167.

¹² This formulation of the steps of salvation is obvious in speeches made at Lectureships sponsored annually at Abilene Christian University. These Lectureships, now in their sixty-eighth year, are representative of mainline Churches of Christ theology. William S. Banowsky, *The Mirror of a Movement* (Dallas: Christian Publishing Company, 1965), pp. 186-189.

¹³ Brownlow, "Because It Teaches That a Child of God Can So Sin As to Be Eternally Lost," pp. 143-153.

¹⁴ Banowsky, pp. 146-164.

¹⁵ Brownlow, "Because It Teaches That the Miraculous Manifestations of the Spirit Have Ceased," pp. 159-167.

¹⁶ Ross W. Dye, "We Shall See the Dead Again," in *Sorrow and Joy*, J.D. Thomas, ed. (Abilene: Biblical Research Press, 1963), pp. 22-25. The Platonic view of the soul is that it is immortal by which is

meant that the individual soul has always existed. It is infinite in time. The standard Christian position is that the soul comes into existence at the moment God creates it, but once created exists without gap from that point on.

[17] A classical graphic illustration of this position, which has wide circulation in traditional churches, may be found in Dickie Hill, *Death and Dying* (Abilene: Quality Publications, 1982), p. 85.

[18] Turner, pp. 47-52, does not fine tune "Tartarus" and "Gehenna" inasmuch as they are not used in a precise manner in the New Testament. He calls the intermediate place of the dead "Hades," the realm for the righteous "Paradise," and that of the wicked "Hell," and separates these two regions of "Hades" with a "Great Gulf."

[19] John Allen Hudson, *How to Read the Bible: Historic Interpretation* (Fort Worth: The Mauney Company, 1958), pp. 121-133. On Satan, *Compend*, Humbert, ed., p. 221. *The Devil You Say? Perspectives on Demons and the Occult,* John Allen Chalk, et al. (Austin: Sweet Publishing Co., 1947), pp. 19-23.

[20] Ibid., p. 28.

[21] The designation for sin after conversion is popularly "backsliding." The sermon "Backsliding Preventatives," from a book of sermons popular in the 1950s makes this point. Fred E. Dennis, *Fifty Short Sermons* (Grand Rapids: Wm. B. Eerdmans, 1944), pp. 100-102.

[22] K. C. Mosier was a precursor for this view. K. C. Mosier, *Galatians* (Austin: R.B. Sweet Co., 1965), p. 66.

[23] This is demonstrated by Rex Kyker's refusal to speculate on why people die young other than in cases where they brought about their own death. The section "Services for Those Young in Years," is especially pertinent. Rex Kyker, *God's Man in Time of Death: A Ministry of Comfort* (Abilene Christian Bookstore, 1982), pp. 23-36. Also Turner, *Life, Death*, pp. 25-29.

[24] A hymn by Charles Albert Tindley written about 1905. The first line is "Trials dark on every hand." The title is sometimes listed as "By and By."

[25] John T. Willis, "Suffering: A Universal Human Experience," in *God and Man: Then and Now* (Austin: Sweet Publishing Company, 1974), pp. 19-24.

[26] Kyker, *God's Man*, p. 80, expressed a preference for the funeral chapel unless other factors prevail.

[27] This standard formulation is set out by Leslie G. Thomas in *What the Bible Teaches* (Austin: Firm Foundation, 1962) Vol. II, p. 208.

[28] Kyker mentions military or masonic rites without impunging them. Kyker, *God's Man*, p. 87.

[29] Leslie G. Thomas, *What the Bible Teaches*, Vol. II, p. 69f.

[30] The reading of the obituary contained almost all the personal references about the deceased. The sermon contained much of the exhortatory remarks from regular sermons designed to impress the auditors with the need to get right with God, because one can never predict the time of death.

[31] I heard funeral sermons of this sort in the 1930's. In unusual circumstances Rex Kyker makes remarks which imply that the deceased has not accepted the Gospel. His approach, however is non-judgmental and indirect. *God's Man*, pp. 28-31.

[32] These emphases are obvious in Kyker's funeral remarks. See especially *God's Man*, pp. 37-69. See also the suggestions in *Sorrow and Joy*, ed. J. D. Thomas (Abilene: Biblical Research Press, 1963), pp. 1-181.

[33] Whether a visitation is arranged depends on how many friends or relatives of the deceased remain. Kyker, in *God's Man*, does not discuss the matter.

[34] Kyker mentions the changing custom of taking food to the fellowship room of the church rather than to the home. He makes a case for this development. Kyker, *God's Man*, pp. 75f.

[35] Kyker in *God's Man*, mentions repeatedly the need to respond to the wishes of the family and to tailor the remarks to the circumstances and the situation of the deceased.

[36] J. J. Turner argues for a resurrection of the physical body, but does not discuss the implications for such a resurrection as it respects embalming, autopsies, etc.

[37] I have heard the matter of cremation discussed very little in church situations. Perhaps one reason is that few members of the Churches of Christ go that route. I have never been involved in or attended a funeral of a member of the Churches of Christ in which cremation was involved. I have heard of a few. Kyker in *God's Man*, p. 16, rejects cremation, but respects the wishes of those who prefer it.

[38] Kyker in *God's Man*, p. 80 recommends abiding by the wishes of the family.

[39] The change in matters appropriate for discussion are vivid to me from having contrasted conversations I heard in my childhood with those in the 1980's. Kyker tells of his conversations with the bereaved and always highlights words of comfort. Hill in *Death and Dying*, offers suggestions about how those in sorrow may be

assisted, as does Turner in *Life, Death*, pp. 87-91. Turner especially stresses the importance of not being judgmental.

[40]   Leslie G. Thomas, *What the Bible Teaches*, Vol. II, p. 19. "The judgment at the last day...will be the time for meting out rewards and punishments, upon both the righteous and unrighteous." Guy N. Woods, *The Second Coming and Other Sermons* (Memphis: Guy N. Woods, 1948), p. 15.

[41]   John David Stewart, *A Study of Major Religious Beliefs in America* (Austin: R. B. Sweet Co., 1964) pp. 17f. See also J. J. Turner, *Life, Death*, pp. 7f.

[42]   G. E. Woods, *Sermons in Outline* (Union City, TN., 1949) p. 142.

[43]   Proposed by W. G. Pollard, "Science and the Bible," *The Interpreter's Dictionary of the Bible*, Supplementary Vol. Keith Crim, ed., (Nashville: Abingdon, 1976), pp. 289-294. Pollard is an Episcopalian.

[44]   A recent clarion call for every baptized believer to be included under the rubric "churches of Christ" has been issued by Rubel Shelly, *I Just Want to Be A Christian* (Nashville: 20th Century Christian, 1984). Shelly presents the other view and quotes several historical documents.

[45]   Leslie G. Thomas, *What the Bible Teaches*, Vol., 1961. See also Hill, *Death and Dying*, p. 99f, who raises the problem and Turner, *Life, Death*, pp. 61-65.

[46]   Turner, *Life, Death*, has a chapter "Heaven: The Eternal Home," pp. 79-84.

THE CHURCH OF
JESUS CHRIST
OF LATTER-DAY SAINTS

Richard M. Eyre

Background of the Faith

While they are often called "Mormons," members of The Church of Jesus Christ of Latter-day Saints know that the full name of the church is both more accurate and more descriptive of the distinctive claim made by the faith. That claim is that there are three organizational categories of Christian churches in the world: 1) Catholic, 2) Protestant (which came about as a result of a reformation), and 3) The Church of Jesus Christ of Latter-day Saints, which is, as the

name suggests, the original Church of Jesus Christ, lost
from the earth during the dark ages, and now restored by
God in modern or "latter" times.

Mormons then, agree with Protestants that there was a
great apostasy through which many of the "plain and precious" parts of Christ's gospel, along with His authority or
priesthood, were lost. However, unlike Protestants, Mormons believe that more than a reformation by men was
required to reconstitute Christ's church once it was lost.
They believe it required an actual restoration by God.

In this context, Joseph Smith was not a reformer, or even
the Church's founder. Rather, he was a messenger or a
prophet called by God to be a vehicle or conduit through
which things that were lost could be restored. The process of
truth being lost from the world and then being returned by
God has occurred frequently in scripture. Enoch, Noah,
Abraham, and Moses—each was a prophet to whom a separate dispensation or restoration of truth was given. While He
lived on the earth, Christ himself again restored truth after it
was lost. A great apostasy followed the death of Christ and
His apostles. Rome first persecuted Christianity, then
adopted it, making it a religion of politics and pageantry. In
the process, doctrines were changed and compromised and
the true authority of God was taken from the earth. The Dark
Ages that followed are aptly named. The Renaissance and
Reformation then opened men's minds and prepared the
world for the restoration that God brought about through
His prophet Joseph Smith beginning in the year 1820.

Mormons believe in living prophets and think that it is
illogical and inconsistent to believe that a just and loving
God called prophets anciently but does not do so today when
our need for truth and guidance is as great as it has ever
been. When Joseph Smith was killed by a mob, Brigham
Young, leader of the Church's twelve apostles, became the
second prophet-president of the Church. Mormons believe
that this chain was continued and that there is a living
prophet on the earth today.

Thus the restoration that occurred through Joseph Smith
is consistent both with sacred history and with the world's

ongoing need for living prophets. Many of the great reformers who preceded Joseph Smith recognized this need. Calvin, Wesley, Luther, and Roger Williams, among others, indicated that they, while doing all they could to reform Christianity, were awaiting a more complete restoration by God himself. Mormons simply believe that this awaited restoration did occur, and that it occurred through the prophet Joseph Smith, beginning in 1820 when he prayed for guidance and received a vision of God the Father and Jesus Christ, who told him that the original Church of Jesus Christ would be reconstituted in these latter times.

The things that were restored might be put into three categories: 1) Accurate doctrine or information about the nature of God and man, and about where we came from, why we are here, and where we are going after death. 2) The Priesthood or true authority of God. 3) Additional scripture and ancient records which support and enhance the Holy Bible and lend further clarification to our knowledge of Christ and His gospel.

Let us deal with these three categories in reverse order so we can end with the main subject matter of this article, which is the Mormon belief in eternity and in life after death.

Additional scripture. Joseph Smith was directed by God, through an angel, to a set of ancient records, inscribed in a form of hieroglyphics on thin sheets of gold, which contained the religious and secular history of earlier inhabitants of the American continents. This record was called the Book of Mormon, named after a man who collected and abridged the thousand-year history of his people.

The record, which Joseph Smith was empowered to translate, tells of a man named Lehi, who left Jerusalem about 600 B.C. and came with his family by boat to Central America. A long succession of different generations of writers then give their accounts of their period of history. The people of the Book of Mormon, who are some of the ancestors of the modern American Indians, passed through many cycles of righteousness and wickedness. They had among them, at times, prophets of the Lord who taught God's commandments and who prophesied the coming of Christ.

In perhaps the most important and fascinating part of the book, an account is given of the coming of Jesus Christ to the Americas. Immediately following His crucifixion and resurrection, He descended from Heaven to the people of this hemisphere, taught them His gospel, called apostles and established His church and told them that they were the "other sheep" whom he had told His followers in Palestine he must also visit (as recorded in John's Gospel).[1]

The teachings of the Book of Mormon complement and, in some cases, clarify those of the Bible. Mormons view the Book of Mormon as a "fifth gospel"—as a further witness of Christ and of His divinity. The subtitle of the book is "Another Testament of Jesus Christ." They use the book hand-in-hand with the Bible and believe that it is, in fact, the "stick of Joseph" that Ezekiel spoke of and prophesied would become "one in thine hand" with the stick of Judah (the Bible).[2]

Mormons believe that Christ was and is the Savior of the entire world and that it is therefore logical that He visited more than one small part of the earth. He said that He had come to the whole House of Israel. The people in the Americas, having come originally from Jerusalem, were of the House of Israel.

The nickname "Mormon" of course, comes from the belief of The Church of Jesus Christ of Latter-day Saints in the Book of Mormon. Additionally, Mormons use two smaller books of scripture called *The Doctrine and Covenants* and *The Pearl of Great Price*. These books contain additional revelations received by Joseph Smith.

Priesthood or authority. Mormons believe that ordinances like baptism for the remission of sins and the laying on of hands for the gift of the Holy Ghost must be done with the true priesthood or power of God to be effectual. Part of the restoration was the returning of this priesthood to the earth. God sent Peter, James, and John, Christ's three chief apostles, back to the earth as angelic messengers. They laid their hands on the head of Joseph Smith and an associate, Oliver Cowdery, and gave them the authority by which they could perform God's ordinances and once again organize His church. This organization consisted of twelve apostles, of bishops, elders, teachers, deacons, pastors and evangelists—indeed, of the exact organization that Christ established His original church (see Eph. 4:11-13).

The Church of Jesus Christ of Latter-day Saints was officially organized in 1830. Since then it has become one of the fastest growing Christian churches in the world and today includes some six million members. When nineteen years of age, most young men in the Church elect to serve a voluntary, unpaid "mission" for the Church. They are called to go somewhere in the world (very often where they must learn a foreign language) for two years and preach the Gospel of Jesus Christ to whomever will listen. Young women in the church also often serve missions.

Mormons believe that the "fruits" of the Church of Jesus Christ (fast growth, low divorce rate, longer life expectancy, high level of education, efficient world-wide welfare system, etc.) are testaments of the truth of the restored gospel (see Matt. 7:16).

Doctrine and Information about the Nature of God and Man

In his first vision, Joseph Smith relearned much of what man had forgotten about God. He learned that God the Father and Jesus Christ, His son, are separate and distinct individuals. He learned that they both have bodies of flesh and bone and that man is literally created in their image. He learned that they are one in purpose, in spirit and in testimony and witness. They are one in the same way that they desire us to be one with them (see John 17:11, 21).

Some time after the organization of the Church of Jesus Christ of Latter-day Saints, Joseph Smith was asked to summarize the fundamental beliefs of the Church. He did so in what is called the "Articles of Faith":

Article 1.   We believe in God, the Eternal Father, and in His Son, Jesus Christ, and in the Holy Ghost.

Article 2. We believe that men will be punished for their own sins, and not for Adam's transgression.

Article 3. We believe that through the Atonement of Christ, all mankind may be saved, by obedience to the laws and ordinances of the Gospel.

Article 4. We believe that the first principles and ordinances of the Gospel are: first, Faith in the Lord Jesus Christ; second, Repentance; third, Baptism by immersion for the remission of sins; fourth, Laying on of hands for the gift of the Holy Ghost.

Article 5. We believe that a man must be called of God, by prophecy, and by the laying on of hands by those who are in authority to preach the Gospel and administer in the ordinances thereof.

Article 6. We believe in the same organization that existed in the Primitive Church, namely, apostles, prophets, pastors, teachers, evangelists, and so forth.

Article 7. We believe in the gift of tongues, prophecy, revelation visions, healing, interpretation of tongues, and so forth.

Article 8. We believe the Bible to be the word of God as far as it is translated correctly, we also believe the Book of Mormon to be the word of God.

Article 9. We believe all that God has revealed, all that He does now reveal, and we believe that He will yet reveal many great and important things pertaining to the Kingdom of God.

Article 10. We believe in the literal gathering of Israel and in the restoration of the Ten Tribes; that Zion (the New Jerusalem) will be built upon the American continent; that Christ will reign personally upon the earth; and, that the earth will be renewed and receive its paradisiacal glory.

Article 11. We claim the privilege of worshiping Almighty God according to the dictates of our own conscience, and allow all men the same privilege, let them worship how, where, or what they may.

Article 12. We believe in being subject to kings, presidents, rulers, and magistrates, in obeying, honoring, and sustaining the law.

Article 13. We believe in being honest, true, chaste, benev-
olent, virtuous, and in doing good to all men;
indeed, we may say that we follow the admonition of Paul—we believe all things, we hope all
things, we have endured many things and hope
to be able to endure all things. If there is anything virtuous, lovely, or of good report or
praiseworthy, we seek after these things.

Joseph Smith[3]

Through the process of the restoration, both in his translation of the Book of Mormon and through other visions and
revelations he received, Joseph Smith learned more of the
nature of God and man and of the answers to the three key
questions of the ages: Where did we come from? Why are we
here? And where are we going?

Perhaps we can briefly summarize the answers to these
three questions by quoting from a Church film called "Man's
Search for Happiness." Following the quote we will present
more detail:

Sometimes, in your search for happiness you ponder the
meaning of your life.

You sift your memory for beginnings; you send your mind
ahead for directions, but all you really know is now. And you
are lost in the present.

Who am I? How did I come to be? Time—where does it take
me? Toward death? And then what? *Who am I?* Where did I
come from?

To understand why you are here, you must first understand
your beginnings. At birth you did not suddenly flare into
existence out of nowhere. You have always lived.

In pre-earth life you were with your Heavenly Father. There,
as his spirit sons and daughters, you lived until you were
ready to come to earth.

As the poet Wordsworth said:

> Our birth is but a sleep and a forgetting;
>   The soul that rises with us, our life's star,
> Hath had elsewhere its setting,
>   And cometh from afar;
> Not in entire forgetfulness,
>   And not in utter nakedness,
> But trailing clouds of glory, do we come
>   From God, who is our home.

Upon entering mortal life, the memory of your life before birth was blotted out that you might live by faith and further prepare for the everlastingness of life.

This mortal body in which your spirit now dwells is subject to pain, to difficulties, to death. For it is through opposition that you grow in strength of character. You must know pain to appreciate well-being, difficulties to develop courage, death to understand eternal life.

You then, whoever you are, are related not only to every person upon this earth who lives, who has lived, who will yet live, but to God, the Father of us all, and to his son, our Savior.

With your acceptance of the responsibility of earth life, you were given a wondrous mortal body in the likeness of God.

"So God created man in his own image; in the image of God created He him, Male and female created He them."[4]

"And the spirit and the body are the soul of man."[5]

As sons and daughters of God, is it any wonder that *you* are an eternal part of his plan and purpose? And coming from such a noble heritage, that you have possibilities far beyond your greatest dreams?

Be assured that your personal search for happiness has real purpose. Be assured that your life is worth living.

Life offers you two precious gifts—one is time, the other freedom of choice, the freedom to buy with your time what you will. You are free to exchange your allotment of time for thrills. . .

You may trade it for base desires. . .

You may invest it in greed. . .

You may purchase with it vanity. . .

You may spend your time in pursuit of material things. . .

Yours is the freedom to choose. But these are no bargains, for in them you find no lasting satisfaction.

Every day, every hour, every minute of your span of mortal years must sometime be accounted for. And it is in *this* life that you walk by faith and prove yourself able to choose good over Evil, right over wrong, enduring happiness over mere amusement. And your eternal reward will be according to your choosing.

A prophet of God has said: "Men are that they might have joy"[6]—a joy that includes a fullness of life, a life dedicated to service, to love and harmony in the home, and the fruits of honest toil—an acceptance of the Gospel of Jesus Christ—of its requirements and commandments.

Only in these will you find true happiness, the happiness which doesn't fade with the lights and the music and the crowds.

God has placed you on earth without memory of your premortal past, but he hasn't left you without hope or without faith in life after death.

This he has promised you: "I am the resurrection and the life; he that believeth in me, though he were dead, yet shall he live."[7]

One of the best attested facts of sacred history is the resurrection of the Lord Jesus Christ. Three days following his crucifixion the disciples were gathered together as recorded in scripture:

"Then the same day at evening, being the first day of the week, when the doors were shut where the disciples were assembled. . .came Jesus and stood in the midst, and saith unto them, 'Peace be unto you'.

"And when he had so said, he showed unto them his hands and his side. Then were the disciples glad, when they saw the Lord."[8]

Just as you lived before mortal birth, just as you now live in this life, so through the love and sacrifice of your Savior do you continue to live after death.

Like every member of the human race, you were born and you must die. Your birth is a matter of record—you take it for granted. But death, that uncertain door that leads ahead, has been for man an awesome mystery.

Life's greatest test comes with the death of a loved one, and without faith in the immortality of the soul, the separation of death looms forever comfortless.

After death, though your mortal body lies in the earth, you—your spirit self—being eternal—continue to live. Your memory of this life will remain with you, and the knowledge of your life before birth will be restored.

Like coming out of a darkened room into the light, through death you will emerge into a place of reawakening and find loved ones waiting to welcome you.

There with your loved ones you will await the resurrection, which is the reuniting of your spirit and your body. There you will continue toward the limitless opportunities of everlasting life.

So here you are on earth, with no memory of what went before, and only faith to whisper what comes after. . .

Be assured that you are here, not by accident or chance, but as part of a glorious everlasting plan.

By a still, small voice within you and through revelation to his appointed prophets, God our eternal Father guides the affairs of his children. . .

Today as in the past.

In 1830 God re-established his Church and restored the fullness of his Gospel once more among men through a modern prophet. . .

Joseph Smith.

By revelation our Savior made known again the plan of salvation, and exaltation.

Salvation comes as a gift to every man through Jesus the Christ, but *exaltation*, which is the highest of eternal opportunities, you must earn.

It is not enough just to believe in Jesus Christ. You must work and learn, search and pray, repent and improve, know his laws and live them.

This is the way to peace and happiness and the fullness of everlasting life. It is your Heavenly Father's way.

Life before birth.   Mormons do not believe in a "one-way eternity." They believe that there is a "forever backward" as well as a "forever forward." This belief, however, should not be confused with reincarnation. We believe that we have always lived, but always as *ourselves*, never as someone else or in another life-form. We do not pass from one identity to another. Rather, we remain ourselves and pass through one place and phase of existence after another. We lived with our Heavenly Father who, as part of His plan for our growth and happiness, created this earth for us and, much as a wise father who sends his children to a fine school, allowed us to come here and become more like Him through the process of being tested, gaining physical bodies, and becoming parents and having families of our own.

In the pre-mortal existence before any of God's children had come to live on this earth, God's plan for our growth through agency and self-choice was presented to us all by the Firstborn Spirit of our Heavenly Father who was Jesus. The plan, which allowed mortal mistakes, was made workable by Jesus' willingness to perform His atoning sacrifice. Lucifer, another spirit-leader, presented an amendment to this plan which offered man coercion rather than freedom, and which conferred upon Lucifer the glory and power. One-third of the hosts of heaven followed Lucifer, who became Satan, and who tempts man today and tries to lead him away from God.

The understanding of our life before birth is a good example of a doctrine that was taught by earlier prophets, but which was distorted and lost during the apostasy. The Bible contains many references to our earlier spiritual life (see Jer. 1:5, John 17:3, John 3:13, Job 38:7, Eph. 1:4, Eccl. 12:7), but the references are vague and oblique enough that they have been ignored or misinterpreted. It is points like this that were clarified by the additional scripture and revelation given through Joseph Smith.

Belief in a pre-mortal existence is important for many reasons. It helps explain the feelings of "deja vu" that all experience—and the longings we feel and our sensation that there is more "in us" than just the results of this one short mortal life. It helps us believe in the fairness and justice of God over the course of eternity, even though we see great inequality here and now on this earth. But most importantly, our belief in a pre-mortal existence helps us better understand why we are here, and how this life ties in with God's eternal plan for His children.

Plan of salvation. This mortal life is a portion of God's

plan for the salvation and exaltation of His children. The experiences and choices we face here present us with opportunities for growth and learning that make us more like God.

When this life ends, our spirits leave our physical bodies and we go to a post-earthly spirit world where we continue to grow and progress and where we await the resurrection and judgment. In this spirit world, all people who have not had an opportunity to hear the full Gospel of Christ receive that chance. As recorded by Peter, this is the place that Christ went to preach to those who had lived during the wicked time of Noah and therefore had no opportunity to know of the true God and His laws.[9]

Those spirits who accept Christ and His Gospel in the spirit world can receive the same blessings, even the blessing of baptism, as those who accept the Gospel in mortality. Since baptism is an earthly ordinance involving water, it is done by proxy by someone on this earth for and in behalf of one who has died and is in the spirit world. This "baptism for the dead" is referred to in the New Testament[10] and is God's way of "linking" people, particularly families, with each other by allowing the living to perform works of love for their ancestors and others who died without knowing of the full Gospel of Christ. This proxy baptism would not be effective for a spirit who did not accept the Gospel in the spirit world.

These vicarious works are performed in the temples of the church and are one reason for Mormons' intense interest in genealogy. Spirits who accept the full gospel in the spirit world but do not have a descendent on earth who is baptized for them will have this work done during the millennium, the 1,000-year period in which Christ will reign personally on earth after His second coming.

The resurrection (a literal physical resurrection of *all* men) will continue with the Lord's second coming in connection with the judgment. This will be essentially a self-judgment, with each person going to dwell with those who are most like him or to where he is most comfortable. Those who have been obedient to God and valiant in their belief in Christ will be comfortable in living with God and will dwell with Him in the Celestial Kingdom.

Mormons believe in the three general divisions of heaven that Paul describes in Corinthians. The highest "degree of glory" (the Celestial) is compared with the sun. The second degree (Terrestrial) is compared to the moon, and the third level (Telestial) is compared to the stars.[11] All three are kingdoms of glory, and the principal punishment of those in the lower degree will be the regret and realization of what they could have done. The only persons who will not participate in any of the three degrees of heaven will be those who received a sure knowledge and then willfully sinned against the Holy Ghost by rejecting it. This relatively small number will be in outer darkness, becoming numbered among Satan's followers.

Within the highest or "Celestial" degree of glory there will be a "highest level" where families will continue. Thus, in Mormon temples, marriages are performed not "til death do you part" but "for time and all eternity." The eternal nature of marriage and the family is a fundamental belief among Mormons and is partly responsible for the strong family orientation of the church.

Civil marriage (or "til death do you part" marriages) are recognized as legal by the church, but "celestial marriage" performed in the Temple is seen as preferable because it binds families together beyond the grave.

The continuation of marriage and family relationships after death is seen as important, not only because of the happiness and joy it will bring to individuals but because it allows people to be more like God himself who is our *Father* in Heaven and thus continues to be surrounded by His family.

In connection with their belief in "eternal progression," Mormons believe that, as they progress, they become gradually more and more *like God. . .like* their Heavenly Father. This belief (in a loving and personal Father God who wants his children to progress toward what He is) is not unique among Mormons. Dr. Scott Peck, in his bestselling book *The Road Less Traveled*, concludes that "all of us who postulate a loving God, come to a single terrifying idea—God wants us to become Himself. We are growing toward Godhood."[12]

While many individuals share this view, the Church of Jesus Christ of Latter-day Saints may be the only church that carries an official doctrinal belief in a God who desires that we become as He is. Mormons view God as a loving Heavenly Father who wants His children, in the distant eternities, to become gods themselves.

Funerals, in the context of eternal families' eternal progression are sad in the sense of the departure of a loved one, but *happy* in the sense that that person is with God and that those left behind can someday join him there. Funeral services usually dwell on the comforting and reassuring of those left behind with the conviction that it is we on the earth who suffer the most grief, not the departed spirit who is now continuing on his or her journey of eternal progression.

To further clarify and elaborate the Mormon belief in life after death, let me, for the balance of this chapter, quote selectively from a book I co-authored called *The Birth That We Call Death*.[13] In it I quote extensively from priesthood authorities in the Mormon Church:

When a loved one has passed on, two kinds of comfort are available. One comes with condolence and love of friends, the soothing words of poet and philosopher, and the comforting presence of the Holy Spirit.

The other lies in knowledge and insight—knowledge of where the loved one is and insight into what he is doing.

Through revelation to his appointed prophets, our Heavenly Father has given us this knowledge. Because of his love for us and his understanding of our need for comfort, he has told us with positive clarity and strong assurance where our loved ones go.

By studying his revealed word, we can be sure of six things:

1. That the spirits of all men, immediately upon death, go to the spirit world to await the resurrection.
2. That, for the righteous, the spirit world is a place of joy and peace.
3. That it is also a place of continued progress and a

144 HOW DIFFERENT RELIGIONS VIEW DEATH

place of missionary work, where those who have received the gospel can teach it to those who have not.

4. That our departed loved ones are changed only in that they are temporarily separated from their physical bodies; that in personality, character, and characteristics they remain the same; that the spirit does not change.

5. That the spirit world is not far removed from us but close by, though invisible to our mortal eyes.

6. That some departed spirits know and understand our thoughts and feelings; that they are aware of us and retain their love for us.

The following statements of prophets give us this knowledge and assurance. Note how positive and precise they are, how specific and complete they are.

Behold, it has been made known unto me by an angel, that the spirits of all men, as soon as they are departed from this mortal body, yea, the spirits of all men, whether they be good or evil, are taken home to that God who gave them life. And then shall it come to pass, that the spirits of those who are righteous are received into a state of happiness, which is called paradise, a state of rest, a state of peace, where they shall rest from all their troubles and from all care, and sorrow.[14]

When the spirits leave their bodies they are in the presence of our Father and God; they are prepared then to see, hear and understand spiritual things. But where is the spirit world? It is incorporated within this celestial system. Can you see it with your natural eyes? No. Can you see spirits in this room? No. Suppose the Lord should touch your eyes that you might see, could you then see the spirits? Yes, as plainly as you now see bodies, as did the servant of Elijah. If the Lord would permit it, and it was his will that it should be done, you could see the spirits that have departed from this world, as plainly as you now see bodies with your natural eyes.[15]

—Brigham Young

The spirits of the just are exalted to a greater and more glorious work; hence they are blessed in their departure to the world of spirits. Enveloped in flaming fire, they are not far from us, and know and understand our thoughts, feelings, and motions, and are often pained therewith.[16]

—Joseph Smith

When a person who has always been good and faithful to his God lays down his body in the dust, his spirit will remain the same in the spirit world. It is not the body that has control over the spirit, as to its disposition, but it is the spirit that controls the body. When the spirit leaves the body, the body becomes lifeless. The spirit has not changed one single particle of itself by leaving the body.[17]

—Heber C. Kimball

Imagine for a moment that you are about to cross the country on a train. You get on board, and as the train starts you find yourself sitting next to a fine person who is making the same journey that you are. Since the trip usually takes almost four days, you begin a serious attempt to get to know each other. You find that you have much in common, and by the time the train steams into the darkness at the end of the first day, you feel a remarkable closeness and begin to feel that the relationship you are forming may be the most important part of your journey.

After a sound night's sleep in the Pullman car, you rejoin your friend and the two of you spend another day relating to each other and experiencing the journey together. Your rapport grows still stronger, and you find yourself feeling a little sorry that the day passes so fast. By the second night your train is deep into the flat middle plains, and as you fall asleep you are thinking about the things you want to find out and talk about with your friend the next day.

In the morning you return to your seat and find, to your dismay, that your friend is gone. When you inquire, someone tells you that he got off during the night.

Got off during the night? But he had a destination very near your own, and you had planned on having the next two days with him, and there was so much more left to say! Suddenly you realize that you never did find out quite where he came from or just who he really was, and that you never did learn why he was on the train or exactly where he was going. Worst of all, you realize that you don't know whether you'll see him again—that you don't know how to find him or contact him.

The feeling is a mixture of sadness and frustration which together produce something in between bitterness and anger. Why did he have to leave? Did someone or something make him leave? Should you be upset at him for leaving or at someone else who made him go against his will? It's not so much that he's gone, it's that you don't know *where* he's gone and you want so much to see him again.

At that point the porter comes down the row to your seat. The message he leaves is very simple, but it changes night into day and bitterness into joy. He tells you that your friend was indeed going to the same place as you—that he was going there to see his father. During the night the train received an emergency message which instructed your friend to get off the train at the next stop and catch a plane to get home more quickly, because his father needed him right then. The porter leaves you a phone number so that you can contact your friend as soon as you arrive.

The simple message of the porter turns your frustration into peace. You are still sorry to miss the two days of discussion you had anticipated with your friend, but your sorrow is no longer bitter or blind; rather, it is sweet with the knowledge of where he is and the assurance that you will see him again.

The sorrow we taste with the loss of a loved one can be bitter or sweet, depending on one ingredient—the ingredient of knowledge—the simple, pure knowledge of our origin, our purpose, and our destination. The restored gospel gives us this knowledge. It tells us our origin; it reveals our purposes on earth; and it teaches us of the life hereafter, assuring us that loved ones will meet us there and that death is a temporary separation and not an utter loss.

As in the imaginary journey on the train, the sense of temporary separation that comes to one who knows the plan of salvation does not carry the sting and panic of permanent loss.

Benjamin Franklin once said:

> Our friend and we were invited abroad....His chair was ready first, and he is gone before us. We could not all conveniently start together; and why should you and I be grieved at this, since we are soon to follow, and know where to find him.[18]

Any dear possession, if separated from us for good purpose, and if returned in even better condition, produces joy rather than agony and peace rather than frustration.

One man loses his billfold containing a large sum of money. Another, with the same amount, sets goals and makes a planned investment. Both are now separated from their money, but one feels the bite and bitterness of permanent loss, while the other anticipates the day when he will retrieve his investment and enjoys the knowledge that it will probably grow in the meantime.

A loss we cannot comprehend or accept (and a loss that is considered permanent) is bleak and stark and comfortless; but a temporary separation as a part of a goal and plan is acceptable and, in a way, even joyful. The loss of a loved one—the parting of the spirit from the physical body—is not a permanent loss, neither is it a separation we cannot accept or comprehend. Rather it is indeed an indispensable part of the goal and plan of God.

In the comprehension of the goal and plan of God lies true and lasting comfort and the ability to view death as the Book of Mormon Prophet Jacob did: "...Death hath passed upon all men, to fulfill the merciful plan of that great creator...."[19]

God is the literal father of our spirits, and Christ the Firstborn, is our eldest spirit brother. We stood with them in the pre-earthly existence and may have heard our Father state his goal: "For behold, this is my work and my glory, to bring to pass the immortality and eternal life of man."[20]

God The Father had achieved immortality and eternal life in a perfected, resurrected body. His goal was that we should become like him. As an infinitely wise father he had achieved ultimate joy, and as an infinitely good father he wanted us to become like him and thus to share that joy.

In that pre-earthly existence there were three broad differences between ourselves and our spirit Father, differences that had to be overcome if his plan were to be fulfilled and we were to become like him. First, God had a body, a glorified, perfected physical body that gave him certain capacities that we did not have. Second, he had power and intelligence and knowledge far beyond ours. Third, he was perfect and had great characteristics that we had not.

We realized, as he did, that we could begin to overcome these differences only through the experience of a mortal existence on a physical earth. This realization and the prospect of gaining physical bodies and experiencing earth life, aroused within us such gratitude and elation that, according to the Old Testament, we and all the hosts of heaven "shouted for joy."[21] There in the pre-earthly existence we must have had certain insights that we lack now, insights into the great value of earth experience and into the importance of that experience in God's plan of eternal progress.

We anticipated the joy of being able to relate to both spiritual and material things. We knew we needed physical bodies to feel with, to learn with, to react with.

Having defined both his goal (that we should become like him) and the vehicle for that goal (a physical earth), God ordained a plan, a plan that would bring about his goal, a plan for the salvation of his children.

Another direction was presented—by Lucifer, sometimes called a son of the morning. It must have had the appealing, safe sound of a guarantee, for Lucifer's promise was, that he would redeem all mankind, that not one soul could be lost.

Apparently he would do this through coercion, making sure we all did what was necessary for salvation. Hence his plan contained no opportunity for failure nor for growth and development. And all he asked for himself was everything— the full credit, the whole glory.

While Lucifer's power-play was rejected, the Father's plan was wholeheartedly accepted by Jehovah (Jesus Christ), the Firstborn. It called for agency and initiative. It included free choice and the opportunity for both success and failure. Because of its freedom, the plan offered the possibility of pleasure but also of pain, of virtue but also vice.

Because it was realistic, it anticipated sin and error which, unatoned for, would permanently separate men from God. Thus Jehovah offered to be that atoner, to come to earth himself, to gain a physical body and, as Jesus Christ the Only Begotten Son of the Father, to willingly sacrifice his life for the redemption of the world.

As spirits we realized that through the operation of this great plan of salvation Adam would fall, bringing spiritual death and physical death (mortality) upon mankind. Jesus Christ would atone for Adam's transgression so that, in Paul's terminology, just as all men would die, all would subsequently be made alive,[22] and thus physical death and physical resurrection would become two automatic transitions in eternity. Christ's atonement would also be, in John's words, the propitiation[23] or payment for everyone's sins so that, as we would repent, those sins could be removed, thus allowing us to overcome spiritual death as well as physical death.

There is as much comfort in the knowledge of a "forever backward" as there is in a "forever forward." Knowing where a loved one came from, why he was here, and that he achieved the basic purpose of his earth life, turns death from "the terrible unknown" to a necessary step in the attainment of an immortal body and in the achievement of our eternal goal.

If, in the pre-mortal existence, we looked forward to birth, which was the leaving of our Father and our eternal family, how much more we must have looked forward to death, which would be a later and essential step in the coming home!

Mortality is the prerequisite to immortality; it is by passing the tests and gaining the progress of this world that men obtain eternal life. Thus death (passing from time into eternity) is as important and as wonderful as birth (passing from eternity into time), and both are among the essential transitions in the Father's plan for our salvation.

President Brigham Young said:

> There is no period known to them (the dead) in which they experience so much joy as when they pass through the portals of death, and enter upon the glorious change of the spirit world.[24]

On this earth we view death from the perspective of one who stays behind, much as a man views a long journey when he is sending someone else off rather than going himself. He puts his friend on the train or plane and waves good-bye, only able to imagine what the trip is like and what the friend will find when he gets where he is going.

If we could glimpse, for even a moment, the glory and excitement that a departed one faces when his eyes close on time and open on eternity—if only we could glimpse this, perhaps there would be more understanding in our sorrow and more joy in our grief.

We know almost enough, through scripture and revelation, to imagine what death's awakening may be like. Lift yourself for a moment from your own shoes and into the role of one who is departing from this earth. You close your eyes for the last time on the sights of this world and become aware that you are being pulled and lifted up and out and away from your physical body. You feel somehow lighter, perhaps both in weight and in illumination. Your eyes, this time spiritual eyes, now become open, and you are aware that you see and hear and feel and sense things which were closed to you while on earth.

Because you somehow have powers you lacked before, you can see the realm of spirits which you now enter. You recognize some of those you see. There is great rejoicing as they reach out and you embrace in the light of love and peace. You already miss your physical body, and somehow you now understand its importance, but you know it will be returned to you in the resurrection; and so you go forth meeting and remembering those you knew before.

President Joseph F. Smith said:

> ...Those from whom we have to part here, we will meet again and see as they are. We will meet the same identical being that we associated with here in the flesh. . . . Deformity will be removed; defects will be eliminated, and men and women shall attain to the perfection of their spirits, to the perfection that God designed in the beginning.[25]

President Brigham Young said:

> We cling to our Mother Earth and dislike to have any of her children leave us. . . . But could we have knowledge and see into eternity, if we were perfectly free from weakness, blindness and lethargy with which we are clothed in the flesh, we should have no disposition to weep or mourn. . . . It is true it is grievous to part with our friends. We are creatures of passion, of sympathy, of love. . . . Should we not. . .rejoice at the departure of those whose lives have been devoted to doing good. . . .?[27]

Thus, we know that the spirits of all men, as soon as death occurs, go directly to the spirit world where they await the resurrection, the final redemption and the judgment. As the Book of Mormon Prophet Alma says, "There must needs be a space betwixt the time of death and the time of the resurrection."[28]

In general terms the spirit world, to which all spirits go at death, is divided into the abode of the righteous (paradise) and that of the wicked.[29] After his death, the Savior bridged the gulf between them by bringing the gospel to the spirits in

prison.[30] Since that time, righteous spirits have been called
to minister and teach the gospel to those who did not have it
on this earth. Thus the spirit world is a place where those
who had no opportunity to hear and accept the gospel on
earth will have that opportunity, so that they can "be judged
according to men in the flesh, but live according to God in the
spirit."[31]

It has been said that all truly deep and meaningful happiness stems from one of two sources: (1) service, helping, and
giving to others; and (2) anticipation, looking forward to and
waiting for something important or fine. If indeed these are
the two key sources of joy, the spirit world must offer great
potential happiness, because it contains the greatest con-
ceivable opportunity for service and holds in its future the
event most worthy of eternal anticipation. A righteous spirit
in paradise can teach other spirits the most important and
indispensable knowledge in the universe and anticipate the
greatest event: the glorious resurrection which makes possible the continuing eternal progression of the righteous.

Speaking of the great service and mission being performed
by the righteous in the spirit world, President Brigham
Young said:

> Compare those inhabitants on the earth who have heard the
> gospel in our day, with the millions who have never heard it,
> or had the keys of salvation presented to them, and you will
> conclude at once as I do, that there is a mighty work to
> perform in the spirit world.[32]

If you can imagine the happy anticipation of a boy who
has been away at a severe and demanding boarding school
and who now returns to the beautiful home of his father
whom he loved dearly—if you can imagine that happiness
and then magnify it a million times, then perhaps you can
glimpse the joy of a righteous spirit awaiting his glorious
resurrection.

The joy we anticipate in the spirit world will come into full
fruition in the resurrection, when our spirits will reunite with
perfected resurrected bodies, our own physical bodies, which

we will rejoice in finding again and which will be immortal and incorruptible.

No two facts are more clearly and explicitly stated in sacred scripture than these—the reality of Christ's resurrection and the certainty of ours. The apostles witnessed the wound in Christ's resurrected body and watched him eat the fish and the honeycomb. They went forth testifying, as he had, that, just as all men would die because of Adam, so also all men would live because of Christ.

President David O. McKay said:

> If Christ lived after death, so shall men, each one taking the place in the next world for which he is best fitted. Since love is as eternal as life, the message of the resurrection is the most comforting, the most glorifying ever given to man; for when death takes a loved one from us, we can look with assurance into the open grave and say, "He is not here," and "He will rise again."[33]

In the resurrection the spirit will re-enter its physical body, which initially will be in exactly the same state as when the spirit left it. Bodies that were sick, infirm, or deformed will then be restored to health and perfection, apparently almost instantly—as Amulek says, to a "proper and perfect frame." (Alma 1:43, in the Book of Mormon.) Nor will he at time of death determine a resurrected being's appearance. President Joseph Fielding Smith said:

> Old people will not look old when they come forth from the grave. Scars will be removed. No one will be bent or wrinkled.... Of course, children who die do not grow in the grave. They will come forth with their bodies as they were laid down, and then they will grow to the full stature of manhood or womanhood after the resurrection, but *all* will have their bodies fully restored.[34]

In his supreme wisdom and in his sublime love, God has laid out before us a plan of such excitement and such beauty that it is difficult, while in the flesh, to fully comprehend it.

As we learn it, though (by outward study of the word and inward study of our souls), we are lifted to higher realms, we face more easily the trials of our lives, and we feel the joy that can go with the sorrow of bereavement.

The Lord said to the Prophet Joseph Smith, "Wherefore, fear not even unto death; for in this world your joy is not full, but in me your joy is full."[35]

Notes

1   John 10:16.
2   Ezekiel 37:15-17.
3   *The Pearl of Great Price.*
4   Genesis 1:27.
5   *Doctrine and Covenants* 88:15.
6   2 Nephi 2:25—*The Book of Mormon.*
7   John 11:25.
8   John 21:19.
9   1 Peter 3:18-19, 1 Peter 4:6.
10 1 Corinthians 15:29
11 Ibid., pp. 40-42.
12 M. Scott Peck, *The Road Less Traveled*, N.Y., NY: (Simon and Schuster, 1978), p. 269.
13 Richard M. Eyre and Paul H. Dunn, *The Birth That We Call Death*, (Salt Lake City), Utah, Bookcraft, Inc. 1976.
14 Alma 40:11-12, *The Book of Mormon.*
15 Eyre and Dunn, op. cit., p. 27.
16 Ibid., p. 27.
17 Ibid., p. 27.
18 Ibid., p. 33.
19 2 Nephi 9:6, *The Book of Mormon.*
20 Moses 1:39, *The Pearl of Great Price.*
21 Job 38:7.
22 1 Corinthians 15:22.
23 1 John 2:2.
24 Eyre & Dunn, op. cit., p. 53.
25 Ibid., p. 54.
26 Ibid., p. 54.
27 Ibid., p. 55.

28 Alma 40:6, *The Book of Mormon.*
29 Alma 40:11-14, *The Book of Mormon.*
30 See 1 Peter 3:18-21, Moses 7:39, *The Pearl of Great Price; The Doctrine and Covenants*, Section 138.
31 1 Peter 4:6.
32 Eyre & Dunn, op. cit., p. 56.
33 Ibid., p. 57.
34 Ibid., pp. 57-58.
35 *Doctrine and Covenants* 101:36.

HINDUISM

Swami Adiswarananda

This chapter is based on the teachings of Vedanta as embodied in the major Hindu scriptures—the Upanishads, the Bhagavad Gita, the Brahma Sutras, and others—and interpreted by Sankaracharya, the exponent of non-dualism. According to non-dualism, the Ultimate Reality of every- is Brahman, the non-dual pure consciousness, and It alone exists. The universe of beings and things is merely an appearance of Brahman in time and space. The individual soul and Brahman are absolutely non-different. The root cause of all bondage is the soul's ignorance of its true nature.

Liberation is union with Brahman attained through Self-knowledge. The two other interpretations of Vedanta are qualified non-dualism and dualism. The chief exponent of qualified non-dualism is Ramanuja and of dualism, Madhva. Qualified non-dualism maintains that Brahman, though non-dual pure consciousness, transforms Itself into God, the universe, and the world of souls, and that the transformation is real. God is the whole and the individual soul is the part. The bondage of the individual soul is due to its alienation from God, and liberation is communion with God. Dualism believes that God is a personal being who creates the universe and the world of souls. The creation is real and the created beings and things are different from and dependent on God. The bondage of the soul is due to its forgetfulness of God, and liberation is communion with God.

Background of the Faith

Hinduism, considered the oldest religion of the world, is today practiced by over 500 million people in India and other countries. The word "Hindu" is a distorted form of "Sindhu," the Sanskrit word for Indus, the river that flows into the Arabian Sea. This mispronunciation is attributed to the Persians who invaded India at the end of the sixth century B.C. Later, during the Greek invasion of India (326 B.C.), the Greeks described the river Sindhu as "Indos," which was sometime afterward changed to "Indus." Since then, the country east of the river Indus has come to be known as India, its people as Indians, and their religion as Hinduism. The original name of Hinduism is *Sanatana Dharma*, which means "eternal religion." It was also known as *Vaidika Dharma*, or the "religion of the Vedas." The European traders and Christian missionaries who came to India at the beginning of the seventeenth century signified Hinduism as "Brahmanism."

A federation of many systems of thought, Hinduism is based not on any fixed sets of creeds and dogmas but on certain eternal principles. It was not founded by any historical personality. Many prophets, saints, mystics, and philosophers, both ancient and modern, have contributed to its growth, development, and perpetuation. The great teachers of Hinduism are Sri Rama (of the Ramayana), Sri Krishna (of the Bhagavad Gita), Sri Sankaracharya (A.D. 788-820), Sri Ramanuja (A.D. 1017-1137), Sri Madhva (A.D. 1199-1276), Sri Chaitanya (A.D. 1485-1533), and in modern times, Sri Ramakrishna (A.D. 1836-1886), and Swami Vivekananda (A.D. 1863-1902). Their lives demonstrate the validity of the spiritual teachings of Hinduism. Hinduism derives its authority primarily from the four Vedas: the Rig-Veda, the Yajur-Veda, the Sama-Veda, and the Atharva-Veda. Each Veda consists of four parts: the *mantras*, or hymns in praise of Vedic deities; the *brahmanas*, or the section dealing with rituals and ceremonies; the *aranyakas*, or philosophical interpretation of the rituals; and the Upanishads, or the concluding portions of the Vedas (known as Vedanta), which describe the profound spiritual truths. Hinduism derives its authority secondarily from another group of scriptures—the Ramayana, the Mahabharata, the Bhagavad Gita, the Puranas, and others. Of the two groups of scriptures, the Vedas along with the Upanishads are known as *srutis*, while the others are called *smritis*. *Sruti* is revelation and *smriti* is tradition.

The Ultimate Reality

Hindu scriptures describe ultimate reality as Brahman. Brahman is non-dual pure consciousness, indivisible, incorporeal, infinite, and all-pervading like the sky. Brahman is of the nature of existence-knowledge-bliss-absolute—the ground of all existence, basis of all awareness, and source of all bliss. It is the reality of all realities, the soul of all souls, one without a second, the constant witness of the changing phenomena of the universe. From the absolute point of view, Brahman alone exists. Brahman has two aspects: transcendent and immanent. In Its transcendent aspect, Brahman is devoid of name and form, sex and attributes. But in

Its immanent aspect, Brahman is endowed with them. The Upanishads designate the transcendent Brahman by the word "It" and the immanent Brahman by the word "He." Through Its inscrutable power called *maya*, the transcendent Brahman appears to be conditioned by time and space and to manifest itself as personal God, the creator, preserver, and destroyer of the universe. The Upanishads describe God as the supreme person:

> His hands and feet are everywhere; His eyes, heads, and faces are everywhere; His ears are everywhere; He exists compassing all.[1] The heavens are His head; the sun and moon, His eyes; the quarters, His ears; the revealed Vedas, His speech; the wind is His breath; the universe, His heart. From His feet is produced the earth. He is, indeed, the inner Self of all beings.[2]

The various Godheads of Hinduism, such as Shiva, Vishnu, Brahmā, Kali, and Durga, are but different facets of Brahman. The supreme Brahman assumes various forms for the fulfillment of the individual spiritual seekers. All concepts and forms of God, according to Hinduism, are what we think of Him and not what He is to Himself. Again, various seekers of God, depending upon their advancement, perceive God differently. For example, to the beginner God appears as an extra-cosmic creator; to the more advanced seeker as inner controller; and to the perfect knower of God, God is everywhere and in everything. Still another manifestation of the conditioned Brahman is the incarnation of God—God's taking human form. According to Hinduism, God incarnates Himself to fulfill the needs of the universe, whenever and wherever such a need arises. In the Bhagavad Gita Sri Krishna says:

> Whenever there is a decline of *dharma* (righteousness), O Bharata, and a rise of *adharma* (unrighteousness), I incarnate Myself. For the protection of the good, for the destruction of the wicked, and for the establishment of *dharma*, I am born in every age.[3]

Thus, according to Hinduism, the supreme Godhead is both formless and endowed with many forms.

The Universe

Hinduism maintains that the universe is beginningless and endless. It subscribes to the theory of manifestation and non-manifestation of the universe, of evolution of cosmic energy into names and forms and its involution. The Vedas describe this process as the outbreathing and inbreathing of Brahman. The Upanishads say that just as the hair and nails grow on a living person, as the threads come out of a spider, as sparks fly from a blazing fire, as melodies issue from a flute, or as waves rise on the ocean, so also does the universe come forth from Brahman. Brahman is both the material and the efficient cause of the universe.

This manifestation of Brahman as the manifold universe is not real but apparent. Through its inscrutable power of *maya*, Brahman appears as the world of matter and souls, and as endowed with the activities of creation, preservation, and dissolution. *Maya* veils the ultimate reality and in its place projects various appearances. *Maya* is change and relativity. It is neither real nor unreal nor both. If the world of *maya* were real, then it could never be changed. On the other hand, it cannot be unreal because the sufferings of life are felt tangibly. As long as it is not known, *maya* is delusive; but when known, *maya* is nothing but Brahman. *Maya* is comprised of the three *gunas*, or qualities: *sattva, rajas,* and *tamas. Sattva* is balance or equilibrium; *rajas* is restlessness or imbalance; *tamas* is inertia or darkness. The three *gunas* are present in varying degrees in all objects, gross or subtle, including the body-mind complex of an individual. For example, when *sattva* prevails in an individual, the light of knowledge begins to shine through his body and mind. When *rajas* prevails, he is stirred by unrest. And when *tamas* prevails, he is taken over by inertia. When the universe is in a period of non-manifestation, the three *gunas* remain in a state of non-differentiation, or equilibrium. Manifestation begins when the equilibrium of the *gunas* is disturbed.

According to Hinduism, the process of manifestation and non-manifestation of the universe follows a cyclical pattern. In each cycle there is a recurrence of the same material phenomena, and the same recurrences continue throughout eternity. No energy can be annihilated; it goes on changing until it returns to the source. Nature presents both movements—from the subtle to the gross and back from gross to subtle. Evolution presupposes involution. Only that which was involved before can be evolved afterwards. Evolution of the physical universe follows a graduated process. The first element to evolve at the beginning of a cycle is *akasa*, or the ether, in its subtle form. Then gradually evolve four other elements: air, fire, water, and earth. In the beginning, the five elements remain unmixed. Then, through their various combinations, the elements take their gross forms. From out of the basic gross and subtle elements are produced all objects, gross and subtle, including the body-mind complex of all living creatures.

According to the Puranas, each world period is divided into four ages, or *yugas*: *Satya, Treta, Dwapara*, and *Kali*. The *Satya yuga* abounds in virtue, with vice being practically non-existent. But with each succeeding age, virtue gradually diminishes and vice increases, making the age of *Kali* the reverse of *Satya*. The approximate duration of each *yuga* has been described as: *Satya yuga*, 1,728,000 years; *Treta*, 1,296,000 years; *Dwapara*, 864,000 years; and *Kali*, 432,000 years. These four *yugas*, rotating a thousand times, make one day of Brahmā, the creator, and an equal number of years, one night. Thirty such days and nights make one month of Brahmā, and twelve months make one year. After living for a hundred such years, Brahmā dies. Brahmā, too, like all other entities of the phenomenal universe, has a limited life span, although this life span seems nearly endless from the viewpoint of human calculations.

The Human Individual

According to Hinduism, man is essentially a soul that uses its body and mind as instruments to gain experience. What is the nature of the soul? Hinduism maintains that the macrocosm and the microcosm are built on the same plan, and that Brahman is the soul of both. As the soul of man, Brahman is known as *Paramatman.* The Upanishads speak of the two souls of man dwelling, as it were, side by side, within him: the real soul (*Paramatman*) and the apparent soul (*jivatman*). The real soul is the witness consciousness, serene and detached. The apparent soul is the embodied soul, the experiencer of birth and death, and is ever in quest of freedom and eternal life. The apparent soul is the ego self— the reflection of the real soul. The real soul has been described as Self and the apparent soul as non-Self. Hinduism analyzes man in terms of three bodies, five sheaths, and three states. It says that a human individual has three bodies: physical body, subtle body, and causal body. The physical body is produced out of the gross forms of the five basic elements (ether, air, water, fire, and earth), and is subject to a sixfold change: birth, subsistence, growth, maturity, decay, and death. At death the physical body perishes and its five constituent elements are dissolved. The subtle body is made of the subtle forms of the five basic elements that produced the physical body. It is the receptacle of thoughts and memories and continues to exist after death, serving as the vehicle of transmigration. A human individual enters this world with a bundle of thoughts in the form of his mind, and he also exits with a bundle of thoughts, some old and some new. The causal body, characterized by ego-sense only, is finer than the subtle body. All three bodies are for the fulfillment of desires, gross and subtle. The soul is different from these three bodies.

Hindu scriptures further describe the body-mind complex of man as consisting of five sheaths, or layers: the physical sheath, the sheath of *prana* (the vital air), the sheath of mind, the sheath of intellect, and the sheath of bliss. These sheaths are located one inside the other like the segments of a collapsible telescope, with the sheath of the physical body being the outermost and the sheath of bliss being the innermost. The sheath of the physical body is dependent on food for its sustenance and lasts as long as it can absorb nourishment. The sheath of the vital air is the manifestation of the universal vital energy. It animates the gross body, making it inhale and exhale, move about, take in nourishment, excrete, and reproduce. The sheath of the mind is the seedbed of all desires. It is changeful, characterized by pain and pleasure, and has a beginning and an end. The sheath of the intellect is the seat of I-consciousness. Though material and insentient by nature, it appears intelligent because it reflects the light of the Self. It is the cause of embodiment. Finer than the sheath of the intellect is the sheath of bliss, the main features of which are pleasure and rest. It, too, is material and subject to change. The five sheaths are the five layers of embodiment and they veil the light of the Self.

The Upanishads mention that man experiences three states of existence—waking, dream, and deep sleep—and his Self within, the experiencer of the three states, is different from them. Analysis of all three states reveals the true nature of the Self. In the waking state man remains identified with his physical body, in the dream state with his subtle body, and in deep sleep with his causal body. The Atman, or Self, is the monitoring consciousness of all three states and is the basis of their unity. Hinduism contends that conclusions based only on an analysis of the waking state are incomplete and cannot reveal the real nature of man. In this sense, Hinduism considers the conclusions of physical science as inadequate although not incorrect.

The Problem of Suffering

Why is a soul born on earth, and why does it suffer? What happens to it after death, and what is its destiny? Why are there inequalities between one person and another? According to Hinduism, the idea of complete annihilation of the soul after death is inconsistent with the concept of a moral order in the universe. If everything ends with death, then there is no meaning to life. Nor is the view that the soul is created at birth and then becomes eternal at death reasonable, for anything that has a beginning will also have an end. Further, this view does not explain the obvious inequalities among people. Clearly, all are not born equal. Some are born with good tendencies, some with bad; some strong, and some weak; some fortunate, and some unfortunate. Moreover, all too often the virtuous suffer and the vicious prosper. One cannot attribute these injustices to the will of God or to some inscrutable providence, because such a concept belies any belief in God's love for His beings. These glaring differences cannot be considered the mere results of chance happening; for if such were the case, there would be no incentive for moral or material improvement. Then, heredity and environment, although they explain the physical and mental characteristics of an individual partially, do not explain inequalities satisfactorily. Nor does the doctrine of eternal happiness in heaven, or eternal suffering in hell, answer this question. Everlasting life in terms of time is self-contradictory. The dwellers in heaven, endowed with subtle or spiritual bodies, are still subject to embodiment and therefore cannot be immortal. The idea of eternal damnation for the mistakes of man's brief earthly career contradicts justice and reason. The inequalities and sufferings of life cannot be set right by readjustments after death, because what happens after death cannot be verified. The conditions on the two sides of the grave are different, and the dead never come back to testify to their afterlife conditions.

Rebirth and the Law of Karma

Hinduism contends that the cause of suffering and inequalities must be sought not in what happens after death, but in the conditions before birth, and puts forward the doctrine of rebirth. Rebirth is the necessary corollary to the idea of the soul's immortality. Death is a break in the series

of continuing events known as life. Through death the individual soul changes its body: "Even as the embodied Self
passes, in this body, through the stages of childhood, youth,
and old age, so does It pass into another body."[4] A knower of
the Self can witness the passing of a soul from one body to
another at the time of death: "The deluded do not perceive
him when he departs from the body or dwells in it, when he
experiences objects or is united with the *gunas*; but they who
have the eye of wisdom perceive him."[5]

Rebirth, Hinduism maintains, is governed by the law of
karma. According to this law, man is the architect of his own
fate and maker of his own destiny. *Karma* signifies the way
of life, that is, what we think, say, and do and it brings
conditioning of the mind, the root cause of embodiment. It is
the mind that produces bodies, gross or subtle. Remaining
identified with the body-mind complex, the soul, though
ever-free, follows its destiny and, as it were, experiences all
pairs of opposites, such as birth and death, good and evil,
pain and pleasure. Patanjali (the teacher of the Yoga system), in one of his aphorisms, describes the causes of suffering as five: ignorance, ego-sense, attachment, aversion, and
clinging to life.[6] Reality is neither good nor evil. There is
nothing in the universe which is absolutely good or absolutely evil, that is to say, good or evil for all time. Good and
evil are value judgments made by the individual mind in
keeping with its inner disposition caused by past *karma*. If
one asks, why does God permit evil, then the question will
come, why does God permit good? According to the Hindu
view, good is that which takes us near to our real Self, and
evil is that which creates a distance between us and our real
Self. The law of *karma* is the law of automatic justice. It tells
us that no action goes without producing its result. The
circumstances of our present life, our pains and pleasures,
are all the results of our past actions in this existence and in
countless previous existences. As one sows, so shall one
reap. This is the inexorable law of *karma*. *Karma* produces
three kinds of results: (a) results of past actions which have
produced the present, body, mind, and circumstances; (b)
results which have accumulated but are yet to fructify; and

(c) results that are being accumulated now. Over the first category of results no one has any control; these are to be overcome by patiently bearing with them. The second and third kinds, which are still in the stage of thoughts and tendencies, can be countered by education and self-control. Essentially, the law of *karma* says that while our will is free, we are conditioned to act in certain set ways. We suffer or enjoy because of this conditioning of our mind. And conditioning of mind, accumulated through self-indulgence, cannot be overcome vicariously. A Hindu is called upon to act in the living present, to change his fate by changing his way of life, his thoughts and his actions. Our past determines our present, and our present will determine our future. He is taught that no change will ever be effected by brooding over past mistakes or failures or by cursing others and blaming the world or by hoping for the future. To the contention that the law of *karma* does not leave any scope for the operation of divine grace, Hinduism's answer is that the grace of God is ever flowing equally toward all. It is not felt until one feels the need for it. The joys and suffering of a human individual are of his own making. Good and evil are mind-made and not God-created. The law of *karma* exhorts a Hindu to right actions, giving him the assurance that, just as a saint had a past so also a sinner has a future. Through the doctrine of rebirth and the law of *karma*, Hinduism seeks an ethical interpretation of life. The theory of the evolution of species describes the process of how life evolves. But the purpose of this evolution can be explained only by the doctrine of rebirth and the law of *karma*. The destiny of the soul is immortality through Self-realization. Existence-knowledge-bliss-absolute being its real nature, nothing limited can give it abiding satisfaction. Through its repeated births and deaths it is seeking that supreme fulfillment of life.

The Ideas of Heaven and Hell

According to the Hindu Puranas, there are fourteen worlds in the universe—the seven upper and the seven lower. The seven upper worlds are *Bhuh, Bhuvah, Swah, Mahah, Janah. Tapah,* and *Satyam*; and the seven nether worlds are *Atala, Vitala, Sutala, Rasatala, Talatala, Mahatala,* and *Patala.* The region known as *Bhuh* is the earth where we dwell, while *Swah* is the celestial world to which people repair after death to enjoy the reward of their righteous actions on earth. *Bhuvah* is the region between the two. *Janah, Tapah,* and *Satyam* constitute *Brahmaloka,* or the highest heaven, where fortunate souls repair after death and enjoy spiritual communion with the personal God, and at the end of the cycle attain liberation, though a few return to earth again. The world of *Mahah* is located between *Brahmaloka* and *Bhuh, Bhuvah,* and *Swah. Patala,* the lowest of the seven nether worlds, is the realm where wicked souls sojourn after death and reap the results of their unrighteous actions on earth. Thus, from the viewpoint of Hinduism, heaven and hell are merely different worlds, bound by time, space, and causality. According to Hinduism, desires are responsible for a person's embodiment. Some of these desires can best be fulfilled in a human body, and some in an animal or a celestial body. Accordingly, a soul assumes a body determined by its unfulfilled desires and the results of its past actions. An animal or a celestial body is for reaping the results of past *karma,* not for performing actions to acquire a new body. Performance of *karma* to effect any change of life is possible only in a human body, because only human beings do good or evil consciously. Human birth is therefore a great privilege, for in a human body alone can one attain the supreme goal of life. Thus, in search of eternal happiness and immortality, the apparent soul is born again and again in different bodies, only to discover in the end that immortality can never be attained through fulfillment of desires. The soul then practices discrimination between the real and the unreal, attains desirelessness, and finally realizes its immortal nature. Affirming this fact, the Katha Upanishad says: "When all the desires that dwell in the heart fall away, then the mortal becomes immortal and here attains Brahman."[7]

Death and Life Beyond Death

Death, according to Hinduism, is a series of changes through which an individual passes. The Brihadaranyaka Upanishad describes thus the passing of a soul:

When the soul departs from the body, the life-breath follows: when the life-breath departs, all the organs follow. Then the soul becomes endowed with particularized consciousness and goes to the body which is related to that consciousness. It is followed by its knowledge, works, and past experience. Just as a leech supported on a straw goes to the end of it, takes hold of another support, and contracts itself, so does the self throw this body away and make it unconscious, take hold of another support, and contract itself. Just as a goldsmith takes a small quantity of gold and fashions another—a newer and better— form, so does the soul throw this body away, or make it unconscious, and make another—a new and better—form suited to the Manes, or the celestial minstrels, or the gods, or Virat, or Hiranyagarbha, or other beings. . .As it does and acts, so it becomes; by doing good it becomes good, and by doing evil it becomes evil—it becomes virtuous through good acts and vicious through evil acts.[8]

Hinduism speaks of the four courses that men follow after death. The first, called *devayana*, way of the gods, is followed by spiritually advanced souls who lead an extremely pure life, devoting themselves to wholehearted meditation on Brahman, but who have not succeeded in attaining complete Self-knowledge before death. They repair to *Brahmaloka*, the highest heaven, and from there in due course attain liberation. The description of this path in the Chhandogya Upanishad is as follows:

Now, such a one—whether his after-death rites are performed or not—goes to light, from light to day, from day to the bright half of the month, from the bright half of the month to the six months during which the sun rises northward, from the months to the year, from the year to the sun, from the sun to the moon, from the moon to the lightning. There he meets a

person who is not a human being. This person carries the soul
to Brahman. This is the divine path, the path of Brahman.
Those proceeding by this path do not return to the whirl of
humanity.[9]

The second course, known as *pitriyana*, way of the fathers, is
followed by ritualists and philanthropists who have cher-
ished a desire for the results of their charity, austerity, vows,
and worship. Following this path, they repair to *Chandra-
loka*, the lunar sphere, and after enjoying immense happiness there as a reward for their good actions, they return
again to earth since they still have earthly desires. The third
course, which leads to hell, is followed by those who led an
impure life, performing actions forbidden by the scriptures.
They are born in sub-human species. After expiating their
evil actions, they are again reborn on earth in human bodies.
The fourth course is for those who are extremely vile in their
thoughts and actions. They are reborn again and again as
insignificant creatures such as mosquitoes and fleas. Eventually, after the expiation of their evil actions, they too
return to human bodies on earth. When a soul assumes a
human body, it takes up the thread of spiritual evolution of
its previous human birth and continues to evolve toward
Self-knowledge. According to Hinduism, all souls will ultimately attain Self-knowledge. The four courses do not apply
to those souls who attain Self-knowledge before or at the
time of death. For these souls there is no going to any realm.
Upon their death, their souls become absorbed in Brahman,
and the elements of their body-mind complex return to their
original source.

From the point of view of Hinduism, dying may be compared to falling asleep and after-death experiences to dreams.
The thoughts and actions of the waking state determine the
nature of our dreams. Similarly, after death the soul experiences the results of the thoughts it entertained and the
actions it performed during its life on earth. After-death
experiences are real to the soul, just as a dream is real to the
dreamer, and may continue for ages. Then, when the soul
wakes up after this sleep, it finds itself reborn as a human

being. According to the Hindu scriptures, some souls after death also may be born as human beings without going through the experiences of heaven or hell. There is no real break in the spiritual evolution of the soul toward Self-knowledge. Even the soul's lapse into sub-human birth from human life is a mere detour. A dying man's next life is determined by his last thought in the present life. The Bhagavad Gita says: "For whatever objects a man thinks of at the final moment, when he leaves the body—that alone does he attain, O son of Kunti, being ever absorbed in the thought thereof."[10] And the last thought of the dying person inevitably reflects his inmost desire. These different courses after death have been described to warn people against neglecting the path of Self-knowledge, which alone can confer immortality and eternal peace and happiness.

Funeral and Disposal of the Dead

Life, according to Hinduism, is a journey toward perfection. Its stages are marked by performances of specific sacraments, or *samskaras*, such as sacraments for birth, initiation into spiritual life, marriage, and death. When a person dies, the survivors consecrate the event of his death by funeral rites for his future good and felicity. Baudhayana (sutras) says:

> Death is inevitable in the case of the man who is born. Therefore one should not be happy at birth, nor mourn death. A creature comes from the unknown and goes to the unknown; so the wise regard birth and death as equal. Such being the fact, people give their dues to their mother, father, preceptor, wife, son, disciples, cousin, maternal uncle, agnates, and cognates, and consecrate their cremation with proper sacrament.[11]

The belief in life after death, and the wish to secure happiness for the departed and the final liberation of his soul from all repeated birth and rebirth, prompt the Hindu to perform funeral rites. The most prevalent way to dispose of the body is cremation, although in special cases burial and water burial are also followed. Fire is considered to be sacred and is regarded by the Hindus as the messenger between this life and the afterlife. The following are the prescribed rites and ceremonies at death:

(1) *Approach of death.* The person whose death is imminent bids farewell to his assembled friends and relatives and the world. Prayers are then offered and alms and gifts are distributed for his welfare. It is the general belief among the Hindus that after death the body should be cremated as soon as possible, and that under no circumstances should the dead body be carried or touched by any except those belonging to the same caste. Embalming of the body is not the practice among the Hindus. The cremation ground is considered sacred because it is here that the transitoriness of life is tangibly revealed.

(2) *Predisposal rites.* Oblations are offered into the sacrificial fire that had been maintained by the dying person. It is also customary to put holy water of the Ganges and holy Tulasi leaves into the mouth of the dying.

(3) *The bier.* A special oblong frame is constructed to remove the dead body to the place of cremation, and the body is formally laid on it with the words: "Give up the clothes that you have hitherto worn and remember your *ista* (sacrifices) and *purta* (acts of philanthropy and charity)."

(4) *Removal of the dead body.* In ancient times the bier was put on a bullock cart with a recitation of the prayer: "May this cart with two bullocks carry you to the realm to which the virtuous resort." The bier is usually carried by the nearest relatives and friends as an act of honor to the dead.

(5) *The funeral procession.* It is usually led by the eldest son of the dead person, and followed by relatives and friends.

(6) *Gift of a cow.* Often a cow is given as a gift, or let loose, in the belief that his act helps the departed in crossing

the ocean of mortal existence.

(7) *Cremation*. The dead body is washed and dressed, the last prayers are offered for the soul, and then the body is put in the flames of the funeral pyre with the chanting of the following Vedic hymn: "O fire, consume not this body to cinders, nor give it pain, nor scatter about its skin and limbs. O Jataveda, when the body is fairly burnt, convey its spirit to its ancestors. May the organs of vision proceed to the sun; may the vital air merge in the atmosphere; may thou (deceased person), according to thy virtuous deeds, proceed to heaven or earth or the regions of water, whichever place is beneficial to you."[12]

(8) *Offering of water*. After the body has been reduced to ashes, the funeral pyre is extinguished by pouring water on it.

(9) *Consoling the family*. The family members console themselves by recounting the good deeds of the departed and listening to readings of the scriptures that describe the transitoriness of life.

(10) *Period of mourning*. A period of mourning is observed by the family of the dead, during which time they practice austerity in food, clothing, and comforts, remembering the departed soul and offering prayers for his spiritual welfare. The mourning period varies from ten days to one month or more, according to the person's caste rules and tradition.

(11) *Collecting the remains*. A portion of the remains is collected and put in the holy waters of any sacred river.

(12) *Symbolic monument*. As a mark of remembrance a mound of earth is often raised over the remains of the dead at the place of cremation.

(13) *Peace rite*. After the period of mourning, a special ceremony called *shraddha* is performed, at which prayers are offered, worship is done, and gifts are made for the benefit of the departed soul.

(14) *Final sacrament*. At the end of one full lunar year, the family members observe the last sacrament with special prayers and rites for the welfare of the departed.

The dying person may be taken to the bank of a sacred river or brought in front of the family worship room in order that he will die with thoughts of God. Chanting of the holy texts and of the holy name of God is done so that the person about to depart will forget everything else and put his mind on God. Expiation ceremonies in the form of special worship may be performed for one who is about to die and who has had many lapses from righteous conduct, or who is suffering from incurable disease.

While the ceremonial disposal of the dead body and the funeral observances are mandatory from the point of view of Hindu religious law, philosophically speaking such rites and ceremonies are more for the consolation of the survivors than for the benefit of the dead, whose destiny is determined by his past *karma*. The dead body is like a cast-off garment, and the departed soul is not affected in any way whether or not the body is disposed of ceremonially. There is therefore no bar to a Hindu's bequeathing his body to any humanitarian cause. An ancient text says: "Since death is certain for the body, let it be used for the good of all beings." There is the example mentioned in the Rig-Veda of the sage Dadhichi, noted for his piety, purity, and Self-knowledge, who voluntarily gave up his body for the benefit of the gods: The demon Vritra once seized the heavenly realm and could not be defeated by the gods by any means. Seeing the predicament of the celestials, Brahmā, the creator, advised them that Vritra could be defeated only by a thunderbolt made from the bones of Dadhichi. When they approached the sage and made their request, he joyfully gave up his body in the state of *yoga* for the benefit of the gods, men, and the universe. In the same spirit, Hinduism does not prohibit a Hindu from doing any act of unselfish service to humanity, including the funeral ceremony of a non-Hindu, if such a need arises. Caste rules and funeral injunctions of the Hindu law-givers are meant to be guidelines for righteous living. They do not prevent a Hindu from performing any unselfish act of service by seeing God in man.

The Goal of Life

The supreme goal of life, according to Hinduism, is *moksha*, or liberation. Liberation is the realization of the soul's identity with Brahman, the absolute reality. It is not merely the cessation of suffering; it is the positive experience of great bliss. Hindu scriptures designate this realization as Self-knowledge. Hinduism holds that Self-knowledge alone can conquer death. The Katha Upanishad says:

> What is here the same is there; and what is there, the same is here. He goes from death to death who sees any difference here.[13] Having realized Atman, which is soundless, intangible, formless, undecaying, and likewise tasteless, eternal, and odorless; having realized That which is without beginning and end, beyond the Great, and unchanging—one is freed from the jaws of death.[14]

Self-knowledge and immortality are synonymous, says the Brihadaranyaka Upanishad:

> Whosoever in this world, O Gargi, without knowing this Imperishable, offers oblations, performs sacrifices, and practices austerities, even for many thousands of years, finds all such acts but perishable. Whosoever, O Gargi, departs from this world without knowing this Imperishable is miserable. But he, O Gargi, who departs from this world after knowing the Imperishable is a knower of Brahman.[15]

Immortality is not the result of any spiritual discipline. It is a revelation. Spiritual disciplines purify the heart, and in the mirror of the pure heart the immortal Self is reflected.

Self-knowledge is not miraculous, nor can it be achieved vicariously. It is a burning realization that totally transforms the person. The knower of Brahman becomes Brahman. Hinduism speaks of three things that, taken together, can verify Self-knowledge: *sruti*, or faith in the scriptures; *yukti*, or reason; and *anubhuti*, or personal experience.

Scriptures, according to Hinduism, are only compendiums of the direct experiences of past sages and saints. Blind belief in them makes a person dogmatic. Then reason, Hinduism contends, begins with doubt and ends in doubt, and it cannot prove or disprove Self-knowledge. A person who depends solely on reason always remains a doubter and may even turn into a cynic. Personal experience can be deceptive and delusive, and therefore it cannot give decisive proof of Self-knowledge. Self-knowledge, in order to be authentic, must be negatively corroborated by reason, testified to by the scriptures, and also felt as a deep experience of life. According to Hinduism, there are three further tests of Self-knowledge: First, it is *avadita*—an experience of enlightenment that is not contradicted by any other subsequent experience. Second, it is *aviruddha*—an experience that does not come into conflict with our everyday experience of the world of reality, just as our adulthood experiences do not negate those of our childhood. Third, it is *sarve bhute hiteratah*—always conducive to the welfare of all beings.

Self-knowledge, the Upanishads point out, must be attained in this very life. One who dies in bondage, will remain bound after death. Immortality, in order to be real, must be experienced before death. The Katha Upanishad says: "If a man is able to realize Brahman here, before the falling asunder of his body, then he is liberated; if not, he is embodied again in the created worlds."[16] Self-knowledge is the consummation of all desires. According to the Hindu scriptures, one should give up individual self-interest for the sake of the family, the family for the sake of the country, the country for the sake of the world, and everything for the sake of Self-knowledge.

The liberated soul is the free soul, who through his life and actions demonstrates the reality of God. Free from all desires and egotism, and ever-established in the knowledge of the immortal nature of his soul, he regards the pain and pleasure of all others as his own pain and pleasure. Though living in the world of diversity he is never deluded by it. He never makes a false step or sets a bad example. Virtues such as humility, unselfishness, purity, and kindness, which he practiced for self-purification, now adorn him like so many jewels. He does not seek them; they cling to him. A free soul wears no outward mark of holiness. As a fish swimming in water leaves no mark behind, as a bird flying in the sky leaves no footprint, so a free soul moves about in this world. While living in the body, he may experience disease, old age, and decay, but having recognized them as belonging to the body, he remains undisturbed and even-minded. For him, the world is a stage and his own life is a play. He enjoys the play and the stage, knowing them to be so.

The Values of Life

Hinduism speaks of four values of life, of which *moksha*, or liberation through Self-knowledge, is the fourth. The other three are *dharma*, or practice of righteousness; *artha*, or attainment of worldly prosperity; and *kama*, or enjoyment of legitimate pleasures. Practice of *dharma* calls for an individual to perform the duties of life in accordance with the laws of morality, ethics, and righteousness. *Artha* implies acquisition of wealth, necessary for the preservation of life and the promotion of the welfare of others. *Kama* is the enjoyment of legitimate pleasures, without which life becomes joyless and dry. The first three values must find their fulfillment in the fourth, Self-knowledge. Moral perfection when not for the sake of Self-knowledge becomes nothing but enlightened egoism. Wealth and prosperity when not used for the sake of Self-knowledge breed delusion and attachment. Art and esthetics that do not reflect the light of the Self degenerate into voluptuousness and promiscuity. Knowledge of science and technology when not directed to the attainment of Self-knowledge proves to be a dangerous weapon of Self-destruction. Therefore, the acquisition of wealth and the enjoyment of pleasures must be guided by *dharma*, or righteousness, and governed by the goal of *moksha*, or Self-knowledge.

The Stages of Life

In keeping with the four values of life, Hinduism speaks of the four stages of life: *brahmacharya, garhasthya, vanaprastha,* and *sannyasa.* In *brahmacharya,* the first stage, the individual is asked to acquire knowledge, both secular and spiritual, and to conserve energy through the practice of austerity and self-control. In the second stage, *garhasthya,* he enters family life through marriage. Marriage is neither a concession to weakness nor a confession of sin. The householder's life is the bedrock of society. Any society that ignores the sanctity of marriage ultimately undermines its entire moral foundation. The individual personality finds its expression through participation in family life, the training ground for unselfishness. The third stage, *vanaprastha,* is the stage of retirement from the compulsive obligations and duties of family life. As sense pleasures grow stale, the individual feels the call of the spirit more and more, and devotes himself to a life of non-attachment and contemplation. The last stage, *sannyasa,* is the stage of renunciation of everything for the sake of Self-knowledge. In this stage a person is alone. Alone a person comes, and alone he goes.

The Four Castes

Hinduism places great emphasis on spiritual qualities, and divides society into four castes in order to preserve the spiritual ideal. It realized that, although all are potentially equal in their divinity, there is an inborn inequality between man and man with regard to intellectual and spiritual evolution, and each could develop his spiritual potential through performance of duties in accordance with his own inner disposition. The four castes are: *brahmins, kshatriyas, vaishyas,* and *sudras.* The *brahmins,* devoted to self-control, austerity, and purity, are the custodians of spiritual culture. The *kshatriyas,* known for their heroism, generosity, and fearlessness, preserve the social laws. The *vaishyas* engage themselves in agriculture, trade, and industry; and the duty of the *sudras* consists of service. A person's caste is never hereditary. A person belongs to a particular caste in keeping with his or her inner disposition, character, and qualities. The division of society into four castes in Hinduism has nothing to do with the superiority or inferiority of a particular group. Working in harmony, the four castes ensure the equilibrium and perpetuation of the Hindu social structure. The welfare of one caste depends on the welfare of all others. The Vedas compare the four castes with the four important parts of the body of the cosmic person: the *brahmin* represents the head, the *kshatriya* the arms, the *vaishya* the thighs, and the *sudra* the feet.

Society, according to Hinduism, is not only men and women but also all beings above them, such as gods and angels, and all beings below them, such as animals and plants. Hinduism maintains that an individual is indebted to all of them for his own existence. For example, he is indebted to his ancestors for his present life, to the vegetable and animal worlds for food, to the saints and sages for moral guidance, to fellow human beings for protection, and, above all, to God for His grace. So he is asked to perform daily the following five sacrifices: worship of God; offerings to the deities; making of oblations to the Manes (dead and deified ancestors); offering of food to animals; and hospitality to chance guests. "He who does not feed the deities, chance guests, the beasts, the Manes, and his own self, each day, by performing the five great sacrifices, is a dead man, even though he breathes," says Manu.[17]

The Paths to the Goal

Hinduism advocates freedom in the practice of religion. It maintains that the path to God-realization cannot be the same for all. Spiritual disciplines can never be standardized, because all men do not have the same inborn tendencies and temperament, and each must follow his or her own path.

According to Hinduism, there are basically four types of mind: emotional, active, mystical, and philosophical. And in keeping with the four types of mind, Hinduism prescribes the practice of four different paths known as *yogas*: *bhakti-yoga, karma-yoga, raja-yoga,* and *jnana-yoga.*

Bhakti-yoga is the path for the emotional type. Following this path, the seeker worships a specific aspect of a personal God or a divine incarnation. Or he may worship the ultimate reality as a deity who is without form but with divine attributes. He establishes a human relationship with God, regarding Him as father, mother, master, friend, or beloved, according to his temperament. He directs all his emotions to God and worships Him through the performance of various rituals and ceremonies. The watchword of *bhakti-yoga* is "Thy will be done," which indicates absolute self-surrender to God. Through self-surrender and ecstatic love the seeker ultimately attains to God-vision.

The path prescribed for the active type is *karma-yoga* or the *yoga* of selfless activity. The watchword of this path is "work is worship." The seeker following this path performs all his actions regarding himself as the instrument of God and surrenders the results of the actions to Him. The seeker may be a worshiper of a personal God or look upon the ultimate reality as the impersonal absolute dwelling within him as the soul. *Karma-yoga* is non-attachment in action. The practice of non-attachment purifies the heart, and purity of heart leads directly to God-vision or Self-knowledge.

For those who are mystical by nature, Hinduism prescribes *raja-yoga*, the *yoga* of concentration and meditation. The seeker following this path looks upon the ultimate reality as his inmost Self. The Self remains unperceived because of the mind's restlessness, which is overcome by ceaseless concentration and meditation on the Self. The watchword of this path is "know thyself." Through uninterrupted concentration and meditation the seeker ultimately realizes the true nature of his Self—pure, perfect, and immortal.

The path of *jnana-yoga* is for those who are philosophical and rational in temperament. It is the path of relentless self-analysis, discrimination, and complete renunciation.

The watchword of this path is "This Self is Brahman." The seeker practices discrimination, renunciation, and self-control, and develops intense longing for liberation. He hears about the Self, reflects on It, and meditates upon It. Through ceaseless meditation on the Self the seeker attains union with it.

However, a seeker may follow any of these *yogas* or a combination of two or more of them for the realization of his spiritual goal.

The four main themes of Hinduism are: non-duality of the Godhead, divinity of the soul, oneness of existence, and harmony of religions. God as the ultimate reality is always one, and all seekers, regardless of their religious beliefs and traditions, are calling on the same God. "Truth is one: sages call It by various names," says the Rig-Veda.[18] The various Godheads of different religions are but various facets of one and the same God. The soul of man is divine, and its divinity is neither created nor derived nor borrowed. The goal of religion is to manifest this divinity already in us. All our prayers and worship, penances and austerities, are intended to arouse faith in our divinity. Oneness of existence is the basis of all ethics, morality, love, and sympathy. An act is regarded as ethical only if it is conducive to the welfare of all, and ethical actions are considered good because they lead us to realize the oneness of existence. Different religions are but different paths leading to the common goal of God-vision or God-realization, and there is an underlying harmony among them—the harmony of the goal. The paths vary because of the variety of human temperaments, but they all lead to the same goal. So Sri Ramakrishna says: "As many faiths, so many paths." Harmony of religions is to be realized by a seeker by deepening his God-consciousness.

Overall Message of Hinduism Regarding Death and Afterlife

(a) Hinduism attaches more importance to life before death than to life after death, because the afterlife is determined by the way the present life is lived. One who has no "here" will have no "hereafter." (b) Death is not the end, because it is followed by rebirth. The idea of rebirth is a great solace for those who think in terms of annihilation at death or eternal suffering in hell. Rebirth creates new opportunities for an individual's self-correction and self-improvement. (c) Death is not without meaning; it is a necessary event of life. Life without death, like good without evil, is not possible. (d) Immortality is never the perpetuation of physical or psychical individuality. It is a spiritual realization. A mortal soul can never become immortal. Neither can an immortal soul ever become mortal. The attainment of immortality means that the soul realizes its immortal nature. Further, immortality, in order to be real, must be attained while living. (e) Immortality is the inevitable destiny of all. Knowingly or unknowingly, all living beings are moving toward that goal. Immortality being the very nature of the soul, it can have no abiding peace and security in anything limited. (f) How to conquer death has been the concern of mankind from the beginning of time. Fear of death is at the root of all fears and anxieties. Some try to forget the question of death, thinking it to be a morbid idea. Others accept death as a bitter but unavoidable end. And many feel depressed even to think of it. Hinduism teaches a person to face the question of death with courage and equanimity of mind. Knowing death is certain, one must learn to face it; and one can face death only by being grounded on the deathless Self. Self-knowledge alone can conquer the fear of death. Affirming this, the seer of the Upanishad says: "I know the great Purusha (Brahman, the supreme person), who is luminous like the sun, and beyond darkness. Only by knowing Him does one pass over death; there is no other way to the supreme goal."[19]

Notes

[1] *The Upanishads*, Vol. II (*Svetasvatara Upanishad*, III.16.), trans. by Swami Nikhilananda, Ramakrishna-Vivekananda Center, 1975, p. 103.

[2] *The Upanishads*, Vol. I (*Mundaka Upanishad*, II.i.4.), trans. by Swami Nikhilananda, Ramakrishna-Vivekananda Center, 1977, p. 282.

[3] *The Bhagavad Gita* (IV. 7 and 8.), trans. by Swami Nikhilananda, Ramakrishna-Vivekananda Center, New York, 1979, p. 126.

[4] Ibid. (II.13.), p. 72.

[5] Ibid. (XV.10.), pp. 319-20.

[6] *Yoga Aphorisms of Patanjali*, II.3. (see *Vivekananda: The Yogas and Other Works*, ed. by Swami Nikhilananda, Ramakrishna-Vivekananda Center, 1971, p. 647).

[7] *The Upanishads*, Vol. I (*Katha Upanishad*, II.iii.14.), p. 187.

[8] *Brihadaranyaka Upanishad*, IV.iv.2-4. (translation from *Hinduism: Its Meaning for the Liberation of the Spirit*, by Swami Nikhilananda, 1958, Ramakrishna-Vivekananda Center, New York.

[9] *Chhandogya Upanishad*, IV.xv.5. (translation from *The Bhagavad Gita*, trans. by Swami Nikhilananda, note on pp. 209-10).

[10] *The Bhagavad Gita* (VIII.6.), p. 199.

[11] *Baudhayana-Pitrimedha Sutras*, III.2.3. (translation from *The Cultural Heritage of India*, Vol. II, Ramakrishna Mission Institute of Culture, Calcutta, 1962, p. 411).

[12] *Rig-Veda*, X.16.1. (translation from *The Cultural Heritage of India*, Vol. II, Ramakrishna Mission Institute of Culture, Calcutta, 1961, p. 412).

[13] *The Upanishads*, Vol. I (*Katha Upanishad*, II.i.10.), p. 165.

[14] Ibid. (*Katha Upanishad*, I.iii.15.), p. 156.

[15] *The Upanishads*, Vol. III (*Brihadaranyaka Upanishad*, III.-viii.10.), trans. by Swami Nikhilananda, Ramakrishna-Vivekananda Center, New York, 1975, p. 232.

[16] *The Upanishads*, Vol. I (*Katha Upanishad*, II.iii.4.), p. 182.

[17] *Manu Samhita*, (III. 68-72).

[18] *Rig-Veda*, (X.114.5).

[19] *The Upanishads*, Vol. II (*Svetasvatara Upanishad*, III.8.), p. 99.

ISLAM

Jane Idleman Smith, Ph.D.

Background of the Faith

Islamic faith in the life after death is based directly on the twin messages of the Qur'an, which were the earliest revelations to the Prophet Muhammad: the oneness of God and the inevitability of the day of resurrection and judgment. Because God is one, human beings are enjoined to live lives of integrity (integratedness), of ethical and moral responsibility, and it is on the quality of that ethical and moral life that final judgment is rendered by God. Thus, those who have

earned a place of reward in the Garden of Paradise are called
"*ahl al-tawhid*," people who affirm God's unity.

Islam itself signifies both the vertical dimension of personal response to God and the horizontal dimension by
which the community of believers is designated. Thus it is at
once the act of submission to the divine and the recognition
that all those who so submit are joined in community
(*ummah*). Insofar as it refers to the basic human impulse
toward the divine, Islam is understood by Muslims to be
primordial, natural, and innate in all humans. As the conscious adoption of divine revelation from God through the
Prophet Muhammad, forming the basis for a universal
community of believers, Islam officially "began" as a religion in 622 c.e. in the heart of Arabia.

The Prophet Muhammad, himself unlettered and as the
last in a succession of prophets and messengers, received
and preached God's message to a then polytheistic society.
This final revelation was recorded by the believers as the
Prophet recited it, and after his death in 632 it was collected
into a book entitled the Qur'an (Koran). Its literal meaning,
"The Recitation," suggests its dynamic and oral character.
The Qur'an, along with the message of divine oneness and
the reality of human responsibility and judgment, also contains clear guidelines for individual and communal behavior. Thus from the dictates of the Qur'an, supplemented by
reports from and about the Prophet himself, developed the
Shari'ah, or law that governs both the personal and the
social life of the ideal theocratic Islamic society.

During Muhammad's lifetime, the new religion spread
throughout Arabia, and within a century of his death,
moved northeast into Iraq, Persia, and adjacent areas, and
then south and west across North Africa and Spain into
Southern France. Today it is a world-wide faith shared by
some 800,000,000 adherents. Despite pervasive elements of
commonality, there exists today and have always existed a
wide variety of practices, beliefs, and interpretations. And,
as is inevitably the case with such a cultural and demograph-
ic spread, there are various identifiable sects and groupings,
as there have been from the earliest days.

The major sectarian distinction in Islam is between the Sunnis, comprising some four-fifths of the Muslims, and the Shi'ites, who are located primarily in Iran and parts of Iraq. The split began originally over the issue of community leadership after the Prophet died leaving no designated successor. Those who considered themselves as followers of the way (*sunnah*) of the Prophet, the so-called Sunnis, thought that the leader should be elected by the consensus of the community on the basis of appropriate moral and leadership qualities. Such a leader was called the Caliph, literally the one who comes after the Prophet himself. The task of interpreting religious law was assigned to the *ulama*, persons learned in questions of theology and jurisprudence. The Sunni world was technically headed by a Caliph until the office was abolished by Attaturk in Turkey in 1924.

Others in the young Muslim community felt that leadership should come not by election but through membership in the family of the Prophet. Such a leader they designated Imam. The Imam is understood to have innate knowledge by virtue of his bloodline, and thus to be able to give both political leadership and authoritative interpretations of the Qur'an and traditions. The cousin and son-in-law of the Prophet, Ali b. Abi Talib, was recognized as the first Imam by a group who broke away from the main body of believers. They were known as the Shi'a or Shi'ites, partisans of Ali. The succession of Imams is believed by the Shi'ites to have continued through seven—as believed by those known as Ismailis, today followers of the Aga Khan—or through twelve—as held by the Ithna Ash'ari or Twelver Shi'ites. For the Twelvers, the group dominant in Iran, the twelfth Imam is believed to have gone into occultation or hiding, to emerge at a penultimate time to lead his community again to a state of perfection. (It should be noted that Imam has also been used by both Sunnis and Shi'ites to refer more generally to a learned leader.)

This specific eschatological expectation in Shi'ite Islam suggests that a fuller treatment is needed to do justice to the Shi'ite understanding of time and history than is possible in this brief essay. For the most part, the following discussion will center on those elements of the afterlife beliefs shared by all Muslims. Another significant movement in Islam which has been an identifiable phenomenon since the very early centuries is that of the Sufis or mystics. This movement began with individuals who, influenced by Christian and Jewish communities in the area, desired an intense personal relationship with God through means of asceticism and devotion. By the twelfth century, Sufism, a path to the divine adopted by certain individuals of both the Sunni and Shi'ite communities, had become a very significant phenomenon and was organized into major paths or *tariqas*, many of which are still active today. For some Sufis, the eschatological impulse is translated from a historical context, which sees judgment and consignment to the Garden or the Fire as a future event, to include an understanding that the merging of divine and human as the ultimate eschatology is potentially realizable at any moment. Again, as with the particulars of Shi'ite eschatology, the complexity of the Sufi interpretation deserves greater attention than is possible here.

The Main Tenets of Islam

For all Muslims, men and women, certain duties and responsibilities are clearly set forth. It is primarily on the basis of these responsibilities that one's life will be assessed in the final reckoning when judgment will be rendered. These are generally understood to be five in number: (1) Giving verbal testimony based on assent of the heart that there is no God but God (acknowledging divinity in any being or reality outside the one God is the greatest sin in Islam and leads with certainty to damnation) and that Muhammad is the Prophet of God. This is the *shahadah*, the basic testimony of faith. (2) Participating in the public prayer (*salat*) at five regularly scheduled times during the day. (3) Participating in the fast (*saum*) observed during one month of the year (Ramadan). (4) Sharing one's material goods with the needy of the community through paying the alms-tax (*zakat*). (5) Joining with other members of the community at least once in a lifetime in the great pilgrimage (*hajj*) to the holy cities of Mecca and Medina.

There is a very clear and direct connection in Islam between this world (*al-dunya*) and the next world (*al-akhirah*). Muslim children are taught from an early age that life on this earth has no purpose if it is not to prepare oneself specifically for life in the next, and that to live ethically in recognition of God's oneness is virtually to assure a felicitous hereafter in the gardens of paradise. In this sense, there is no distinction in Islam between faith and works (although, as in Christianity, scholastic theologians have disputed the relative merits of each). One of the main concerns of contemporary Muslim theological writing about the afterlife is to underline its intellectual plausibility. "Thus the Qur'an has explained the life hereafter in a manner acceptable to the intellect and has called for faith in it," says Muhammad al-Mubarak of the University of Mecca.[1]

Aside from unity or oneness, the central characteristic of the divine, God is understood in Islam to have an infinite number of attributes, often described as 99 in number to signify infinity. Of these, the most often cited are omnipotence, omniscience, justice, and mercy. Because of the great emphasis put on judgment at the last day and the just dispensation of souls, justice has often been seen as overriding in the Islamic conception of the divine. In fact, all of the 114 chapters of the Qur'an but one begin with the invocation "In the name of God, the merciful, the compassionate." With the requirement to live lives of ethical obligation is also the Qur'anic understanding that as humans we will err, and that the mercy of God is abundant.

As part of God's creation, humans can be assured of two things: first, that there is a virtually limitless distinction between humanity as created and God as creator, and that our best efforts succeed only insofar as God wills it; second, that behind all events is a divine plan and order. Humans are created from clay and put on the earth for a specific time (*ajal*) known beforehand only by God. But despite our lowly origins, we have, because of our intellect, potential to be vice-regents on earth.[2] Humans are not described in Islam as inherently evil or misguided, although Adam and his wife did foolishly succumb to the temptations of the serpent in primordial time. We are often subject to error, but always have the potential to recognize the truth and to act accordingly. The only real "fallen" creature is Iblis, an archangel ejected from paradise by God for insubordination and residing eternally as the chief denizen of the underworld. Iblis is occasionally portrayed as a temptor, but does not attain the proportions of a full-blown devil as in Christian thought. He is accompanied by numerous other demons and tempting spirits who contribute to the tortures of the damned in the fires of punishment.

Essential to an understanding of the Islamic view of the afterlife is a consideration of the flow of time and history. Time in the overall perspective has a beginning and an end. All of human history moves from the creation to the eschaton. Looking structurally at the overall conception of time in the Islamic understanding, one sees the pattern of collective time, that lasting from creation to eschaton, juxtaposed over that of individual time, the specific events of each individual existence. For the individual, the sequence runs inevitably from birth to death, followed by the existence of the soul in the grave (or elsewhere) awaiting the resurrection, to participation in a series of eschatological events experienced by everyone together. Collective time encompasses everything from the creation of the world through the passing of history to the warning of the impending judgment, the events of the day of resurrection, the final consignment, and passing into eternity. Let us turn to the particulars of these individual and collective events.

Death and Burial Practices

Because Muslims participate in such a variety of cultures, it is inevitable that funeral and burial practices will differ somewhat. On the whole, however, a general pattern can be identified which is based on a common understanding of the meaning of death and on the advice given by the Prophet as to what is fit and proper.

When it appears to those accompanying a dying person that death is near and certain, someone is called to read verses of the Qur'an. Normally this is a person specifically trained in that function. Among the traditions of Islam is one describing the visit of Iblis to the one who is dying, tempting him or her to deny faith in God and adherence to Islam by offering water to the parched victim. To help in the struggle against such temptation, drops of water (or, as in India, honey) are placed in the mouth of the dying. At the moment of death, the eyes are closed and the jaw is bound up, and the body is carefully arranged while waiting for a physician's examination.

One of the most important components of the funerary process is the washing of the body. Cleanliness and ritual purification are essential in Islam; prayer is always preceded by ablutions. Embalming is not practiced, as it is believed that the body should be allowed to quickly return to the earth whence it came.[3] The washing is done by a professional washer at home, at a hospital, or in a special place outside the mosque. All items involved in the ablution must be newly purchased, and the water, thought to be polluted after use, must be disposed of carefully. During the washing ceremony, verses from the Qur'an are usually recited. After the body is dried, cotton plugs are placed in body orifices and the body is carefully wrapped in a shroud. Normally it is put into a simple wooden coffin, narrow at the feet and wider at the shoulders, and borne to a mosque.

Attending a funeral, and in particular helping to carry the dead in the funeral procession, is considered an act of piety. The coffin is usually carried by relays of male relatives and friends. In some places, the coffin precedes the mourners, as in Lebanon, while in other places such as Egypt, it comes after them. Also, local custom dictates whether or not women participate in the procession. At the mosque, a funeral service is held, often attended even by those who did not know the deceased. On completion of the service, the body is either carried or taken by hearse to the graveyard. Burial takes place within 24 hours of death.

The body is usually taken out of the coffin before it is buried in order to speed decomposition. The shroud is loosened, and the corpse is put into the grave with its face toward Mecca. Always the body is handled with extreme care out of belief that it is still able to experience pain. Because of this belief, and because Muslims understand that the agonies of the fire are for God alone to prepare for the sinful, cremation is not practiced. While the body is being buried, until the grave is filled with earth, prayers are continually recited. In some cases, a brief sermon is preached. Usually plants rather than cut flowers are placed on the grave, which is marked by flat or sometimes rounded markers of wood or stone. In some instances, dome-like structures are erected over the grave.

The question of mourning for the deceased is an interesting one in Islam, and it is clear from the traditions that the Prophet forbade it. Nonetheless, grieving normally does take the form of clear and outward lamenting, sometimes loud and prolonged wailing. Traditionally, this has been a role played by women. On certain occasions, professional mourners are engaged. Generally, it is understood that while mourning should not be taken as a sign of lack of faith in God's goodness or in a felicitous hereafter for the righteous, communal grieving is an important sign of support and caring for the loved ones of the deceased. Differing according to locale, certain rites and ceremonies, grave visitations, and communal meals are held at specified times, after the burial.

There are opportunities for intercessory prayers for the dead. Repeating the Fatihah (the brief opening chapter of the Qur'an) when visiting or passing a grave, for example, is considered efficacious. In general, however, the community must take solace in the knowledge that the departed one is in God's charge and that in the fullness of time, justice and mercy will assure an appropriate station.

Between Death and Resurrection

Chapter 23:100 of the Qur'an describes a partition (*barzakh*) or barrier separating the land of the living from those who have died.[4] The interpretation of this has been that the deceased will in no way to be able to return to the earth. There is nothing in the Qur'an to support the idea of reincarnation or multiple births; its message is clearly that we have one life on earth and our future existence will be determined on the basis of the quality of that life. With rare exceptions in some splinter sectarian groups, Islam has consistently rejected the notion that human souls could or would be reincarnated in different bodies for the purpose of working off past debts or accumulating further merit.

If we return again to the time outline discussed above, we see that the expectation of a day of resurrection and judgment of necessity means that there is a kind of waiting period of individuals between death and that day when resurrected bodies will be joined with souls to pass through detailed eschatological events. The term *barzakh* has also come to be applied to the place/time in which the dead wait for the day of resurrection in a variety of conditions. Precisely what happens to souls during this period of waiting is not discussed at all in the Qur'an and consequently has been a subject of great speculation. Islamic tradition has willingly filled in a great many of the details, with varying degrees of authenticity and reliability.[5]

Contemporary Muslim writers vary in the degree to which they accept much of this traditional material as descriptive of what will actually happen, but it is certainly the case, as documented in recent studies,[6] that many if not most Muslims accept that certain events are inevitable. The theme of prefiguration of joys and torments to be experienced at the time of final judgment by the righteous and the faithless respectively is repeated in a variety of ways as one follows the sequence of death and afterdeath events. Often there is a welcome given by the grave to the one who has just died, and it is obvious that the form of this greeting is determined by the relative virtue of the deceased. In some instances, the grave greets the faithful by promising an expansion of vision and a continuing look at the gates of the Garden of Paradise. Far more narratives, however, describe the agony to be endured by the faithless. The grave is said to warn such persons that it is a place of darkness, isolation, and loneliness.

One of the most commonly accepted narratives is that describing immediate events after the death of an individual. The soul, now separated from the body, embarks on a journey. Apparently it is modeled on the mystical journey (mi'raj) undertaken by the Prophet Muhammad during which he ascended to the heavens and was able to look down into the layers of hells. A good soul is said to slip easily and painlessly from the body, and wrapped in perfumed coverings, it is led by the angel Gabriel through the seven layers of heaven to see what will eventually be its abode. The end of the journey is a vision of God, after which the soul returns to the grave.[7] Wicked souls, or those of persons who have not followed God's command in life, leave the body painfully and wrenchingly. They are foul smelling, and they are rejected from even the lowest levels of the heavens. Given a vision of what awaits them at the day of judgment (glimpses into the fires of punishment), they also return to the grave.

One very commonly accepted event is the visit of questioning angels.[8] Sometimes they are identified by the names of Munkar and Nakir, appellations that are non-Qur'anic and appear rarely in the canonical traditions. Their descriptions vary slightly from one account to another, but in general they are understood to be fearsome to behold, black in appearance with green eyes, with voices like thunder and eyes like lightning. Their long fangs rend the ground. They ask the deceased about his or her knowledge of God, the Prophet Muhammad, and Islam. One's ability to answer these questions, easy for the righteous and impossible for the faithless, determines the quality of one's stay awaiting the day of judgment.

Sometimes it is said that, for the good soul, windows will be opened in the top of the tomb so that one can feel the sweet breezes from the Garden, and that for the evil soul a similar opening on the bottom will allow the hot stench of hell to penetrate. Or, respectively, graves will be expanded for greater comfort or straightened so that the suffering soul will shriek in agony. Muslim superstition has it that animals passing through graveyards can sometimes hear the piercing cries of the tormented damned. One of the particular sins for which punishment in the grave is said to occur is suicide. The giving and taking of life in the Islamic understanding is for God alone.

While the blissful rewards are sometimes mentioned, punishment in the grave has received by far the greater attention in theological writings and in folk traditions. It is interesting to note that while no Muslim would doubt the reality of the disintegration of the body in the earth (with the exception of saints, whose bodies remain intact), it is also the case that the punishments and pleasures of the grave are understood in a very physical way. Along with the narratives suggesting that the soul is experiencing joy or pain in the grave, are those which indicate that it is in fact apart from the tomb and going through appropriate pleasure or purgation elsewhere. Souls of the damned, for example, are sometimes said to already be in the fire, or suffering somewhere in pits of snakes and other loathsome creatures. Souls of the righteous, on the other hand, are sometimes said to be free to wander through the spheres at will, or to be at the right hand of Adam, or to be waiting at the gates of the Garden of Paradise. Some traditions suggest that the righteous are very much aware of life on earth while waiting for the resurrection; sometimes they are described as praying for the living or even attempting to greet us.

The Coming of the Day of Resurrection

As we move through the time sequence of after-death events, we come to that period dramatically portrayed in the Qur'an in which the natural order will be disrupted and cataclysmic events will occur, signaling the resurrection of the bodies (*ba'th*). The first warning of the impending cosmic upheaval in traditional and in many contemporary accounts is actually a disruption of the ethical/moral order. Some of the signs of this are that liars and traitors will be trusted and the righteous belied; usury will be acceptable; a man will disobey his parents and obey his wife (thereby upsetting the family structure); wine-drinking will be commonplace, and the like. Many accounts say that this time of moral chaos will conclude with the arrival of a guide (*madhi*) who will then reign over a millennial period of justice and peace. This figure is sometimes identified in Sunni Islam with the person of Jesus, and is to be understood more a leader than a savior.

The actual arrival of the day of resurrection is made known to all upon earth and in the heavens through a series of events that are clearly cosmic in nature. According to the understanding of the Qur'an, this is a day when the heavens are split apart, when the earth will be rent asunder, when the mountains will be set moving, when heaven will be rolled up like a scroll, and many other specific signs will be given indicating the reversal of the natural order and a disintegration of the structure of the universe.[9] The drama of the Qur'anic description is captured in this excerpt from al-Ghazali's famous medieval treatise on eschatology, *al-Durrah al-Fakhirah*, describing the events after the angel Israfil sounds the trumpet heralding the imminent end of the world:

> Then the mountains will be scattered and will move like the clouds; the seas will gush forth one into the other and the sun will be rolled up and will return to ashes; the oceans will overflow until the atmosphere is filled up with water. The worlds will pass into each other, the stars will fall like a broken string of pearls and the sky will become like a rose balm, rotating like a turning millstone. The earth will shake with a tremendous shaking. . .until God orders the stripping off of the spheres. In all of the seven earths and the seven heavens, as well as the vicinity of the Throne, no living being will remain.[10]

After the final cosmic disintegration, we then have a dramatic description of what Islamic tradition has seen as God's absolute oneness in the universe. Here God is not only the sole God, he is all that remains in the universe. An ethical disintegration, a cosmic disintegration, and finally the stunning vision of God's absolute aloneness. Were this the end of the story, we would have to conclude that human claims on immortality are temporary at best, confined to a reflection of divine oneness through the expression of faith and works. But as the drama unfolds, we see that after the manifestation of absolute aloneness comes the return to a focus on human accountability. God brings all humanity back to life in the resurrection of bodies, the ingathering and infusing of new life as the first step in the process of calling human beings to an accounting for their earthly deeds.

Resurrection and Judgment

The fact of the resurrection of the body has been of continuing importance to Muslims. It was not really a point of issue for early Islam, but came to be hotly debated among theologians and philosophers. Contemporary Muslims are firmly convinced that bodily resurrection is basic to the Qur'anic message. The first mortal to be raised is generally said to be the prophet Muhammad. The stress on the importance of Muhammad's resurrection before the other believers is related not only to his recognized status as the seal of the prophets, but also to the general understanding of his role as the intercessor for his community.

The Qur'an, along with later eschatological writings, describes in great detail the day of judgment as one in which even the most pious will be afraid. The resurrection itself is scarcely pictured as a time of joy or gratitude on the parts of those to whom life is given again. Medieval manuals delight in elaborate portrayals of individuals awaiting in terror the actual judgment, standing in sweat up to their ankles, their waists, their shoulders. It is at this time that souls experience most graphically the results of their deeds and misdeeds on earth.

The Qur'an makes it clear that each individual alone is responsible for his or her past deeds and that one will have to encounter those deeds and their consequences in very graphic form on the day of judgment. On that day the record will be revealed to each person individually, the result of the reckoning obviously predetermined by one's being ordered to take the book in either the right or the left hand. For the heedless, this revealing of the record will come as a tremendous shock.[11]

References in the Qur'an and the elaborations of tradition have added several other events to the picture of the last day. The Qur'an mentions the *mizan* or balance, which in the singular means the principle of justice. The plural has the clearer eschatological reference of the scales by which deeds are weighed. The image of a specific weighing has thus been adopted as one of the modalities of judgment. Another such modality is the bridge (*sirat*), adopted into Islamic tradition to signify the span over Gehenna, the top layer of the Fire. It is said that both the saved and the condemned must pass over the bridge, although the judgment process actually has been completed at the point at which the bridge is mentioned in most narratives. Those judged guilty of sin but still considered to be believers fall from the bridge into the Fire, but only for a limited period of purgation. Those who have neither faith nor good deeds to their credit, however, find that the *sirat* has become sharper than a sword and thinner than a hair, and that their fall into the Fire of everlasting punishment is inescapable. The faithful, on the contrary, move easily and swiftly across a broad bridge, led by the Prophet himself.

Intercession

This raises the issue of intercession and whether or not it is recognized in Islam. Technically the Qur'an says that there is no possibility of intercession, although some verses lend themselves to more flexible interpretation. No intercession would be in keeping with the dominant conception of a God of absolute justice. As mercy has been understood to be one of God's primary characteristics, however, so the possibility of an intervening being has come into the Islamic picture of eschatological realities. Aside from some possibility of intercession by saints, the main figure credited with the intercessory function is the Prophet Muhammad. Sometimes intercession is said to take place at the bridge; more often it occurs at the basin or pond (*hawd*) at which Muhammad will meet the members of his community. Its general location is somewhere near the balance and the bridge. The Qur'an leaves no question whatsoever that divine justice will prevail on the day of judgment and that no one can bear the burden of anyone else's actions. With the possibility of intercession, however, one sees a softening of the formula of unrelenting retribution; sometimes it is said that even the smallest deed registered to one's credit may in the long run be sufficient to bring one to salvation.

The Garden or the Fire

The Qur'an leaves no doubt that the alternatives for each individual at the day of judgment are two: the bliss of the Garden or the torment of the Fire. One reference in the Qur'an to what is called "the heights" (*al-ac raf*) in verse 7:46 has led to the development of what some have called the "limbo" theory of Islam, or the supposition that there is a place for an intermediate class of people who do not automatically enter the Garden or the Fire. While there are a variety of interpretations of this verse, most exegetes have said those on the heights are persons whose good deeds keep them from the fire and whose evil deeds keep them from the Garden—i.e. those whose actions balance in terms of merit and demerit, and who are therefore the last to enter the Garden.

Because of the full and graphic descriptions of the Garden and the Fire in the Qur'an, Islam has often been accused of a very materialistic conception of the afterlife. As with the modalities at the hour of judgment, the Muslim community has expressed a variety of interpretations about whether or not the rewards and punishments of the life to come are to be understood in their most literal sense. While the dominant understanding has been an affirmation of the reality of physical torment and pleasure, proponents of this view generally have not insisted that the realities of the next world will be identical with those of this world. While clearly physical, recompense in the ultimate sense is generally understood to have a reality beyond what we are able to comprehend.

The Qur'an itself does not offer a detailed plan of the realms of the Fire or the Garden. The term *Gehenna* is sometimes used to refer to the totality of the Fire and sometimes only to the top-most circle. In the Qur'an (15:43-44), Gehenna is described as having seven gates; this led to the popular notion that the Fire consists of seven descending layers of increasing torment. An elaborate structure of relative punishments came to be worked out around the seven layers of Fire, and later tradition supplied each of the gates with guardians who torture the damned. At the bottom of the lowest level grows the dreaded tree Zaqqum (37:62-68) with the heads of demons for flowers. The Qur'an offers a number of specific indications of the tortures of the Fire: its flames crackle and roar; it has fierce boiling waters, scorching wind, and black smoke; the people of the Fire are sighing, wailing, and wretched.

In some ways the divisions of the Fire directly parallel those of the Garden, although the Garden is sometimes said to have eight rather than seven layers (and at other times is described as being of four portions). The opposite of the tree Zaqqum is the lote tree at the top of paradise. Garden (*jannah*) is the general name for paradise, although the Qur'anic descriptions are of gardens in the plural. The most spacious and highest part of the Garden is directly under the throne of God, from which the four rivers of paradise flow. Qur'anic references to the joys awaiting the dwellers in the Garden are sufficiently rich that tradition has done little but amplify and elaborate on them. The faithful are content, peaceful, and secure; they enjoy gentle speech, pleasant shade, and fruits neither forbidden nor out of reach, as well as cool drink and meat as they desire; they sit on couches facing each other, wearing green and gold robes of finest silk. One of the joys afforded to the inhabitants of the Garden is the companionship of young virgins with eyes like guarded pearls. Some traditions suggest that families will be reunited in the Garden, but this is not discussed in the Qur'an. While the Qur'anic descriptions do not mention God, the clear understanding of Muslims is that the faithful will gaze upon his face, a joy which the inhabitants of the Fire are denied.

For the most part, Islamic theology has not concerned itself with questions about the location and structure of the Garden and the Fire, on the understanding that only God knows these particulars. Theologians have, however, speculated at great length on the question of whether or not they are already in existence. Orthodoxy has concluded that they are created and do exist, awaiting their inhabitants on the last day.

On the basis of the Qur'anic assurances in descriptions of the Gardens as well as a firm faith in God's justice in addition to his mercy, neither the theologians nor the traditionalists have questioned the eternal nature of the Garden and the residence of the faithful in it. The question becomes more problematic in relation to the Fire, however. The majority have held to the view that despite the Qur'anic indication that sinners will stay eternally in the fire, it is not only possible but even likely that at some future time all sinners will be pardoned and the Fires of judgment will be extinguished forever. Equally complex has been the issue of whether or not non-Muslims will be able eventually to enjoy the Garden. The general conclusion is that they will, but only after a period of purgation.

It is clear, then, that afterlife beliefs in Islam are a blend of Qur'anic description, traditional elaboration, theological speculation, and popular belief. There is much in the general Islamic understanding that is intended to comfort the bereaved as well as to reassure and challenge the community as a whole. Many contemporary Muslim writers do not deal directly with issues of life after death because they see the basic affirmation of the Qur'an as so natural and reasonable as to require no defense or elaboration. To the extent they do, it is generally to affirm to the Muslim community and the world at large that the strength of Islam lies in the faith that the fruits of today's labor will be reaped in the hereafter, and that God will reward all in justice and mercy in the world to come.

Notes

[1]   Muhammad al-Mubarak, *Nizam al-Islam* (Beirut, Dar al-Fikr, 1970), 148.

[2]   Qur'an 2:29-30.

[3]   "He has made all that he has created good. And He began the creation of man from clay..." (Qur'an 32:7).

[4]   "...behind them is a barrier (*barzakh*) until the day when they are resurrected."

[5]   Much of this material is contained in eschatological manuals which ordered the many traditions that came into circulation in the Muslim community concerning life after death. While descriptive in effect, the function of these manuals as a whole is didactic and homiletic, intended to encourage the hearer to redouble efforts to live ethically and justly.

[6]   See esp. Sayyid Uways, *al-khulud fi hayat al-Misriyin al-muasirin* (Cairo, al-Hay 'at al-Misriat al-Aam lil-Kitab, 1972).

[7]   This vision of God is often described in extremely vivid terms, as in this passage from the *Durra al-fakhira* of the medieval theologian and mystic, al-Ghazzali: "Then they penetrate the coverings affixed to the Throne of Mercy. There are eighty thousand pavilions of the Throne, each pavilion having eighty thousand believers and each balcony having a moon radiant upon God, glorifying Him and venerating Him." (Scholars Press, 1979), 14.

[8]   See, e.g., contemporary writers such as Ahmad Fa'iz, *al-Yawm al-akhir fi zilal al-Qur'an* (Beirut, Dar Maktabat al-Hayat 1975); Ibrahim al-Bayjuri, *Sharh al-Bayjuri ala'l-jawhara* (Cairo, Matbaa al-Taqadam al-Alamiya 1964).

[9]   See especially Qur'an 81:1-4.

[10]   *Op. cit.*, 38-39.

[11] "As for the one who is given his book in his right hand, he will say: Take and read my book. I knew that I would be called to account. And he will be in a blissful condition...But as for him who is given his book in his left hand, he will say: Would that my book had not been given to me and that I did not know my reckoning!...(and it will be said) Seize him and bind him and expose him to the burning Fire!..." (Qur'an 9:19-31).

JUDAISM

Rabbi Alan L. Ponn

Background of the Faith

The Jewish faith can be described as the first noticeable
step away from paganism. The ancient peoples feared the
powers in the universe, but speculated widely about the location and the nature of those powers. Groping for answers,
the pagans drew initial conclusions about the supernatural
based on primitive assumptions, superstition, and magical
explanations.

The pagans assumed a world of spirits, both good and bad, constantly permeating their living space. They worshipped every natural object that seemed impressive to them: the sun, moon, stars, high trees, imposing animals such as lions and bulls, and constructed great idols and symbolic poles of their own, which they worshipped in the sacrificial ways of animal and food offerings. Nowhere did they see a oneness in God, a unity of the various deities, or a kindly personal god who cared for humankind.

Judaism, 5744 years ago according the tradition made a breakthrough in experiencing a revelation of God's oneness, and of God's personality as a divine parent, both loving and just, a creative presence both inside and outside the inhabited world.

Although the Bible begins with the appearance of Adam and Eve, it is Abraham who is known as the first Jew, for the great revelation of God's oneness first appeared to him. Jewish tradition emphasizes that Abraham broke the idols and false gods of his father's household by smashing them to pieces. Little by little Abraham began to receive words and promises from God that formed the basis of a mutual agreement called a covenant. Religious scholars assume that God was seeking out Abraham who was able to use his reason and intuition to search for God. The covenant that was concluded promised God's blessings and concern for all people in return for their acceptance, faith, and belief.

The original Jews consisted of the close-knit patriarchal families of Abraham, Isaac, and Jacob. Each was motivated and transformed by this covenant with God. Judaism was begun, maintained, and transmitted by families, and family unity and closeness is one of the most important Jewish tenets even today. God, in his early covenantal promises, promised that Abraham's progeny would be numerous like the stars in heaven, that Abraham would be the father of a multitude of nations, and that his seed would someday possess the land of Canaan.

In times of famine in their often parched land, the Hebrews were accustomed to going down to Egypt in search of food. From Abraham's time on, this practice led to a considerable population of Jews developing a residence there. Ultimately feared and envied by Pharaoh Rameses II, the Jewish people were then subjugated into degrading slavery. They endured many hardships, and they may have been assigned to build monuments and pyramids for the Pharaoh.

This episode of slavery, the rise of Moses, and God's redemption of the enslaved Hebrews led to the most monumental change in this emerging civilization. No longer a small group of patriarchal families, the Hebrews were transformed into a national and spiritual entity. They, like the proverbial clay in the hands of the potter, stood ready to be trained, organized, and galvanized for the spiritual odyssey that lay ahead.

Into the pagan world of religious anarchy came God's authoritative words of instruction: His law, and rules of proper living. The Ten Commandments were only the starting point of elaborate law and ritual that was meant to define explicit religious practice and moral conduct that would assure the peoples salvation and preservation. Assurances of God's love were also contrasted with stern warnings about the punishments for misbehavior and disloyalty to the covenant.

From Moses's day on the Hebrews traveled along this pathway from paganism to religious civilization and moral idealism. Many were their failures and backslidings. Guided by efforts of strong kings and eloquent prophets, Judaism became an enduring entity.

Judaism's essential doctrine is simply this: following God's suggested way of life can bring a deepening joy and fulfillment. Judaism does not stress belief in God as much as acceptance of God and the way of life that God has set forth for the adherent. Therefore, there is no emphasis on doctrinal formulations.

God is understood as a divine parent, with personal care and concern for humankind. God gave the world law first because the pagan world was in a state of anarchy and needed the direction and discipline that only law could bring. The law was of two kinds. Ritual law and moral law are both distributed throughout the Torah and the rest of the

Old Testament. God also expressed his love and compassion for his creatures in the Torah, and God's emotional words of love and attachment to his creation alternate with legal expression. Therein, these ritual and ethical laws form the basis of the pathway to salvation. Worship of God, good deeds, and charitable acts are thought to be the main vehicles of religious expression. Now Judaism retains the Hebrew language and the ancient scrolls as a mark of identity to these ancient Jewish roots. Prayer and songs in the synagogue retain these features.

Jews believe that the purpose of life is to glorify God on earth by expressing their higher selves, or spiritual selves. They consider that they have been made in God's image; yet they are also half animal, and they are mortal. The religious challenge is therefore to direct personal efforts to the good, or higher inclinations, and away from the bad, or evil inclinations.

God's destiny and that of humans are intertwined. Jews define the partnership as one that requires our ultimate loyalty and dedication as human beings. God, the divine parent, is the epitomy of justice and compassion, the source of both good and evil, creation and destruction, knowledge and ignorance. God's purposes are unfathomable, but Jews are loyal to God through intuitive trust such as that given to a human parent.

This World and the Next World

Although the hope for the fulfillment and redemption of the adherent's life is intended to apply to the span of earthly existence, there is ample recognition in Judaism that life does not abruptly cease when the body has died. Something precious remains at the time of earthly demise, and these doctrines of immortality and resurrection, heaven and hell, accountability and judgment, are found in Jewish teachings and in the prayer books of the Jewish people. But the first and primary responsibility of the Jew is this life and not the world to come.

The fulfillment of laws and commandments are meant to

improve one's life on earth. Devotion to prayer, study, and charity are expected to lead to a meaninful way of life as the life cycle progresses from birth to death. This is clearly a recommendation to each Jew to concentrate on his or her responsibilities on earth and not to speculate or postpone life's opportunities while he or she lives. The idea of subordinating life's opportunities, responsibilities, or challenges to some greater possibilities in the world to come is alien to Judaism. Judaism can thus be characterized as a this-wordly religion, and it is no accident that the pendant often chosen to be worn as a necklace contains the Hebrew inscription *Chai*, which means *life*. *Chai*, or life, is characterized as the supreme religious value.

Life after Death

The belief in life after death, probably the most universal of all of humanity's religious doctrines, grew rather gradually in Jewish thought. During biblical times, only the kernels of the beliefs in an afterworld are to be found. The post-biblical writings, especially the Talmud, put a firm foundation and a complete structure on that slight and tenuous emphasis in the Old Testament concerning the future world. During Talmudic times, Jewish doctrine became more and more specific about resurrection, immortality, heaven, hell, and God's judgment. Accordingly Jewish ritual kept apace. The pattern of the modern Jewish funeral service and the laws of death and burial in the Jewish religion are an elaborate expression of proper preparation for an assured afterworld.

Immortality is a belief that comes naturally with the conviction that God is a divine parent. To be reunited with the divine source of one's being is the hoped-for ending to a pious and dedicated religious life. That God would gather the righteous and sincerely repentant souls around the shelter of his wings is a most yearned for expectation of the Jews.[1]

At such time, it is hoped that the inconsistencies, mysteries, and uncertainties of life will somehow be resolved and reconciled. The deep longing to be reunited with dearly departed relatives will be fulfilled. A peacefulness and tranquility will replace the frustrations and challenges of our earthly existence. For the traditional Jew, immortality will bring resurrection of the soul and the body. For the Reform Jew it will bring a resurrection of the soul only.

Judgment

Jewish tradition emphasizes that God is the true and righteous judge. Each human soul is held accountable before God for the use made of the life given. Thus, our lives cannot be wasted or taken lightly. During the Jewish High Holiday Season (New Year and the Day of Atonement), a chance is given anew each year to redirect the serious goals of one's life. The prayers say: "God records our deeds in a book." This ledger, attributed to God, is called the "Book of Life." In this "Book of Life," God is said to make continual entries concerning the merits of our deeds and the worthiness of each individual to merit continued existence. It is in this context that we read during Yom Kippur, "Choose good, and not evil, that ye may live."[2]

The Jewish religious regimen of the New Year, with its emphasis on the purification and cleansing of the soul, paves the way for the sublimity of character that allows entry into the world to come. The theme of the High Holiday season is that change and growth of character are possible through concentrated effort. Yet even the stubborn and rebellious worshipper can sometimes attain this change and growth through repentance during the latter stages of life. Even at this eleventh hour, such sincere repentance is considered acceptable for entry to the world beyond this one.

The Good Life

Reincarnation is a popular belief that never settled in the

Jewish sphere. Yet the Jewish masses were attracted to it from time to time. With origins in the primitive religions of northern Europe, the reincarnation doctrine spread mostly into the non-Jewish Asiatic centers of population.[3]

The new Jewish prayerbook of Reform Jews, *Gates of Prayer*, states explicitly that "mortality is the tax we pay for the privilege of love, thought, creative work. . . . Just because we are human, we are prisoners of the years. Yet that very prison is the room of discipline in which we, driven by the urgency of time, create."[4] Such a prayer reconciles the worshipper to his apportioned span of life. One lifetime, according to Jewish thought, is sufficient to make good account of ourselves, if we earnestly try. Fragility and mortality become spurs to accomplishment, and creative endeavor. Reincarnation is very much a permanent part of a caste system and of fatalism. Such conditions Jews do not espouse.

First of all, each adherent of the Jewish faith is bidden to develop all parts of himself or herself in one lifetime. If one's occupation is mechanical, one's avocation should be scholarly and intellectual. If one's occupation is scholarly, then one's avocation should stress non-scholarly characteristics. The ideal of the whole person is to be achieved. Such versatility and variety of individual activity is most notably found today in the land of Israel where leaders of high political stature are known to pursue challenging avocations of a contrasting nature.[5] Secondly, fatalism occupies a position of little importance in Judaism. The individual is bidden through prayer and doctrine to accept the active role in God's creative process, to improve God's world, and to make it a better place in which to live.

Satisfaction and fulfillment can come only to those adherents who do their share of good deeds (*Mitzvot*). Fulfillment comes especially to those believers who have fully transmitted the heritage to a future generation. Seeing the young imbued with high ideals for the future brings the deepest satisfaction humanly possible. After a lifetime of such effort, death should not bring discontent. Heaven is reality to the adherent, but he is bidden not to be preoccupied with it while he lives. Fulfilling God's precepts and developing a praiseworthy life take first preference on the human agenda of the believer. Few Jewish sermons entice the worshipper to the glories of heaven or threaten the evils of hell. Although Jewish literature is filled with lavish heavenly pictures and lurid thoughts of the underworld, such descriptions never predominate in Jewish pulpit or pew.

Heaven and Hell

There are some assumptions, however, about the nature of these important future repositories of our souls. Primarily, heaven is pictured as a place where the passions no longer frustrate, conflicts no longer cause suffering, and anxiety and travail are ended. There is a predominance of imagery in Jewish literature of quiet, peaceful, intellectual activity, with perusal of religious texts.[6] Another popular conception is that of family reunion and devotion among those who had been separated by death. There is also a hope for the resolution of the mysteries of life and an aspiration to draw nearer to God's sheltering protection and love.

Although sadistic descriptions of hell do occur in Jewish literature, Jewish worshippers have long assumed that God's real caring nature could rule out an almighty God practicing sadism for any purpose. Firm is the conviction that God's judgment is real, and accountability is as certain as the fingerprints on our hands. Yet the nature of hell is one of the mysteries of Jewish doctrine, and the modern worshipper seems content to let it remain a mystery.

Since Judaism is not a creedal religion, adherence to each doctrine, such as heaven and hell, is not entirely obligatory upon the worshipper. It would not be surprising, therefore, to encounter a few Jews who still hold today the early biblical view that there is no afterworld, since such a view would not be considered heretical in this non-creedal religious approach. The mainstream of Judaism does, by a huge majority, accept the reality of the afterworld as described herein.

How does one gain admittance into the heavenly portals, and who of humankind's creatures qualifies? Entrance is gained by righteous deeds and an ethical living pattern. Behavioral performance and helpfulness to others are regarded as the true test of character. Yet people who lack these qualifications can make a special appeal to God's mercy through sincere repentance even a short time before death itself. If the repentance is sincere enough, it is considered highly likely that God will grant pardon even at that late moment. What if the sinner is unrepentant even at the end of life? If the person led a life devoid of good deeds, he or she would really face the stern test of God's tribunal. He or she would expect to be held to account, and punished, for wasting his or her life, hurting others, and being so callous as to show indifference instead of conscience at the close of his or her mortal days.

What if the person was unaffiliated, an agnostic, or an atheist? What if the person was a non-Jew? Anyone who fulfills the basic commandments of proper relationships with others is still regarded as worthy of salvation, although he or she may not have chosen the Jewish pathway. Fervent Jews deplore atheists and agnostics especially, but none would disagree that proper conduct and behavior is the one standard that can be applied to all humankind, Jews and Gentiles, believers and unbelievers, alike. From this it can be stated that Jews do not feel that their religion is the only pathway to God. It is only the one most suitable for the Jews themselves.[7] This tolerant pattern was set in the days of Noah and the biblical characters who preceded Abraham, the first Jew. God's relationship with them was very much an ethical test, too, based on the Noachide laws prohibiting murder, incest, and adultery. The deeds of men, regardless of their religious beliefs, are the most important admission cards to the world to come, according to the Jewish orientation.

The End of the World and the Messiah

How long will the world itself last? Can we ever expect an end to the existing world as we know it? The Jews have a

distinct interpretation of the scriptural account of the covenant given to Noah directly following the great flood. The
Rainbow Covenant, as it is called today, was meant literally
as a sign that God will never destroy the world again. This is
fervently accepted in all Jewish denominations. Consequently, there is no place among the descendants of Noah for
those who carry placards asserting that the end of the world
is coming soon.

If Jews believe that God will never destroy the world
again, what of messianic belief that is still current in Jewish
hearts? The pulse of long-suffering Jewish hearts and souls
beats rapidly at the daily services in synagogues everywhere
in the hope that a Messiah might yet bring peace. Such a
projected messianic intervention will not bring an end to the
existing world, according to Jewish thought. Rather it will
herald a peaceful age the likes of which the world has never
known. Living, breathing, pulsating life will continue indef-
initely. Life in its existing form is still considered the
supreme value in itself. Its promises and joyful moments are
not to be displaced by the messianic intervention, although
some very early Jewish literature suggested that they might
be.[8]

There is a sifting tendency in Judaism, that is very poorly
understood outside the fold of Jews. In the thousands of
years of evolving tradition, many ideas were placed in Jewish literature, tried, tested, and ultimately rejected. Among
these were thoughts of Satan, dybbuks, original sin, and
many other doctrines. It is for this reason that doctrines of
the imminent end of the world, which had a place in Jewish
literature once, became rejected and disregarded by the Jewish mainstream. This change, and all the others mentioned,
took place because the post-biblical holy books authorized
changes that formed amendments to the biblical authority.
The Old Testament formed the constitution to which amendments were permitted in later ages leading to the present
time.

The Resurrection

It seems only natural that the Jews' love of life on this earth would overflow into a very strong aspiration for an individual's continued existence in the world to come. Early Jewish teachings virtually ignored the subject. By the time that the Jews and the Christians were beginning to separate into two religions, the doctrine of resurrection had permeated Judaism very much indeed. Jesus' ascent to heaven as a resurrected body and soul was in Jesus' day not a new doctrine in the Jewish milieu. Resurrection had become an acceptable amendment to the biblical teachings although the Bible had made little reference to it. Today, it is accepted in all Jewish denominations, except that the reform Jewish denomination asserts that there will only be a resurrection of the soul, not the body.

How did this belief in resurrection become so popular among the Jews? Rabbi Morris Kertzer related it to the time when the Persians dominated Israel. The teachings of Zoroaster were influential among the Jews.[9] Although no specific references in the Bible postulated a definite resurrection, certain biblical characters made indirect references of considerable importance. For instance, in Daniel 12:2 it asserts, "Many of them that sleep in the dust shall awake, some to everlasting life, and some to reproaches and everlasting abhorrence." It was the Pharisees, the progenitors of post-biblical literature, who promoted the doctrine, and the Sadducees, the strict biblical constructionists, who opposed it. The Pharisees, who were the more popular party, sought to prove that the body and the soul really belonged together, and so they needed to be judged together.

The specifics of resurrection are defined in writing. The Talmud declares that those who rise "will be apparelled in their own clothes."[10] The decomposition of the body did not present any difficulty to the sages of the Talmud and the Midrash because resurrection was to be a purely miraculous act of God. The resurrection will take place in the days of the Messiah.[11] Jewish expectations concerning the Messiah differ from the Christian ones. A Jewish precondition for the coming Messiah exists. The Jewish concept of Messiah requires that the world will be brought to a peaceful state as a result of his coming. Until such world peace is demonstrated by the Messiah, complete resurrection must wait!

Purgatory

Purgatory, or limbo, has deep origins in Jewish literature. Although its doctrinal influence declined and mellowed over the years, it was thoroughly described in the texts that also described hell. Then, like many doctrines before it, the idea became generally unacceptable to the populace. Its unacceptability was based on the growing maturity of the Jewish doctrine of the nature of God and God's likely utilization of intelligent, rather than barbaric punishment. Nevertheless, the earlier Jewish descriptions of purgatory were very graphic. The scholarly school of Shammai assigned purgatory to those whose virtues and sins counterbalance one another. The scholars predicted that "they shall go down to Gehenna and float up and down until they rise purified."[12] The Shammaites assumed that the wholly righteous would go directly to heaven, and the wholly wicked directly to hell. How long would purgatory last? The greatest sages, such as Rabbi Akiba, seemed to agree on twelve months. Those souls whose judgment is still not sealed are required to look upon the carcasses of the wicked, the raging fires of hell, and the tortures of the netherworld. Although the belief in purgatory apparently became fundamental in the Roman Catholic Church, it never became an influential Jewish doctrine.

Salvation

Salvation is the dearest goal of any religious devotee. It is the entrance to the gateway of God's sheltering arms. The Jewish pathway to salvation is clearly spelled out in the scriptures and the Talmud. Salvation can be obtained only by active response to the commandments of God. Righteous deeds, charitable acts, service to others, and ethical obedience are all primary vehicles for reaching the destination of heavenly redemption. The Ten Commandments serve as the foundation of the many other laws, and there are 613 major laws in the Bible and Talmud to which the seeker must show obedience. Because the pathway is primarily the ethical deed, salvation is not by its standard open only to Jews, but to any human who truly leads a righteous life. In Old Testament times, sacrificial worship was included in the necessary acts of piety prescribed by law. But since the destruction of the temple, animal sacrifice no longer seemed an appropriate expression of religiosity in the more civilized world of cities and towns.

The struggle to achieve salvation required a supression of the evil inclination (*Yetzer Ha Ra*), and the concentration upon the good inclination (*Yetzer Hatov*). It means that we must win the struggle over our animal natures and channel human energy into a spiritual and ethical plane of activity. Although rejecting original sin, Jewish doctrine recognizes the evil inclination that wars with humans' higher nature. This internal struggle can be aided by proper habits of prayer, the observance of regular rituals, the practice of good, unrewarded deeds (*Mitzvot*), and the diligent habit of study. The last element, that of study, is compulsory for Jews of all ages. Study fosters respect for the law. It defines and explains the ethical requirements and the pathways that have civilized humankind in the past. Study should motivate the Jew to active ethical response and true salvation.

Death Rituals

The Jewish faith provides a firm foundation for death rituals as well as the rituals for life, and the rituals and ceremonies surrounding the funeral service are very elaborate. The ritual guidelines represent the outlook of the faith and facilitate salvation for the dead and healing for the bereaved. Burial must be accomplished as quickly as possible. Early burial has always been Jewish practice. Many reasons in history have been given: it was sensible to bury quickly in a hot climate (Mediterranean); it would prevent dishonor to the dead;[13] it seemed to alleviate the grief of mourners if the burial was accomplished quickly. Exceptions to early burial are allowed when relatives must travel a great distance to the gravesite, or when burial clothes or coffin are not immediately obtainable.

The overall guideline for funeral arrangements is simplicity and modesty of materials and cost in order to avoid embarrassing the poor. Everyone is to be regarded as equal in death. Death is no situation for economic competition. Traditional Jews insist that each person be buried in a simple standard wooden box casket. They allow no lavish fixtures to adorn the casket or to be used as decoration. The funeral clothes are to be plain white shrouds representing penitence and piety. These shrouds are religious garments and are placed upon the body after a ritual cleansing process called *Tahara*, which is usually performed by dedicated synagogue functionaries (*Chevra Kadisha*). The use of flowers and other such expensive decorations are greatly discouraged by orthodox authorities. They have been discouraged, according to Rabbi H. Rabinowicz, because long ago they were so commonplace in the idolatrous rites of ancient peoples. Non-traditional Jews make some compromises with these customs, and although their approach is more individualistic, the principles remain the same. Those non-traditional Jews who choose lavish, expensive caskets have unwittingly fallen into the overall American pattern of funeral arrangements that makes the modern American funeral so costly.

The funeral service itself is a composite of psalms and prayers of comfort, an appropriate eulogy, the solemn *El Mole Rachamim* (God, Full of Compassion) prayer, and the well-known Kaddish prayer at the conclusion. The Kaddish prayer, recited in ancient Aramaic dialect, is really an affirmation of praise and faith in God, and does not mention the dead at all. The Kaddish is effective in lifting up the spirit of the mourner.

The service of the funeral is usually divided into two parts. The first is held at the funeral home or synagogue. The second, or interment service, is usually held at the gravesite. Traditional Jews shovel some dirt from the ground nearby into the grave at the conclusion of the prayers. This allows the mourner to participate in the actual fulfillment of the returning of the body to the earth whence it came (dust returning to dust). In the Jewish service, the casket is closed, and viewing of the body prior to burial is against the custom of the faith. The service is supposed to be a catalyst and a facilitator for the outpouring of natural grief. The atmosphere is arranged to be as realistic as possible without being maudlin or frightening. Vast displays of flowers or elaborate instrumental music are not present even in liberal congregations.

The Jewish funeral is in no sense a happy occasion. The prayers and the eulogy evoke the natural feelings of sadness at the loss. Words and prayers of courage and inspiration are said, and the occasion allows for public expression of the sense of deprivation that mourners are experiencing. It is for this reason that the bereaved almost always enter the funeral service having torn a portion of the outer garment that they are wearing, in symbolic expression of frustrating grief, or they have pinned on themselves a mourning black ribbon, which is symbolically torn to express grief.

It is the custom also to permit no light-hearted conversation to take place near the mourners and to respect fully their sensitivities by refraining from introducing casual subjects in their presence.

The care of the dead in the Jewish religion really begins at the stage when the person is about to die, if such determination can be made beforehand. A person who is dying must be constantly attended to, and not left alone. Small details relating to the comfort of the dying person must be scrupulously attended to. Relieving a dying person's thirst, or hearing a last will and confession are true services that must be provided. Traditional Jews assign dedicated people to help in such blessed tasks, and close members of the family circle bear the most important responsibility for such care.

Once the person has died, there are important rituals to be performed, and those in attendance are expected to perform such tasks right away. The eyes and mouth are to be closed by the son or nearest relative. "The arms and the hands are extended at the sides of the body, and the lower jaw is bound up before rigor mortis sets in. The body is then placed on the floor with the feet toward the door, and is covered with a sheet, while a lighted candle is placed close to the head."[14] Prior to burial, the body must undergo a ritual washing before it is placed in the shrouds for burial. These rituals are intended to form a continuous procedure of care and attention from the time a person is about to die until burial itself. Non-traditional or liberal Jews eliminate many of these customs in the modern day, but the general principles of care, consideration, and constant attention apply as a general rule.

The practice of embalming is against Jewish custom and usage. Very pious Jews will not embalm their dead. Occasionally transportation rules and state laws require modifications of this procedure, and such modifications are permitted. The practice of quick burial, and the aversion of Jewish authorities to showing or viewing the body all reinforce the Rabbis' rules against embalming unless it was required by civil authorities.

Autopsy is a procedure that was forbidden throughout the centuries; however, attitudes towards autopsy are liberalizing even among traditional Jews throughout the world. There are two Jewish values in conflict here. The first value is the physical integrity and wholeness and dignity of the body in preparation for bodily resurrection. The second value is the long-term devotion of the Jews to medical research and the advancement of medical techniques. Some of the world's earliest physicians were Jewish, and Jewish leadership in medicine has been consistent through the centuries.

Cremation has long been against Jewish custom and

practice.[15] This is primarily because it interferes with all the natural preparations to return the body to its natural state and with efforts to maintain it intact for bodily resurrection. Also cremation is a destructive process that does not allow the normal degenerative processes to take over. It is thought thereby to change the mood of the natural mourning process. A few cremations take place among liberal Jews, but they are very few in number. It is difficult to predict whether external conditions might lead to the liberalization of Jewish views on cremation. Such growing problems as lack of space in urban areas and immensely crowded cemeteries in certain localities must be solved. But at the present time, no such liberalization is in the offing. Cremation will likely remain a rarity among Jews.

Judaism has an exceptionally well-developed system of comforting and responding to the bereaved. Right after the funeral the bereaved are required to rest and reside in a "House of Mourning" designated for their recovery from the loss. (In practice the House of Mourning is often the bereaved's own house.) The primary mourning period is seven days for traditional Jews and three days for liberal Jews. Under this system, it is entirely improper for the bereaved to forego this ritual, and resume normal activities without it. Right after arriving at the House of Mourning, the next of kin and close friends minister to the bereaved by attending to all their personal needs. The meal of condolence is prepared by the family circle and loving friends and is served shortly after the funeral to the bereaved and to the visitors who arrive as comforters. A hard boiled egg must be served with this meal, for it signifies life's continuation. In traditional Jewish homes, the mourners sit on low stools rather than the usual comfortable living room furniture. It is the custom also for the traditional Jewish mourner to remove his leather shoes. Cloth, felt, or rubber slippers are allowed instead. No work is permitted, for it is a time of meditation and introspection. Female traditional mourners are allowed to do domestic work around the house, if they so desire. During the first three days of mourning, the traditional mourner does not acknowledge or welcome his or her guests, but remains in virtual silence. This becomes relaxed after the third day. Non-traditional Jews have liberalized many of these rules. They do not sit on low stools nor do they remove their shoes, and they are allowed to greet their guests.[16] It is the usual custom to have religious services in the House of Mourning especially timed for the fulfillment of the daily prayers that are incumbent upon all Jews. When the services are held at the House of Mourning, special mention is made of the individual who has died. Close friends and relatives bring freshly baked breads, prepared dishes of all kinds, and offer their services to clean house, run errands, and remain during late hours if the mourner is alone in the house and needs moral support.

The mourning period is divided into three parts of special nature. The first week is the most intense part of mourning. This is when the mourner must receive the comforters and remain in a state of deep contemplation. The second period is the thirty-day period after the death when the mourner is restricted from attending most entertainment and formal community events.

The third is a twelve-month period of mourning. Restrictions about the timing of remarriage fall within this period, and it is during this latter period, or at its close, that the tombstone is officially dedicated in solemn ceremony.

Many strict customs still apply to the most pious of traditional Jews. For these, it is inappropriate to cut one's hair during the first thirty days, although it may be combed. Also, the wearing of black is a strict rule among very pious, traditional Jews during the first thirty days of mourning. It is a general rule to forbid the mourner from taking a wife during this first thirty-day period. A man whose wife has died is not permitted to remarry until three festivals have elapsed (a period of several months), although exceptions are made in the case of a widower with very young children.[17] A widow is forbidden to remarry until ninety days have elapsed after the death of her husband.[18]

After the funeral service it is customary to light a seven-day *Yartzeit* (Memorial) candle in memory of the deceased.

Yartzeit candles are lit for twenty-four hours in the mourner's home on the anniversary of the death each year, and also memorial wall tablets are lit in the Synagogue on the Day of Atonement, the holiest day of the Jewish holiday cycle. In some modern, non-traditional synagogues, the names of the deceased are read during religious services on the anniversary of the death, and in many synagogues of all types, memorial tablets are erected that list the beloved dead of the congregational family. Charitable contributions in honor of the deceased are an important custom to be carried out by the synagogue family and the local Jewish community. These contributions are often listed in the synagogue bulletin.

The saying of the Kaddish prayer is an essential part of the mourning experience. This famous prayer is distinctive because of its rhythmic cadence, and its use of Aramaic language instead of the customary Hebrew. It is incumbent upon the mourner to recite the Kaddish prayer with meticulous regularity during the year of mourning. In practice, the prayer amounts to a virtual petition or intercession for the welfare of the deceased. The Kaddish prayer is supposed to be recited by the next-of-kin at every regular service during the year of mourning.[19] In the event of a legitimate inability to fulfill this Kaddish prayer recitation, then a surrogate must be appointed to fulfill this act of prayer. Non-traditional Jews have permitted leniencies in this very stringent rule, permitting absences and periods of excused non-compliance. Originally the Kaddish prayer was supposed to be recited by the son only in the situation of the death of a parent. Traditional Judaism entrusts such ritual obligations exclusively to the male. Today the prayer is used for more than parents, and most authorities extend its use for all next-of-kin. Many authorities allow the females to recite this prayer.

During festivals and holy seasons, Jews hold memorial services to remember the dead. The memorial services are added to the roster of prayers normally said on those holidays. The three festivals of Passover, Sukot, and Shavuot, and the Day of Atonement, constitute such occasion. Many synagogues also hold memorial services at the congregational cemeteries during the days of repentance, which occur at the time of the holiest seasons of New Year and Day of Atonement.

An important Jewish procedural rule for care and remembrance of the dead is the fact that no funeral rituals can take place on Sabbaths and holidays. There can be no funeral on the Sabbath or on the first day of a Jewish holiday, and the mourner refrains from mourning during these periods. It is felt that the celebrative holiday mood and the mourning mood simply cannot be reasonably combined. Public memorial services and the reciting of the Kaddish are permitted, but the major acts of personal mourning and the funeral services are prohibited during these periods, the first days of Sabbath and holidays.

It is especially important to emphasize the need of the mourner to fully express his or her grief by the natural act of weeping and expressing personal sorrow; to hold in or to restrain one's grief would be harmful to the process of full recovery that is the hoped-for result of the year's ritual of mourning.

Overall, practices and beliefs surrounding death in the Jewish religion are meant to reflect God's purpose that his creatures have a meaningful and righteous existence, in this world, and in the hereafter. The hallmarks of the funeral service and the burial are simplicity and rapidity. Ostentation and length of the occasion are greatly limited so as not to delay the evolving of the natural expression of grief.

Again, the year of mourning is divided into three parts, and surrounded by ritual prescriptions of all kinds. The mourner should be encouraged to let the tears flow, to sit and grieve while others attend to the necessities of his or her life. The mourner is treated like a sick person who cannot resume normal activities until the spiritual and psychological conditions have righted themselves.

The dead must be honored, loved, and remembered. This process is activated right at the point when the person is dying. Personal attention is given at this point by care and the supervision of the dying so that personal love may be demonstrated and human needs be met. Jewish eulogies are invariably personal, and often quite emotional. Details of the person's life are usually thoroughly presented in the eulogy. The most common form of tribute given by friends and associates is a gift to charity befitting the interests and associations of the departed.

Jewish funerals today most often take place in funeral homes, with a committal service at the cemetery. But in the case of a great scholar or dignitary, the services can begin in the synagogue, where there is special prestige accorded to the event. In the instances of the burial of a very old person, who has few friends and relatives to attend the services, and few survivors in the community, the service is often restricted to a short committal service in the cemetery. Such a service is known as a graveside service. A non-Jewish person may be buried in a Jewish cemetery, but the officiant and the symbols used must be specifically Jewish.[20]

To love, to honor, and to remember the dead is the ongoing obligation of the person who has lost a loved one. By saying the Kaddish prayer during the year of mourning, by lighting the remembrance lamps (*Yartzeit lights*), by fulfilling the rules of the year of mourning, the process of grief gradually ebbs as the year draws to a close. At that point, although the laws permit it earlier, the tombstone is usually marked and dedicated. Unlike the funeral service, the tombstone dedication is attended by the close family and a few friends only and does not contain an emotional eulogy. It is shorter and simpler in every way.

The *Yartzeit* remembrance lights continue to be lit year after year, and the deceased is remembered at the various memorial services of the synagogue in the annual cycle. Very often, the dead are memorialized on memorial tablets which have been placed on a synagogue wall. In special instances donations are given to dedicate portions of rooms or libraries in the synagogue in memory of beloved dead. In many synagogues, the names of the deceased are read aloud on the anniversary of the death. The process of naming children in Judaism also serves to memorialize the dead. Praiseworthy ancestors have always been the ones first considered when children's names must be selected.

In many remote areas, Jews share cemetery space with non-Jews. In such instances, the section is ritually separated and marked off. Inscriptions in Jewish cemeteries invariably contain some of the Hebrew language followed sometimes by English translation. One of the most common inscriptions is: "May the soul be bound up in the bonds of eternal life." At synagogue services when a dead person is mentioned, it is usually said: "May he or she be remembered for blessing" or such and such "of blessed memory."

It is the fervent hope of the Jewish believer that the good influence of the dead will always remain as an inspiration for the next generations.

Notes

[1] *El Moley Rachamim*, "O God, Full of Compassion." This standard funeral prayer petitions God that the soul of the deceased may be brought under the shelter of God's wings.

[2] *Deuteronomy*, 30:15.

[3] Charles Braden, *The World's Religions*, Abingdon Cokesbury Press, 1939, p. 81.

[4] From *Gates of Prayer*, The New Reform Jewish Prayerbook, Central Conference of American Rabbis Press, 1973, p. 625.

[5] "What is the Jewish Attitude Toward Manual Labor"? Rabbi Morris Kertzer, *What is a Jew?* World Publishing Co., 1953, p. 34-35,

[6] Very Rev. Dr. Joseph H. Hertz, (Chief Rabbi or the British Empire), *Sayings of the Fathers*, Behrman House Inc., 1945, p. 119.

[7] Milton Miller, *Our Religion and Our Neighbors*, Union of American Hebrew Congregations Press, 1963, p. 259.

[8] *Encyclopedia Judaica*, Keter Publishing Co., 1971, Volume 11, p. 1412.

[9] *What is a Jew?* p. 13.

[10] Rabbi H. Rabinowicz, *A Guide to Life*, KTAV Publishing Co., 1967, p. 130.

[11] Ibid., p. 130.

[12] *Encyclopedia Judaica*, V. 12, p. 998.

[13] *A Guide to Life*, p. 22.

[14] *A Guide to Life*, p. 18-19.

[15] *What is a Jew?* p. 95.

[16] Frederic A. Doppelt and David Polish, *A Guide for Reform Jews*, KTAV Publishing Co., 1973, p. 87.

[17] *A Guide to Life*, p. 98.

[18] Ibid., p. 99.

[19] *A Guide for Reform Jews*, p. 89.

[20] Walter Jacob, ed. *American Reform Responsa*, Central Conference of American Rabbis Publisher, 1983, p. 340.

LUTHERANS

Daniel E. Lee, Ph.D.

Background of the Faith

Lutheranism is most appropriately understood as a particular expression of Christianity and is envisioned as part of one universal church, rather than as a separate church. Throughout the 450-year history of Lutheranism, Lutherans have joined in the ancient confession, "We believe in one holy catholic and apostolic church."

The Lutheran movement began more by circumstance than by design. As the name suggests, a key figure in the historical development of the movement was Martin Luther,[1] an Augustinian monk born in 1483 in the little town of Eisleben, located not far from Berlin in what is now the German Democratic Republic. After entering the Augustinian cloister at Erfurt in 1505, Luther spent a good deal of time wrestling with a variety of questions related to salvation. The process continued after his transfer to Wittenberg in 1511, where he joined the faculty of the university which had been established there by Frederick the Wise. In time, he came to question a number of the beliefs and practices of the Roman Catholic Church of his time.

Luther was not at all reluctant to express his views on matters that concerned him. On the eve of All Saints Day in 1517, he posted for debate ninety-five theses challenging various of the practices of the church that troubled him. The Ninety-Five Theses were the spark which lit the powder keg that was to become known as the Protestant Reformation. Even though most of the practices challenged in the Ninety-Five Theses were subsequently changed—many of them within Luther's own lifetime—the theses began a chain of historical events from which there was no turning back.

News of the outspoken monk quickly reached Rome. In 1520, Pope Leo X, a member of the influential Medici family, issued a decree giving Luther sixty days to submit to the authority of the church. "Arise, O Lord, and judge thy cause," the preface began. "A wild boar has invaded thy vineyard."[2]

But Luther was not to be quieted. Tossing the papal decree in a fire near one of the gates of the university in Wittenberg, he continued to challenge the beliefs and practices of the church, questioning not only the authority of the pope but sacramental theology as well.

In 1521, in the city of Worms, Luther stood before the young Charles V, a member of the Hapsburg family who had been chosen Emperor of the Holy Roman Empire less than two years before. Again he was asked to recant. Again he refused. Under the circumstances, it is not surprising that he was excommunicated from the church.

The Lutheran movement spread rapidly for a mixture of religious and political reasons. Parishoners were pleased to hear that they could enter heaven without complying with the heavy demands placed on them by the Roman Catholic Church. The princes of the fragmented territories that comprised the Germany of that time (there was no German nation as such) were quick to exploit the opportunity to assert to a greater degree of independence from the Holy Roman Empire, of which they were nominally a part, and from the Roman Catholic Church, with which the empire was so closely allied.

In time, the Lutheran movement spread to the Scandinavian countries, which were to become predominantly Lutheran (aided, in part, by the fact that Lutheranism became the official state religion). Immigrants from Germany and the Scandinavian countries brought Lutheranism to the American colonies prior to the American Revolution. Since a number of these immigrants sided with the British crown during the war for independence, Lutheranism was to set roots in Canada in the years following the war. Subsequent waves of immigrants in the late nineteenth and early twentieth centuries added considerably to the number of Lutherans in the United States and Canada.

Missionary work, primarily in the last century and a half, has spread Lutheranism to other parts of the world. Among the countries with sizable Lutheran populations today is Namibia in southern Africa.

In the United States, there are at present three large organizational groupings of Lutheran congregations and several smaller ones. The three larger churches, each with approximately three million members, are the American Lutheran Church (ALC), the Lutheran Church in America (LCA), and the Lutheran Church-Missouri Synod (LC-MS). Among the smaller organizational groupings is the Association of Evangelical Lutheran Churches (AELC), which consists of a number of congregations previously affiliated with the Lutheran Church-Missouri Synod. The ALC, LCA, and AELC are presently engaged in merger discussions directed toward the formation of a new Lutheran Church.

Lutheran Beliefs

Playing a key role in Lutheran doctrine and beliefs is the doctrine of justification by faith. The Augsburg Confession, compiled in 1530 as an expression of basic Lutheran beliefs, states the doctrine as follows:

> It is also taught among us that we cannot obtain forgive-
> ness of sin and righteousness before God by our own merits,
> works, or satisfactions, but that we receive forgiveness of sin
> and become righteous before God by grace, for Christ's sake,
> through faith, when we believe that Christ suffered for us and
> that for His sake our sin is forgiven and righteousness and
> eternal life are given to us.[3]

Luther tended to view the world as caught in a struggle between the forces of good and the forces of evil—between God and Satan. In his essay "The Bondage of the Will" and elsewhere in his writings, he insisted that apart from God's intervention, human beings, who are born sinful, are totally under the sway of the forces of evil. The will is so vitiated by sin, Luther believed, that it is not possible even to accept the salvation offered by God without divine assistance.[4]

In the Christ of the cross, Luther believed the ultimate price was paid. In the crucifixion and resurrection of Christ, victory over the forces of evil was gained. Thus, Luther believed, as a result of Christ having paid for the sins of all humanity, God extends salvation to the believer (the act of faith itself being a gift from God). Luther put it as follows in his *Small Catechism*:

> I believe that Jesus Christ, true God, begotten of the Father
> from eternity, and also true man, born of the Virgin Mary, is
> my Lord, who has redeemed me, a lost and condemned crea-

ture, delivered me and freed me from all sins, from death, and from the power of the devil, not with silver and gold but with his holy and precious blood and with his innocent sufferings and death, in order that I may be his, live under him in his kingdom, and serve him in everlasting righteousness, innocence, and blessedness, even as he is risen from the dead and lives and reigns to all eternity. This is most certainly true.[5]

A classical expression of Luther's theology is to be found in the words of the well-known hymn he wrote, "A Mighty Fortress Is Our God." In this hymn, he states that "though hordes of devils fill the land," Christ "holds the field victorious."[6]

In the course of the centuries, the apocalyptic nature of Lutheran theology has softened. In the sermons preached in many Lutheran churches today, there is seldom—if ever—any reference to the devil.

Yet the basic doctrine of justification by faith remains central, for Lutherans are unanimous in insisting that salvation cannot be earned by good works but can only be received as a gift from God.

Funeral Practices and Ministry to the Dying and Bereaved

The Lutheran Book of Worship, which originated as a cooperative effort of all major Lutheran groups in the United States and Canada, includes a service for the burial of the dead.[7] Intended primarily to be used in a church with the body of the deceased present, the service is structured so that it may easily be modified for use in other settings such as a funeral chapel, private home, or crematory, and for situations in which the body of the deceased is not present. The liturgy is a service of worship. Ceremonies or tributes of social or fraternal societies are not allowed within the service of worship.

The Service for the Burial of the Dead consists of three parts: the Service of the Word, the Commendation, and the

Committal. The first part of the liturgy—the Service of the Word—typically begins with a procession which forms when the minister or ministers meet the coffin, the pallbearers and the bereaved at the entrance to the church. The order of the procession is as follows: the cross, the paschal candle or torches, the presiding minister, the assisting minister or ministers, the pallbearers with the coffin, and the bereaved.[8]

While the coffin often is open for a last viewing in the narthex (entrance) of the church prior to the service, the coffin remains closed throughout the service. When the service is conducted in some other setting, such as a funeral home or a private home, the expectation is that the coffin will be closed here as well, though some ministers will accommodate the preferences of the family.

When the service is conducted in a church, a white pall (cloth) may be placed on the coffin prior to the procession. The pall is both to symbolize the righteousness of Christ and to assure a measure of equality by preventing the display of a costly coffin or any embarrassment that might be associated with an inexpensive one.[9]

The coffin is placed at the front of the church perpendicular to the altar. An old tradition, still practiced in some churches, suggests that if the deceased is a pastor, the coffin should be placed with the head toward the altar whereas if the deceased is a lay person, the placement should be with the head toward the congregation. This placement has no particular theological significance but is simply intended to reflect the accustomed role of the deceased in the church, with pastors facing the congregation and lay persons facing the altar.[10]

The Service of the Word includes several readings from Scripture and various prayers. Several options are included in the liturgy. Special music often is part of the service. The Apostles' Creed may be said. The Service of Holy Communion may be included.

The service usually includes a sermon. While the sermon may include recognition of the life of the deceased, it is not intended to be a eulogy but rather a proclamation of hope and comfort in Christ and thanksgiving for the life of the deceased. In some cases, relatives and friends may comment briefly on the meaning of the life of the deceased for the community.[11]

When the service is held in a church, it usually concludes with the Commendation, a prayer asking God to receive the deceased in mercy, recalling the last prayer of Jesus on the Cross, "Father, into your hands I commend my spirit." When the body is cremated, the Commendation may be held in the crematory chapel with the Service of the Word being held in the church as a memorial service.[12]

The Committal is a liturgy usually performed at the interment site. If the body has been willed to science, the Committal may, with appropriate modifications, be performed prior to the removal of the body.[13]

When all have arrived at the place of burial, additional prayers may be read. When the coffin is lowered into the grave, handfuls of earth may be cast on the coffin by the assisting minister and those who stand nearby as the presiding minister commits the body to its final resting place.[14]

Many Lutheran ministers believe that it is their duty to conduct a funeral whenever asked to do so, whether by the request of the deceased prior to his or her death or by family members at the time of death. When the deceased is not a member of the congregation, it is usual to omit certain portions of the service that pertain more specifically to those who have been practicing members of the congregation.

Cremation is not widely practiced by Lutherans but is an option encompassed by the liturgy. So also is donation of the body to science, a practice given support by the "LCA Social Statement on Death and Dying" (a position paper adopted at the 1982 National LCA Convention).[15]

The Book of Occasional Services, a cooperative effort of the AELC, the LCA, the ALC, and The Evangelical Lutheran Church of Canada, includes a service for comforting the bereaved.[16] This service is sometimes used at the funeral home at the close of visitation with only family and close friends present.

The church's ministry is understood as including the time prior to death, as well as the time after death. The LCA

Social Statement on Death and Dying observes:

> In death-and-dying situations, the Church's ministry of Word and Sacrament through its members and ordained ministers is of great significance. Remembrance of Baptism renews the Christian's sense of unity with Christ and the Church, and the Sacrament of Holy Communion serves as a reassurance of Christ's living presence and offers hope for the life to come. Simply to be with those for whom death is approaching—to pray with and for them, to listen and to respond, to comfort and to console—is also an essential ministry.[17]

Perspectives on Death and Life After Death

Among Lutherans there is considerable diversity of opinion as to how death should be interpreted. One view, held by numerous individuals in all major Lutheran groups, suggests that death is the result of sin and, accordingly, an intrusion into the natural created order. A document prepared by a Lutheran Church-Missouri Synod working group states this view as follows:

> God created human beings to live and not to die. Death in any form is inimical to what God originally had in mind for His creation. . . . Death is the very negation of what God has given. Had it not been for man's own rebellion against the kind of intended relationship established by having been fashioned in God's image, there would be no death.[18]

A contrasting view, which also has broad support among Lutherans, characterizes death as part of the natural created order. An ALC document states that "death is a natural event in the course of human life."[19] A similar view is expressed in the LCA Social Statement on Death and Dying, which suggests that death is "a natural part of the life cycle."[20]

There is also some diversity of opinion about what happens after death. In theological and philosophical thought, there is a distinction to be made between the doctrine of the resurrection of the body and the doctrine of the immortality of the soul. The doctrine of the resurrection of the body, which is firmly rooted in early Christian thought, suggests that after an interim period of time, those who have died will be brought back to life again. The doctrine of the immortality of the soul, which is Greek in origin, suggests that some aspects of human existence—perhaps including some form of consciousness—continue to exist after the death of the body.

Like many other Christians, the average Lutheran sitting in the pew on Sunday morning tends to blend the two doctrines without distinction. While comprehensive surveys of the views of parishioners on these matters are not available, it is probably accurate to say that the typical Lutheran is likely to believe that some part of the person continues to exist after death but that full restoration to life must await resurrection of the body.

The liturgy of the church, as is evidenced by the Service for the Burial of the Dead, places a strong emphasis on the resurrection of the body. References to the doctrine of the immortality of the soul are somewhat more muted. The Commendation, which, as already noted, is a prayer asking God to receive the deceased in mercy, might be interpreted as implying some type of continued existence. So also might the Apostles' Creed, which speaks of Jesus descending into hell prior to being raised from the dead. (An alternate translation, which is also included in the Lutheran Book of Worship, states that Jesus "descended to the dead."[21])

In keeping with the interpretation of the Sacrament of the Altar (Holy Communion) articulated by Luther, it is not the practice of Lutherans to say masses on behalf of the dead.[22] The early leaders of the Lutheran movement however, did not preclude the possibility of saying prayers for the dead.[23]

In a certain sense, both the Commendation and the Committal in the Service for the Burial of the Dead are prayers on behalf of the deceased. A prayer occasionally used as part of the Service for the Burial of the Dead (though not included in the Lutheran Book of Worship) is even more explicit. This prayer reads, in part:

Lord...
You raised the dead to life;
give to our *brother/sister* eternal life.
        Hear us, Lord
you promised life to those who believe;
bring our *brother/sister* to the joys of heaven.
        Hear us, Lord[24]

In practice, however, prayers for the deceased are exceedingly rare among Lutherans, particularly on occasions subsequent to the funeral. When references in prayers are made to the deceased on subsequent occasions, it is almost always a prayer of remembrance that expresses thanksgiving for the life of the deceased. A commonly used prayer is the following:

> We remember with thanksgiving those who have loved and served you in your church on earth, who now rest from their labors (especially those most dear to us, whom we name in our hearts before you). Keep us in fellowship with all your saints and bring us at last to the joy of your heavenly kingdom.[25]

As noted above, the traditional Lutheran view is that of resurrection of the body and of a life to come. The doctrine of reincarnation does not find support among Lutherans.

Salvation

Traditional Lutheran belief holds that at some unspecified time in the future, Christ will return, the dead will be raised, and a day of judgment will be held. The Augsburg Confession puts it as follows:

> It is also taught among us that our Lord Jesus Christ will return on the last day for judgment and will raise up all the dead, to give eternal life and everlasting joy to believers and the elect but to condemn ungodly men and the devil to hell and eternal punishment.[26]

As previously noted, Luther believed that only those to whom God extends grace will receive salvation and thus be spared eternal punishment. In Luther's view, the fact that someone might go to church regularly and profess to be a Christian was by no means a certain indicator that he or she was a recipient of God's grace leading to salvation and eternal life in heaven. Nor did Luther exclude the possibility that God's grace might be extended to someone lacking in the outward signs of being a Christian.

An equally perplexing problem for Luther (as well as for other Christians) was the question of why a God, who is loving, merciful, and all-powerful, would allow some people to suffer in the torment of hell for all eternity. Also troublesome was the question of why it is just for God to punish people if they are born under the bondage of sin and are totally unable to do anything other than sin. All that Luther could say was that "the light of glory. . .will one day reveal God, to whom alone belongs a judgment whose justice is incomprehensible, as a God whose justice is most righteous and evident. . . ."[27]

As with other aspects of Lutheran theology, beliefs pertaining to the question of salvation and the day of judgment have been softened somewhat in the four and a half centuries since the time of Luther. References to hell and eternal damnation are relatively rare in the sermons preached in Lutheran churches today. Rather, the emphasis is on God's love and mercy. There is some tendency to believe that God extends salvation to all who wish to receive it. Some parishioners go one step further and say that the gift of grace encompasses all persons without distinction.

In a widely read book on the Augsburg Confession, George Forell, a contemporary Lutheran scholar, gives a somewhat temporal interpretation to the reference to a day of judgment in the Confession. In an era in which apprehensions about nuclear annihilation and other fears of impending disaster are widespread, the Augsburg Confession, he suggests, serves to remind us "that the symbol which dominates the final scene of human history is not the cloud but the cross." He continues, "The Christian proclamation in our time is a message of hope rather than despair because Christians believe that history is moving toward Jesus Christ."[28]

Lutherans, like most other Christians, have traditionally understood salvation as being saved from the fires of hell. However, there has been some rethinking in this area as well. Some Lutherans, including several involved in various aspects of counseling, are inclined to view salvation as a healing process involving restoration to wholeness. While there is no consensus as to what wholeness of the person encompasses, it is generally understood as spiritual and psychological well-being, in some combination, and, in some cases, social well-being as well. For example, some would consider working through unresolved grief as a form of restoration to wholeness. Quite obviously, the time parameters for such a view of salvation are somewhat different, with salvation at least potentially occurring here and now, rather than in a life to come. The two views of salvation, it might be added, are not antithetical and can be held concurrently, with salvation envisioned as a multifaceted process.

In most cases, suicide is viewed as the result of disturbance or illness, rather than as a sin. In the limited number of cases in which suicide is viewed as a sin, Lutherans typically believe that God's love and mercy are of sufficient magnitude to extend forgiveness for this sin, as well as for all other sins.

Heaven

Lutherans have not been given to speculative theology attempting to determine what the nature of heaven might be like, where it might be located, etc. To the extent that Lutherans have a belief, it is usually envisioned as an eternity in the immediate presence of God, joining in unending praise to the Creator and Lord of all that exists. A traditional Norwegian hymn sung by many Lutherans ("Den store hvide Flok"—"Who Is This Host Arrayed in White") paints the following picture of heaven:

Who is this host arrayed in white
    Like thousand snow-clad mountains bright,
That stands with palms and sings its praises
    Before the throne of light?
These are the saints who kept God's Word;
    They are the honored of the Lord.
He is their prince who drowned their sins,
    So they were cleansed, restored.
They now serve God both day and night;
    They sing their songs in endless light.
Their anthems ring when they all sing
    With angels shining bright.[29]

Thanksgiving

In the life and liturgy of Lutheran churches, there is a strong emphasis on the theme of thankfulness for the gift of life that God has created. It is in keeping with this spirit that the LCA Social Statement on Death and Dying concludes with Psalm 107:1:

O give thanks to the Lord, for he is good;
for his steadfast love endures forever! (RSV)

Notes

[1] For a highly readable biography of Luther, see Roland H. Bainton, *Here I Stand: A Life of Martin Luther* (New York: Abingdon Press, 1950).

[2] Ibid., p. 114.

[3] *The Augsburg Confession*, Article IV. Included in *The Book of Concord: The Confessions of the Evangelical Lutheran Church*, trans. and edited by Theodore G. Tappert (Philadelphia: Muhlenberg Press, 1959).

[4] Martin Luther, "The Bondage of the Will," *passim*. Selections from "The Bondage of the Will" are included in *Martin Luther: Selections from His Writings*, ed. by John Dillenberger (Garden City, NY: Anchor Books, 1961), pp. 166-203. The translation of the Dillenberger volume is by J.I. Packer and A.R. Johnston.

[5] Martin Luther, *The Small Catechism*, commentary on the second article of The Apostles' Creed. Included in *The Book of Concord*, trans. and ed. by Tappert, p. 345.

[6] Martin Luther, "A Mighty Fortress Is Our God." Included in the *Lutheran Book of Worship* (Minneapolis: Augsburg Publishing House, 1978), Hymns 228 and 229.

[7] *Lutheran Book of Worship*, pp. 206-14.

[8] Philip H. Pfatteicher and Carlos R. Messerli, *Manual on the Liturgy: Lutheran Book of Worship* (Minneapolis: Augsburg Publishing House, 1979), pp. 356-357.

[9] Ibid.

[10] Ibid., p. 358.

[11] Ibid., p. 360.

[12] Ibid., pp. 362-363.

[13] Ibid.

[14] Ibid., pp. 363-365.

[15] The Lutheran Church in America *Social Statement on Death and Dying* (New York: Lutheran Church in America, Division for Mission in North America, 1982), p. 7.

[16] *Occasional Services: A Companion to Lutheran Book of Worship* (Minneapolis: Augsburg Publishing House, 1982), pp. 108-112.

[17] LCA Social Statement on Death and Dying, p. 6. See also the liturgy for "Commendation of the Dying," *Occasional Services*, pp. 103-107.

[18] Commission on Theology and Church Relations of The Lutheran Church-Missouri Synod, *Report on Euthanasia with Guiding Principles* (October, 1979), p. 18.

[19] Task Force on Ethical Issues in Human Medicine, *Health, Life, and Death...A Christian Perspective* (Minneapolis: The American Lutheran Church, 1977), p. 17.

[20] LCA Social Statement on Death and Dying, p. 1. This issue is discussed in greater detail in my book *Death and Dying: Ethical Choices in a Caring Community* (New York: Lutheran Church in America, Division for Mission in North America, 1983), pp. 1-7.

[21] *Lutheran Book of Worship*, p. 65.

[22] See e.g., *The Babylonian Captivity of the Church in Luther's Works*, Vol. 36, p. 55.

[23] See e.g., *The Apology of the Augsburg Confession*, art. XXIV (included in the various editions of the *Book of Concord*).

[24] Included in Pfatteicher and Messerli, *Manual on the Liturgy Lutheran Book of Worship*, p. 361.

[25] *Lutheran Book of Worship*, p. 53.

[26] *Augsburg Confession*, Article XVII.

[27] Luther, "The Bondage of the Will," pp. 200-202.

[28] George W. Forell, *The Augsburg Confession: A Contemporary Commentary* (Minneapolis: Augsburg Publishing House, 1968), p. 75.

[29] *Lutheran Book of Worship*, Hymn No. 314.

PRESBYTERIANISM

Ben Lacy Rose, Th.D.

Background of the Faith

The faith of the Presbyterian and Reformed churches[1] was brought to fullness during the Protestant Reformation under the leadership of John Calvin in Switzerland where he built on foundations laid by Ulrich Zwingli and others. Feeling that the Roman Catholic Church had distorted the faith of the Bible, Calvin and the other reformers set about the task of uncovering and articulating afresh the teachings of the Scriptures of the Old and New Testaments. Calvin's followers, therefore, do not see him as the founder of their faith, but they see Abraham, Moses, David and Paul as founders, with Jesus Christ as the pioneer and perfecter.

Nor did Calvin see himself as against Martin Luther and his work, though these two theologians differed in many respects. Today Calvin's theology is titled "Reformed" while Luther's is titled "Lutheran."

John Calvin was born in 1509 in France of Roman Catholic parents. He was preparing for a career in law when, around 1533, he was converted to the Protestant cause, which at that time was gaining popularity among the French. Shortly thereafter Calvin left France and settled in Geneva, Switzerland, where he spent most of his life teaching, writing, and preaching. The only positions he ever held were preacher, pastor, and professor, but through these he influenced the life of Geneva in a profound way. Spread primarily by his writings and by his disciples, Calvin's ideas were carried rapidly to Holland, Germany, France, Scotland, and to central and eastern Europe. The Huguenots of France, the Puritans of England, and William of Orange and his followers in the Netherlands were all spiritual children of John Calvin.

Under the leadership of John Knox, who spent several years with Calvin in Geneva, the Reformed faith and Presbyterian policy were adopted by the Church of Scotland. The Westminster Confession of Faith and Catechisms, one of the finest statments of Reformed doctrine, was drawn up by an assembly of divines called together by the English Parliament in 1643.

The Presbyterian and Reformed faith was brought to America by immigrants primarily from Holland, Scotland, France and Germany. Today among Protestants, the Presbyterian and Reformed family is the second largest in the world. The Lutheran family is the largest.

Presbyterian and Reformed people have been prolific in the production of creeds. Dr. John H. Leith in *Creeds of the Churches* declares that "more than sixty creeds would qualify as Reformed."[2] These creeds differ in many details, yet they exhibit a surprising unity regarding the basic elements of the faith.

Main Beliefs of the Faith

Some of the main beliefs of the Presbyterian and Reformed faith are set forth in the following paragraphs:

God has revealed himself in the Scriptures of the Old and New Testaments, which, being uniquely inspired by him, are our only trustworthy rule for believing and living. While it is impossible to describe fully the nature of God, one Reformed creed puts it thus, "God is a spirit, infinite, eternal, and unchangeable in his being, wisdom, power, holiness, justice, goodness, and truth."[3] We joyfully declare that "God is love,"[4] yet at the same time we tremble at his wrath, believing that even in his anger his love is revealed. God is creator, sustainer and sovereign ruler of all his creatures and all their actions. "From all eternity God did by the most wise and holy counsel of his own will, freely and unchangeably ordain whatsoever comes to pass, yet so as thereby neither is God the author of sin nor is violence offered to the will of the creatures, nor is the liberty or contingency of second causes taken away, but rather established."[5] God is personal and has revealed himself as a trinity of Father, Son and Holy Spirit. We do not thus affirm three gods but one God who exists in three persons. God created humankind in his own image and for fellowship with himself. He put men and women on the earth that they might "glorify and enjoy him forever."[6] The glory of God is therefore the purpose of human existence.

Humankind, however, refused to walk in fellowship with God but rebelled against him. Thus they fell from the estate wherein they were created by sinning against God. Possessing now a fallen nature, human beings are basically selfish and prone to sin. Some Presbyterians believe in a literal Devil and some do not, but, all recognize the awful power of evil in the world from whatever source it comes.

In order to redeem humankind and bring them back into fellowship with himself, God sent his only begotten Son, the Lord Jesus Christ, who was born of the Virgin Mary grew up as would any normal boy in a family, preached and taught in the land of Palestine, and was crucified on a Roman cross near Jerusalem during the reign of Pontius Pilate. He was dead and buried, but God raised Jesus Christ from the dead and set him on God's right hand. From there he shall come again at the end of time to judge the living and the dead.

Salvation comes to human beings through faith in the Lord Jesus Christ. The church, which consists of all who believe in Christ together with their children, was created by God to carry the message of God's saving love to all the world. Believers are given the task of witnessing to the faith of Christ and of ministering to persons in his name and spirit. "As servants of the sovereign will of God, Christians are under obligation to their fellowmen and to unborn generations to shape and influence institutions and practices so that the world may be brought more nearly into conformity with the purposes of God for his creation. We believe that our destiny and that of the world are not subject to chance or fate, but to the just and loving sovereignty of God. In this assurance we face the problems of suffering and evil. Faith in the purpose and providence of God assures us of his presence in suffering and of his power to give it meaning. We are confident that no form of evil can separate us from the love of God, that God works in all things for good, and that evil will ultimately be overcome. Therefore, while we cannot fully understand the pain and evil of the present world, we can offer ourselves as active instruments of God's will in their conquest."[7]

Finally we believe in "the resurrection of the body and the life everlasting."[8]

Most Presbyterian and Reformed churches have doctrinal standards which set forth their theology and also manuals of government which contain guidelines by which church affairs are to be ordered. Members are not required to accept all that is affirmed in the doctrinal standards, but ministers are required to accept the essentials.

Presbyterian Funeral

The doctrinal standards and manuals of government of Presbyterian and Reformed churches give very few instructions regarding funerals. No inviolable rules are laid down, no rituals or prayers are prescribed. One manual reads, "Christians should make of the occasion of death a time in which the hope of the gospel is reaffirmed by them with solemn joy. . . . The funeral service, which should be conducted with dignity and simplicity, is a witness to the greatness and goodness of God and to the love he bears all people, a love which strengthens and supports even in the midst of grief."[9] Most funerals are conducted within two to four days after the death, with the body of the deceased present during the service. Services are held in the church sanctuary more often than in a funeral home, but the use of the latter is growing. Sometimes in Presbyterian circles a private interment is conducted with only the family present and a public memorial service is held later in the church.

Treatment and Interment of the Body

Presbyterian and Reformed churches give no authoritative instructions regarding the disposal of the body. Members and ministers are left free to follow their best wisdom in such matters. Embalming is almost universally used. Autopsies and cremation are neither encouraged nor discouraged. The donation of the body to science is advocated by many ministers. One Book of Order says, "The [funeral] service normally should be held in a church and the casket should remain closed. . ."[10] but this is not mandatory. Sometimes the casket is opened so that the body may be viewed before the service begins in the church, but all churches make a practice of closing the casket during the funeral service. Sometimes the family of the deceased will request that the body not be viewed at any time.

Responding to the Bereaved

The role of the concerned member of Presybterian and Reformed churches in responding to the bereaved is one of a ministry of presence. By a visit, a phone call or a letter, the members assure the bereaved of their sympathy and concern. During a visit to the family of the deceased, concerned members are not required to *say* anything, but by their presence a message of love and support is sent. Members simply stand by one another in a time of grief. Our churches prescribe no mourning rituals.

Burial of Non-Believers

Presbyterian and Reformed ministers often conduct funerals for persons who are not of their faith. Whether or not a minister will conduct such a service is for the minister alone to decide. There are few if any requirements placed on our ministers or our members regarding burials.

General Presbyterian Beliefs about Life After Death

Presbyterians believe that, after death, those who believe in Jesus Christ and love the things of his kingdom will dwell with him forever in blessedness and peace, while those who reject Christ and do not love the things of his kingdom will experience everlasting suffering and misery.

While holding firmly to the *fact* of life after death, we have been reluctant to attempt any description of the *nature* of that life. We recognize that when speaking of that other world even the Bible must use symbols and figures such as "gates of pearl. . .streets of gold" or "fire and brimstone. . . with wailing and gnashing of teeth," which cannot approach the reality either of the glory or the agony. We believe, as the Bible says, that "Eye hath not seen nor ear heard, neither have entered into the heart of man the things which God has prepared for them that love him."[11] We believe also that the torments of the damned are equally indescribable.

Presbyterians believe that what happens in this world determines what happens in that other world, that *that* life is an extension of *this* life, and that those who have loved God, purity, and other people will continue after death to find joy in that, while those who have loved self, sin, and evil will continue to be miserable in that. For this reason Presbyterian and Reformed creeds give a large place to the duties of persons in this world but say very little about the nature of the world to come. We are willing to leave those details to God, for we have full confidence that life after death will be for God's people a life of blessedness and peace, a life of worship and work, a life of growth and increasing knowledge.

Presbyterian Beliefs about Reincarnation

The doctrine of reincarnation (which is understood as affirming that after death a human soul may be reborn in another body or in another form of life), while not discussed in any of the Presbyterian and Reformed creeds, is vigorously denied by Presbyterian and Reformed theologians as contrary to the Christian concept of salvation and of God's deep respect for the individuality of each person.

Presbyterian Beliefs Regarding Heaven and Hell

Heaven is an estate of perfect holiness and joy, and hell is an estate of indescribable misery and suffering. Presbyterians have not tried to locate either heaven or hell as though they could be found on some distant star, but have emphasized that heaven is a realm of blessedness and peace, while hell is a realm of remorse and shame. These are realms of the spirit that cannot be localized in the material world.

According to the Presbyterian and Reformed faith, heaven

is not a trophy to be attained by human effort but a gift of God to be received by faith, and God gives it to all who trust Him enough to accept it. So, heaven is peopled by those persons who are happy to be in the presence of the God and Father of the Lord of Jesus Christ, and hell is peopled by persons who would be miserable in the presence of such a God. "Those who have accepted the forgiving love of God in Christ enter into eternal life in fellowship with God and his people. . . . This new life begins in the present world and continues into the world to come. Those who have rejected the love of God bring upon themselves his judgment and shut themselves outside the fellowship of God and his people."[12]

Presbyterians have never taught that those of their particular persuasion would be the only ones in heaven. Heaven is the home of all who believe in Jesus Christ. But Presbyterians have differed, and still do differ, regarding the eternal destiny of non-Christians. One Presbyterian statement of faith declares "persons, not professing the Christian religion. . .cannot be saved."[13] Many Presbyterians take literally the Scripture that says "There is salvation in no one else [except Jesus Christ], for there is no other name under heaven given among men by which we must be saved."[14]

On the other hand, many Presbyterians utterly reject the statement that all non-Christians will be consigned to hell forever. These Presbyterians differ widely among themselves regarding the eternal destiny of non-Christians, but most of them simply leave non-Christians in the hands of a loving God, sure that the God and Father of the Lord Jesus Christ will deal fairly with all such persons. It is the confidence of all Presbyterians that when the final judgment is passed, no person will be able to say truthfully "God did not deal justly with me."

The Time of the End

On the question of what will happen to the earth at the end

of time, most Presbyterians suspend judgment and are perfectly willing to leave that to God. Our doctrinal statements have seldom dealt with the question. A few Presbyterians believe that a renovated earth will be the final abode of the righteous. Here, they say, will be established the New Jerusalem. Others take literally a passage in the Bible which says, "The day of the Lord will come as a thief in the night, in which the heavens shall pass away with a great noise, and the elements shall melt with fervent heat; the earth also and the works that are therein shall be burned up."[15] Most Presbyterians see this passage as figurative and acknowledge that they do not know what will happen to the earth at the end of time.

Presbyterian Beliefs about Bodily Resurrection

Presbyterians have always been, and still are, strong in their affirmation of a bodily resurrection. But here is another place where Presbyterians differ among themselves—and a place also where many Presbyterians depart from the statements of their creeds.

A typical statement from one creed reads: "The souls of believers are at their death made perfect in holiness and do immediately pass into glory, their bodies being still united to Christ, do rest in their graves until the resurrection."[16] In this, as in most of the early Presbyterian and Reformed creeds, it is affirmed that, for a time after death, the souls of believers are disembodied spirits in the presence of Christ waiting for the resurrection of their bodies and, at the end of time, there will be a resurrection when their bodies will be reunited with their souls. Many Presbyterians today find this view unsatisfactory.

Presbyterians differ among themselves regarding the meaning of the term "the resurrection of the body." Very few hold that this term refers to the same physical body that was laid in a grave. Some Presbyterians believe that at death believers go immediately into the presence of Christ, who then and there gives them a new body, a spiritual body which is like their old body but remade in the likeness of Christ's resurrection body. With this new body they begin immediately to enjoy the blessings of heaven. At the final judgment, those already in heaven will be "openly ack-nowledged and acquitted" and will have confirmed to them the blessings of God for eternity. On the other hand, these Presbyterians affirm that at death the wicked enter imme-diately the torments of hell. About the "resurrection of the unjust"[17] most Presbyterians are vague.

Still other Presbyterians hold that death is real and that body and soul die together. The body returns to the dust and the spirit ceases to be. But, these same persons declare, at the resurrection, which will take place at some future time, God will give to each of his children a new body and a new spirit.

Others find biblical support for the view that after death, while the body ceases to be, the soul enters a period of "sleep" from which it is awakened at the resurrection and given a new and spiritual body.

Thus, while Presbyterians believe in a bodily resurrection, they differ widely concerning the nature of such and the time of such. In this matter of faith, Presbyterians continue to search the Scriptures for enlightenment.

Presbyterian Beliefs about Purgatory or Limbo

Presbyterian and Reformed creeds have with one voice rejected the Roman Catholic doctrine of purgatory, a place where souls that are not ready for heaven remain until they have been purged. Most Presbyterians today do not believe in purgatory. However, in recent years some Presbyterians have moved toward the belief that ultimately the love of God will prevail, and that somewhere down the corridors of eter-nity all persons will come to acknowledge Christ and will enter heaven. This belief requires that there be some kind of an intermediate state where unbelievers will come to know and accept the grace of God in Jesus Christ.

Presbyterian Concept of Saving Faith

When a jailer in Philippi asked the Apostle Paul, "What must I do to be saved?" the Apostle replied, "Believe in the Lord Jesus and you will be saved."[18] For Presbyterians it is as simple and as profound as that. Numerous books have been written on the meaning of "saving faith," but in its essence the Presbyterian creeds describe it as "receiving and resting upon Christ alone for justification, sanctification, and eternal life."[19] Saving faith includes repentance, which means that the believer turns from his sin and strives to do the will of God as that will is made known in Jesus Christ. Without the desire and the effort to do God's will, saving faith is incomplete. Saving faith is shown to be genuine by works of goodness and mercy. But the sinner is not saved by the works but by the faith. Persons are saved by faith in Jesus Christ and not by their good works, but a person who produces no good works cannot be saved.

This saving faith is shared by numerous other Christians besides those of the Presbyterian and Reformed family, and it is to them, as us, effective for gaining salvation. We are confident that God will save all who possess this faith. Whether he will save any who do not possess it is for God alone to decide.

Recognition of Friends and Family in the Next World

While our creeds have not dealt with the subject, most Presbyterians believe that persons in heaven will know and recognize friends and relatives. The disciples of Jesus recognized him in his resurrection body, and we believe that we shall be raised in his likeness. We shall not in heaven be more ignorant than we are here, and we know one another here. We argue that if we do not know loved ones, then we will have been deprived of our memory, and without our memories we are not ourselves.

In heaven family relationships will be remembered, but all relationships there will be lifted to a higher level. The redeemed will be in a loving and trusting relationship with all other persons in heaven, so that the importance of and the need for family relationships will be superseded.

Sequence of Events at the Moment of Death

Most Presbyterians believe that at death the souls of believers go immediately to be with God. Regarding the souls of the damned, our creeds tend to say little, but most Presbyterians believe that the punishment of unbelievers also begins immediately at death.

Presbyterian Beliefs about the Second Coming

Presbyterian and Reformed creeds, almost without exception, affirm the second coming of Christ, but they give very few details regarding the same. One statement reads, "As Christ came in humility, he will return in glory for the final judgment and for the consummation of his universal kingdom. The work and promises of Jesus Christ give assurance that the age-long struggle between sin and grace will, in God's holy, wise and loving purpose, be accomplished."[20]

A few Presbyterians hold the pre-millennarian position which offers a detailed account of what will happen when Christ comes again. Most Presbyterians, however, do not attempt to give a chronology of those events. Acknowledging that before Christ shall accomplish his holy purpose for the world, he will break into human history in some manner as he did before, we are willing to leave the details of that event to the Lord himself. We see it as our duty to be faithfully doing his work now without watching the clock.

Prayers for the Dying and the Dead

Presbyterians believe firmly in intercessory prayer for the dying, but none of our creeds has encouraged or approved prayers for the dead. Presbyterians have tended to see the dead as beyond the reach of our prayers. Our doctrinal standards have said nothing at all about whether those in the afterlife are aware of us who are still in this life—or whether they can or do pray for us. Consequently individual Presbyterians hold differing opinions on those questions.

Suicide

Nor have our doctrinal statements dealt with the subject of suicide, but most Presbyterians believe that suicide is not an unpardonable sin, and that one who takes his own life is not, at that moment, himself or herself. One who takes his own life will be judged, not merely by the one act that terminated his life, but by the overall faith that prevailed in his heart.

A Final Word

The primary message of the Presbyterian and Reformed faith regarding the afterlife is: Trust Christ, and be not afraid. The God who raised Jesus from the dead will also raise up those who love him to be with him forever. Strive to do God's will here and now, and leave worry about the life beyond to him. *That* life will be indescribably wonderful and full of all blessings, but you can leave the ordering of its affairs to the Lord. Do not get lost in contemplation of that other world or worry much over about its details lest you fail to deal fully with the tasks God has assigned to you in this world. By worship and prayer and Bible study, renew regularly your faith in Christ so that you will be saved; and then in the light of that faith-commitment, get on with the business of living a life in which God is glorified and enjoyed.

Notes

[1]   Instead of the term "Presbyterian faith," it is more correct to speak of "the faith of the Presbyterian and Reformed churches," since Presbyterians share a common faith with those denominations that use the title "Reformed," e.g., The Reformed Church in America, The Reformed Church in Hungary, etc. The term "Presbyterian" refers only to a form of church polity, i.e. government by presbyters or elders, while the term "Reformed" refers to a system of doctrines. Most Presbyterian churches are "Reformed" in their doctrine, and most Reformed churches are "Presbyterian" in their polity.

[2]   *Creeds of the Churches*, John H. Leith (Atlanta, 1963), p. 127.

[3]   The Westminster Shorter Catechism, Q.4.

[4]   I John 4:8.

[5]   The Westminster Confession of Faith, Chapter III.

[6]   The Westminster Shorter Catechism, Q.1.

[7]   A Brief Statement of Belief, adopted by the General Assembly of the Presbyterian Church U.S. in 1962.

[8]   The Apostles' Creed.

[9]   The Book of Order of the United Presbyterian Church U.S.A.

[10]   Ibid.

[11]   I Corinthians 2:9.

[12]   A Brief Statement of Faith.

[13]   The Westminster Confession of Faith, Chapter XXII.

[14]   Acts 4:12.

[15]   II Peter 3:10.

[16]   The Westminster Shorter Catechism, Q.37.

[17]   Acts 24:15.

[18]   Acts 16:30-31.

[19]   The Westminster Confession of Faith, Chapter XVI.

[20]   A Brief Statement of Faith.

ROMAN CATHOLICISM

Rev. Francis X. Cleary, S.J.

Background of the Faith

Because Christianity powerfully influenced western culture, its basic history, beliefs, and practices have become common knowledge. The Roman Catholic Church, with current membership numbering 841,000,000, is the largest and most widespread denomination within the worldwide Christian community of faith. Tradition plays an important role in all religions that preserve fundamental teachings central to belief while growing and adapting to concrete situations. Roman Christianity traces its roots back to the local Christian church founded in Rome, at that time capital city and center of the far-flung Roman Empire. This community of believers came into existence only a few years after Jesus' death. It remains the oldest "local church" in continuous existence.

Christianity first appeared nearly two thousand years ago in the Near East, spreading first to Antioch (in modern Syria) from its original centers in Galilee and Jerusalem. The founding members of the Church in Rome, like other very early churches, were Jews. What made the Roman Jewish community different was their unique blend of respect for Jewish tradition with openness to the good points of paganism. They maintained close ties with the Jerusalem "mother" city, religious center of worldwide Judaism. Proud of their heritage, Roman Jews-become-Christians preserved the spirit of those venerable practices that were recorded in the Old Testament and kept alive in Jerusalem Temple worship.

This explains Roman Catholic respect for holy persons, holy places, and holy objects. Like the Old Testament priesthood, Catholic priests consciously live as persons set apart, observing distinctive rules governing behavior, dress, and function. The same God uniquely present in the Temple Holy of Holies can be encountered in Catholic shrines and churches. Again under the influence of ancient Jewish Temple practice, Catholics employ a wide variety of religious objects to increase devotion (holy water, incense, cultic equipment). Recent scholarly biblical studies show Roman Catholicism to be more biblical in its life and practice than many realize.

A second crucial influence on present-day Roman Catholicism can be traced back to the Jewish-Christian community in ancient Rome. The New Testament Book of Revelation condemned the Roman Empire as an enemy of God, ripe for terrible judgment. Other books, however, took a contrary view. The Gospels, Acts of the Apostles, and many Letters

(Epistles) view Romans and the Roman Empire very positively. Roman governor Pontius Pilate is presented as only reluctantly sentencing Jesus to death under pressure of Jerusalem's religious leaders. A Roman centurion (military officer) was the first to profess faith in Jesus after his death (Mark); another became the first gentile (non-Jewish) convert (Acts of Apostles).

Not surprisingly, Roman Jewish-Christians showed pride in their heritage as citizens or inhabitants of the Empire's capital city. They acknowledged its remarkable achievements of peace and prosperity and willingly served in the imperial bureaucracy. They admired the Roman genius with its emphasis on order and clarity and its concern for organizational structure and efficiency. Thanks in part to its own clearly delimited hierarchical system, the Roman Church quickly prospered as leader of all other local churches.

Centralized control allows for remarkable openness to local adaptation without diluting essential traditions. Healthy diversity enhances genuine unity. Across the world, on any given day, identical biblical passages are proclaimed and preached and the same required order of worship is faithfully followed. But overall style differs strikingly. The Church is lived differently in Africa, in the Middle or Far East. Even among Catholic Americans, Native Americans, Blacks, and Hispanics maintain their cultural distinctiveness. Parishes reflect local conditions and membership— rural or urban, blue-collar or middle class, German, Italian, Irish, etc. Thus, in spite of potential for abuse, the heritage of appreciation for authority and structure has helped the Roman Catholic Church preserve essential beliefs while adapting to varying conditons.

Main Beliefs

Roman Catholicism's distinctiveness centers on the Bishop of Rome, acknowledged as successor of Saint Peter and supreme leader. As for the rest, at least for mainline Christian denominations, there is much that unites and little that

divides. Differences mainly concern organizational structure and lines of authority, plus inevitable divergences in
prayer and worship customs that shape the concrete practice
of a common faith commitment. Modern scholarly studies
indicate substantial agreement among most Christian denominations about basic articles of faith. This is often demonstrated concretely in the ecumenical movement, when
various denominations come together for prayer and fellowship. The following brief overview of some Catholic teachings basic to issues of death and afterlife would be received
with substantial agreement by many other Christian communities, particularly where biblically based.

First, the nature of *God*. Creation proclaims the glory of
the Lord, its beauty and marvelous complexity reflecting his
own being. But the Bible reveals in a special way God's
inmost "personality," what he is really like. An awesome,
sovereign Lord shows himself marvelously generous and
accepting. He selflessly shares with innumerable creatures
the life that is his alone by right. Upholding the moral law
yet remarkably non-judgmental, the God of the Old as well
as New Testaments returns good for evil, wants to forgive
rather than punish, tenderly loves all creatures, earnestly
desires their eternal happiness. The Christian doctrine of a
three-personed God shows how a selflessly, sharing love lies
at the center of divine being: from eternity the Father gener-
ating the Son, the Holy Spirit proceeding from both Father
and Son.

Second, the nature of *human beings*. Created in God's
image—more like him than anything else that exists—we
are destined to share his own unlimited life and felicity. But
the freedom of self-determination, as well as the accumulating evil in the world, contribute inevitably to universal sinfulness. Apart from special divine help, no one can fully
realize the human potential and live as he or she ought.
Nevertheless, Roman Catholicism insists on the basic goodness of human nature. Consistent with its openness to the
unbelieving world, it acknowledges much that is admirable
in paganism, for even there the effect of God's hidden but
powerful grace can be discerned.

Third, existence of the *Devil* seems essential to Roman Catholic as well as biblical faith. Such a being represents the only explanation for the pervasive evil that infects our world. As a creature, however, the Devil cannot ultimately compromise or frustrate divine sovereignty. The biblical God reigns, supreme and serene, unthreatened by hostile forces. The story of salvation consists of his progressive triumph over all evil powers, human and superhuman. Dualism—two opposed gods, one evil and one good—has no place in traditional Christian faith.

Fourth, the meaning of *suffering*. Biblically based Christianity acknowledges a God who is all-powerful and all-good. Suffering by contrast is both real and evil, in itself the opposite of fulfilled living. And yet, God remains in charge of his creation. He doesn't directly *cause* suffering, which in a mysterious way results from resistance to his loving purpose. But like loving parent, teacher, or friend, he *allows* suffering to exist for its unique potential of furthering human growth. Suffering remains a mystery. People do suffer undeservedly, but the Bible—especially in the example and teaching of Jesus—shows how to deal with it creatively.

What if God sheltered human beings from every encounter with suffering? What would life be like without pain, hurt, loss, failure, and frustration? The result would be persons tragically incomplete and unfulfilled, unable to assume personal responsibility, profoundly unhappy. From another point of view, human society would collapse, undermined by monsters of insensitivity and selfish uncaring. But such disciplinary and educational suffering doesn't work automatically. Having taken all prudent means to eliminate pain, humans must creatively cooperate with what can't be changed. Then only can suffering's hidden potential for good be realized; then only can it serve as a unique means of growth toward full humanity.

Often, however, suffering becomes so overwhelming that the individual does not, cannot, grow personally. Pain too easily crushes the spirit, illness diminishes the body. But even here there is potential for meaning, rather than

meaninglessness—for hope, not despair. Willing acceptance
of handicap, chronic pain, and debility can become empowering grace in others' lives, helping them accept what can't
be changed. This explains the healing and personal growth
many experience in working with retarded or exceptional
children, and with the terminally ill. Personal problems tend
to fall into perspective, complaining yields to fervent gratitude for personal blessings heretofore insufficiently acknowledged and appreciated. Those who accept and live
with handicap or imminent death can inspire others to
renewed living.

Such suffering becomes redemptive. One person's willing
endurance "saves" others, gifting them with fuller measure
of life. Redemptive suffering lies at the very heart of Christianity, which proclaims salvation through Jesus' rejection,
crucifixion, death, and resurrection. Only in the total self-
emptying of martyrdom, selfless surrender of his life in the
fullest possible expression of love, could Jesus offer life in
fullness to a world unable to save itself.

Questions About Death and the Afterlife

1. *Funerals.* Because Roman Catholicism is a religion
that exists in many parts of the world, funeral practices
differ widely and are adapted to local and national customs.
Services for the dead celebrate Christian hope in the midst of
grieving; sadness at loss is tempered by assurance of "eternal rest" for the deceased. During the past several years and
under the influence of Vatican Council II, the Church has
reformed its last rites. By removing accretions to the funeral
service added over intervening centuries, it returned to more
authentic practices of earlier times. "Mass of Resurrection"
with white vestments has thus replaced "Mass of the Dead"
where somber black served as the principal color. Jesus'
resurrection is recalled as assurance of future rising for all
who have died "in Christ" and are intimately united to his
death and resurrection through baptism.

Catholic funeral rituals are structured to acknowledge the

loss suffered by those who mourn, and to assist them in a healthy grieving process. Friends and acquaintances gather to console with their presence and prayers. In the United States, for example, a waking service, held for one or more evenings prior to burial, includes private prayers and a brief ceremony at the funeral home. After the funeral Mass, the hearse is followed to the cemetery for final graveside farewell. In some localities mourners gather again after thirty days for a second memorial Mass. Other American Catholics follow their own customs while preserving essentials— Native Americans (Indians), for example, may gather in a "sweat lodge" ceremony. The official service book includes a wide range of prayers that encourage adaptation to specific situations. Did the deceased die in old age, middle years, or as a child? If a baby, with or without baptism? Is the gathered community crushed by sudden and unexpected death, or resigned and already grieving during long illness? Numerous options allow the officiating priest to respect particular sensibilities.

Instead of wooden, pro-forma gestures punctuated with pious platitudes, Catholic funeral services emphasize supportive love for those who grieve from relatives, friends, and neighbors. Death moreover is considered a public rather than private event. It serves as solemn opportunity for community reaffirmation of faith in life beyond death. Because believers gather to celebrate God's gracious gift of a life ended on earth yet newly begun in Heaven, eulogies of the deceased are out of place. The words spoken emphasize the good news of what God has done, is doing, and will do for us, not the individual's accomplishments during earthly life. Mourning Christians struggle to accept the present while looking back in gratitude and forward in hope.

2. *Disposal of the Body.* A corpse may be disposed of in any way that preserves reverence for what it once had been. Burial in the ground acknowledges our humble mortality— bodies made of dust inevitably return to dust. What happens to the corpse in no way affects afterlife or final-day resurrection. Legal, medical, educational, and charitable purposes

can be served by autopsy, donation of organs, or the gift of the body to medical college. Such options become religiously symbolic, final expressions of loving, self-emptying service to others.

Although it is a practice mostly limited to the United States, embalming can aid the grieving process. On the other hand, attempts at lifelike exhibition that deny the reality of death—for example, a corpse displayed on a couch as though sleeping—are unacceptable. In eighteenth century Europe, cremation publicly stated disbelief in afterlife. Having lost its anti-religious overtones, cremation once again becomes an approved option for Catholics. It may even be required—to hinder the spread of plague, prevent irreverence when a large number have died, preserve valuable land for cultivation of food.

3. *Response to the Bereaved.* Earlier remarks indicated that response to the bereaved represents a principal factor in Roman Catholic funeral practices. Believers are helped to work through their grief, avoiding extremes of death-denial, hopelessness, and despair.

4. *Requirements for Burial.* Since Christian burial constitutes a religious act and public testimony to the dead person's faith in resurrection, unbelievers would not be granted the regular service. But Catholics, including priests, are free to participate in and even lead memorial services for such persons. Reverent burial of the dead, regardless of religious affiliation or lack thereof, has always constituted an important Christian work of mercy. Local customs and regulations determine the response to lapsed or inactive Catholics and to notorious public sinners. In general, the Church tends to permit rather than refuse Catholic burial in such circumstances, lest she be guilty of harsh judgment. In earlier times, funeral Mass and burial in consecrated ground were routinely denied suicide victims for having deliberately rejected God's gift of life. More enlightened church law now acknowledges that suicides represent a pathetic cry for help or desperate attempt to flee unbearable psychological or

physical pain. One's last conscious act doesn't necessarily determine eternal fate; in death as in life, only God reads hearts. The Catholic Church offers full Christian burial to suicides, peace and hope to their relatives and friends.

5. *Life After Death.* Belief in afterlife constitutes the heart of Christian faith. St. Paul preached resurrection of the body, a difficult saying rejected by Greek philosophers who preferred immortality of the soul. Christian belief emphasizes that life after death is not something that comes naturally—something already due by reason of creation. Instead, we receive it as the final, quite undeserved and unmerited, gift from God by reason of Jesus' redemptive death and resurrection. The New Testament speaks of rebirth, of entry into a radically new and different form of existence quite beyond present comprehension. Everlasting, glorified existence that Jesus now possesses will one day become the inheritance of all the faithful—those destined to share his triumph over death.

6. *Reincarnation.* Reincarnation implicitly contradicts basic teaching. Biblical texts emphasize the awesome privilege and responsibility of each person to repent and be reconciled with God *now* rather than tomorrow or in subsequent existences. Neither science nor Christian philosophy can identify any portion of a human being capable of passing over into another earthly life. Moreover, we don't need other lives to work out our salvation through suffering for sins committed in earlier incarnations. Christianity insists that no one earns salvation; it comes only as a free and unmerited divine gift because of what Jesus did.

7. *Heaven and Hell.* Heaven designates a condition rather than place; it is an eternal fullness of life, supreme happiness flowing from intimacy with God. Since glorified bodies exist beyond time and space, heaven is, strictly speaking, nowhere, occupying no location within created reality. The term "heaven" reflects understandable human tendency to locate the divine realm in the heavens, whence come bless-

ings of sun and rain. The Bible prefers God's "Kingdom" or (more accurately) "Kingship," since life can be fully lived and enjoyed only by doing it his way.

Biblical authors refrain from exact description of afterlife. St. Paul, quoting Isaiah 64:3, insisted that "eye has not seen, ear not heard, nor has it so much as dawned upon human-kind what God has prepared for those who love him" (1 Corinthians 2:9). But metaphors comparing heaven to pres-ent experiences provide some insight. Heaven is something *like* life in a glorious garden where people live in complete harmony with self, others, and nature, enjoying privileged intimacy with God (Genesis 1-3). Another and more frequent biblical comparison is the heavenly banquet hosted by God with the saved as honored guests. In the Eucharist (Lord's Supper), Christians sacramentally anticipate this eternal celebration, eating and drinking at the Lord's table. The image of a dinner party acknowledges the bodily component of human existence—we are not spirits temporarily trapped in evil or unworthy matter. The metaphor also stresses our essentially social nature; we are individuals finding fullness not alone but with others. A good meal with close friends surely ranks among life's finest delights.

Christianity insists that humans possess free will—that they are capable of self-determination. God does not compel cooperation with his loving plan for our eternal happiness. The existence of Hell as genuine option guarantees freedom of choice. Like Heaven, it represents a permanent, irreversi-ble state of existence rather than a particular place. Again like Heaven, the Bible can only describe Hell's torments in metaphorical language. Images from our world of experi-ence—fire, worm, the physical and psychological pains associated with burns, despair (gnashing of teeth)—cannot be taken literally, any more than Heaven consists in non-stop eating and drinking. Such word-pictures powerfully describe the total frustration creatures experience when definitively separated from the sole source of all blessings.

God doesn't so much condemn to Hell as ratify human self-determination. A God who *is* love can never hate; he who doesn't directly cause suffering on earth cannot directly inflict eternal punishment. Instead he permits humans to accept or reject his offer of eternal happiness. Already in this world, sinful humans prefer doing things their way in spite of painful consequences. The Catholic Church insists on the reality of Hell, but it has never taught that anyone is actually there—for example, Judas Iscariot or Adolph Hitler. Proposed in earlier centuries but soon rejected is the doctrine of *apokatastasis*, eventual salvation for all, including those in Hell. This denies the seriousness of human, final self-determination upon death. If persons have chosen Hell, they want to be and remain there for eternity.

Jesus intended his Church to help rather than hinder world-wide salvation. In an awesome prediction of the Last Judgment (Matthew 25:31-46), he taught that even the unbaptized accept or reject eternal salvation. These, no less than believers, qualify for admission by serving the Lord Jesus. In their case he remained hidden and unrecognized, intimately identified with the world's needy.

> When the Son of Man comes in his glory, escorted by all the angels of heaven, he will sit upon his royal throne, and *all the nations* [not just Christians] will be assembled before him. Then he will separate them into two groups.... The King will say to those on his right: "Come. You have my Father's blessing! Inherit the kingdom prepared for you from the creation of the world. For I was hungry and you gave me food, I was thirsty and you gave me drink. I was a stranger and you welcomed me, naked and you clothed me. I was ill and you comforted me in prison and you came to visit me." Then the just will ask him: "Lord, when did we see you hungry and feed you or see you thirsty and give you drink? When did we welcome you away from home or clothe you in your nakedness? When did we visit you when you were ill or in prison?" The King will answer them: "I assure, as often as you did it for one of my least brothers, you did it *for me*." (Matthew 25:31-40)

Jesus will announce to "all nations" (not church members) that by caring or refusing to care for the poor, sick, and lonely, each person unknowingly accepts or rejects Jesus

himself and his offer of heavenly life. As for God-fearing
Christians, Jesus repeatedly warned that "last shall be
first," undermining smug presumption and feelings of
superiority.

8. *Eventual Fate of the Earth.* Biblical teaching reas-
sures us that the present world, infected with evil and its
results (suffering and death), will one day be transformed
rather than destroyed. Final-age purification will result in
totally renewed creation. Instead of going up into the sky,
the saved will enjoy fullness of life on a new earth. Once
again, metaphor must not be confused with literal description. However beyond present human understanding, God
intends a bright future for the universe he lovingly created
and happily pronounced "very good" (Genesis 1). His gift of
eternal salvation reaches beyond human beings to include
the whole range of existence. More than this cannot be con-
fidently stated. Christian revelation focuses on this-worldly
living, resisting the impulse to speculate about future, other
worldly conditions. "The world itself will be freed from its
slavery to corruption and share in the glorious freedom of
the children of God" (Romans 8:21).

9. *Bodily Resurrection.* Resurrection of the body means
eternal life as full and integrated persons, not just as separated souls. It contrasts with resuscitation or return of the
dead to this-worldly living. Final-age, perfected existence,
already enjoyed by Jesus in resurrected glory, will be shared
upon his return, when God's promised Kingdom comes in
fullness. Here, too, human concepts and language only
approximate reality. Jesus' resurrected "body" exists outside time, occupies no particular space, and therefore is nowhere within created reality.

10. *Purgatory and Limbo.* Catholic teaching insists on
the reality of Purgatory, a condition (rather than a place) of
transition and adaptation for those entering heavenly beatitude. Even great saints know sin during earthly life and die
affected by selfish self-centeredness incompatible with divine

intimacy. Purgatory describes the passage, at once painful and joyful, into purified existence. Then only can persons accept and return God's overwhelming love without hindrance.

Limbo was originally proposed by theologians as a condition (not a place) intermediate between Heaven and Hell for infants dying unbaptized but without personal sin. Never taught as absolutely certain Catholic doctrine, Limbo is now generally rejected as an erroneous (but logical) answer to a wrong question. It seems reasonable that an all-good God permits persons never fully developed physically—infants, severely retarded—the personal opportunity to choose or reject his offer of eternal life.

11. *Requirements for Salvation.* Christianity firmly insists that no human being, however holy, earns salvation. It comes as a pure gift, graciously bestowed upon the undeserving. God never deviated from his commitment to create a perfect world, but human sinfulness has frustrated this saving purpose. Jesus, sinless Son of God, by giving his life in a selfless act of love effectively neutralized humanity's resistance. Creatures need only accept what Jesus accomplished through intimate union with him in baptism. This sacrament causes what it signifies: death to hopeless existence (going down into baptismal waters), followed by rebirth into newness of life (coming up from the water) as Jesus' follower and sharer in his unique Son-relationship with his Father.

Salvation comes only through Jesus, normally through Baptism and active membership in his Church. The Bible however emphasizes God's universal salvific will; and Jesus now reigns as Lord of everyone, not just Christians or Roman Catholics. Another biblical theme, election for service rather than merit, reminds Christians that they haven't been chosen because they are better than unbelievers. The Church represents a community called to share with the world God's good news of salvation through Jesus. Because the question wasn't raised, or perhaps lest Christians grow negligent in their primary responsibility as apostles biblical and Church teaching doesn't explain in detail how unbeliev-

ers come to salvation. Theologians speculate about "ano-
nymous Christians," unbaptized persons ignorant of Jesus'
life and work or scandalized by misleading witness of less
than perfect church members. Non-believers are open to salvation through Jesus by responding according to their best
lights. Everyone can serve the Jesus who is hidden in needy
neighbors (Matthew 25:31-46; see above section no. 7, Heaven
and Hell).

12. *Social Relations in Afterlife.* Christians look forward
to a radically transformed existence in the afterlife. It will
have a continuity with previous earthly life that nevertheless includes discontinuity. We will be different because perfected, yet will remain ourselves; as much as possible like
God himself, while not ceasing to be creatures. Friends and
relatives will recognize each other in a situation of changed
relationships. The intimacy that close friends and married
couples strive with varying degrees of success to attain in
this life will be completely realized in Heaven in the union of
all persons. "When people rise from the dead, they neither
marry nor are given in marriage but live like angels in
heaven" (Matthew 22:30). Since the entire community of
saved know an intimacy far beyond anything achieved on
earth, private groupings in families and friendships have no
place.

13. *"Particular" and "General" Judgments.* Death represents the end of human growth. At the same time it's a sort of
graduation, when each person finally and fully becomes
what he or she tried to be throughout life. Christian theology
distinguishes "particular" and "general" judgments. The
first takes place immediately at death, when God solemnly
ratifies definitive acceptance or rejection of the salvation
that has been offered everyone. St. Paul longed "to be freed
from this life and to be with Christ, for that is the far better
thing" (Philippians 1:23). Catholic teaching affirms what
Paul hints at—immediate passage into conscious afterlife
rather than a "sleep" until the Last Day.
But salvation has a community as well as individual

dimension. Those already enjoying fullness of life with God experience a certain incompleteness until the whole of creation has opportunity for radical renewal. The Kingdom comes to individuals at the particular judgment, but God's grand salvific purpose will be realized only at final or general judgment.

14. *Jesus' Second Coming.* Ancient religions generally looked to the past for a perfect world, an ideal existence long lost and never to return. Judaeo-Christianity by contrast looks to the future and anticipates a glorious fullness yet unachieved, a time when creation will be completely perfected. This final age becomes reality with the return of Jesus, cosmic ruler and Lord of History. The Bible's most profound revelation of creation's ultimate destiny is found in 1 Corinthians 15:20-28. The scenario described there begins with Jesus' present, though hidden, reign as cosmic Lord. But the real hero is God the Father, who is already at work subjecting all evil forces to his son's authority. "Christ must reign until God has put all enemies under his feet, and the last enemy to be destroyed is death." This ultimate victory takes place at the Second Coming (Return, Parousia) of Jesus.

Christ's triumph will become occasion for his own selfless self-emptying. "When, finally, all has been subjected to the Son, [the Son] will then subject himself to the One [the Father] who has made all things subject to him." Then follows a statement as profound as it is simple, describing what eternity will be like: "...that God [Father] may be all in all," or "everything to everyone." Here in a few words Paul summarized the purpose and goal of creation and redemption. Universal salvation means God's generous sharing of what is his alone: fullness of life, eternal happiness.

15. *Afterlife.* Afterlife in Christian and Catholic understanding isn't something tacked on as a continuation of earthly existence. It's not a reward earned by an elite few who did and said the right things to cajole blessings from a reluctant deity, or a gift limited to those lucky to belong to

one particular religious group. Far more than something
that comes "after," final-age existence represents the culmination, fulfillment, and perfection of created being. Life as
we now know it serves as an incomplete sign and promise of
what could—what will be. Heavenly life corresponds to our
deepest longings, and reflects God's marvelously selfless
love. His firm commitment is to share his being so completely that we become as much like God as possible, while
remaining ourselves. It is offered as the purest of gifts: what
can't be earned, and comes to the undeserving, needs only
grateful acceptance.

16. *Solidarity in Prayer with the Dead and Dying.* Human beings from diverse cultures and religions sense a
solidarity of the living with deceased ancestors, including
relatives and friends. A widow or widower can experience
the presence, mysterious but real and intimate, of the lost
spouse. Religious persons instinctively pray for the dying
that they recover or find easeful death. Also widespread is
the feeling that prayers assist the dead in their life beyond
this world. Roman Catholics share such sentiments. They
appeal for supporting evidence to the Second Book of Maccabees, accepted as part of the Bible (Old Testament) by
Catholics as well as Eastern Orthodox Christians, but not
by Protestants or Jews. Second Maccabees was composed a
hundred or more years before Jesus' birth. It attests to the
intercession of saints in heaven for people living on earth
(15:11-16), and to the power of the living to offer prayers and
sacrifices for the dead ("that they might be freed from sin,"
12:39-46).

Prayer for the dying creates no special problem since
Christians pray to God for themselves and others in times of
need. More complex is prayer that the dead be forgiven their
sins and permitted entrance into eternal happiness. God
needs no prodding or encouragement, having shown himself
eagerly desirous and diligently working to save rather than
condemn. Nor can salvation be forced upon anyone, since
each individual must personally accept the divine offer. But
prayers for the dead fit in with the understanding of Purga-

tory as described above (section no. 10). They serve as expressions of loving support and encouragement during a period of painful but joyful adjustments to heavenly life.

Those now with God in blessedness remain involved and concerned with humans on earth and indeed with the whole of creation. New Testament images such as "body of Christ" and "people of God" apply to both the Church Militant (on earth) and Church Triumphant (in Heaven), so that living and dead form a single fellowship. Those already with the Lord eagerly yearn for the time when everyone and everything can share their fullness. Catholic teaching rejects verbal or other communication with the dead—seances, ouija boards, ghosts. But the intercession of those now in glory, joined with that of the Lord Jesus, assists the living even more effectively than during their time on earth; they help the living in a mysterious way that respects the world's autonomy and integrity.

SEVENTH-DAY
ADVENTIST CHURCH

Robert M. Johnston, Ph.D.

Background of the Faith

The northeastern United States in the "Jacksonian era," which began in 1829, was a time of ferment, restlessness, experimentation, and intense interest in reform of many kinds, but above all, in religion.[1] Old religious groupings and dogmas were breaking down in the cross current of many movements that were sometimes conflicting and sometimes

277

coalescing. There was a pervasive desire to return to primitive Christianity, to rise above denominational differences,
to bring everything into harmony with God's will, to throw
"the traditions of men" out the window, to shake off a past
which was viewed as corrupt or apostate.

It was the genius of Adventism to gather up some of the
more helpful of these impulses and reform causes and fuse
them into what became a distinctive international religious
denomination. The catalytic spark for this was the message
that began to be preached in 1831 by William Miller of Low
Hampton, New York. His earnest study of the biblical book
of Daniel led him to the conclusion that the Second Coming
of Jesus would occur in 1843 or 1844, a calculation that
paralleled similar ones made by various divines and missionaries of the time in England, Germany, Chile, the Near
East, and elsewhere. But it was Miller and the associates
that came to join him who made the greatest impact; and by
the time the movement reached its climax, as many as a
million people in the United States, out of a total population
of seventeen million, were caught up in it.

Jesus did not return to earth in 1844, which became for
Adventists the time of the "Great Disappointment." But the
time of penitent preparation had been a spiritually purifying
experience for many, and there were those who could not
bring themselves to repudiate something which seemed to be
from God, even though there was clearly some mistake about
it. Hiram Edson, of Port Gibson, New York, and some associates concluded that the calculations had been correct but
the event was mistaken: the "sanctuary" referred to in
Daniel 8:14 was not this earth, as Miller had supposed, but
the heavenly temple spoken of in the New Testament epistle
to the Hebrews.[2]

In the meantime other Adventists (as believers in Miller's
announcement were called) became convinced that the true
Sabbath commanded to be kept in the Bible was Saturday,
the seventh day of the week.[3] This view, which can be traced
to the Seventh-day Baptists, was energetically promoted
among Adventists by Joseph Bates, a retired sea captain

who had already had a colorful career as an advocate of temperance and reform of health habits. The keeping of the false Sabbath was identified with the "mark of the beast" spoken of in Revelation 14:9. Adventists have come to regard the "Three Angels' Messages" of Revelation 14:6-12 as epitomizing their special mission in the world: the first angel (vv. 6, 7) proclaims that the hour of judgment has come; the second (v. 8), that the religious world is apostate; and the third (vv. 9-12) warns against false worship.

It was a prominent Millerite preacher, Charles Fitch, who had declared that the various denominations, by their rejection of the message of judgment, had become fallen "Babylon." Fitch is also responsible, along with George Storrs, for popularizing in Adventist circles the doctrine that the dead are asleep until the time of the resurrection, when Jesus comes again.

In 1848, in Connecticut, New York, Maine, and Massachusetts, a series of meetings were held which congealed into a self-conscious group the scattered Adventists who were sympathetic to all these ideas. The most prominent leaders emerging in these meetings were Bates and a newly married young couple, James and Ellen White. James White became the most tireless and dominant personality in the emerging denomination and remained so until his death in 1881. His wife, Ellen, even before her marriage, had frequent visionary experiences, and she has been regarded by Seventh-day Adventists as a messenger of the Lord, having received the gift of prophesy. Until her death, in 1915, she was a strong unifying influence in the denomination and was especially opposed to any manifestations of fanaticism. Her writings, which are voluminous, cover a wide range of topics and have been instrumental in institutionalizing various kinds of reforms as part of the denominational program.

With his wife's encouragement, James White began to publish a periodical in 1849, *The Present Truth*, which became in 1850 *The Advent Review and Sabbath Herald* (now *The Adventist Review*). In 1863 the church was officially organized, in spite of considerable resistance on the part of those who recalled bitter experiences in their former denominations and were reluctant to see their movement become another denomination; and the name Seventh-day Adventist became official, in spite of the wishes of some who would have preferred the name Church of God. An increasing concern for temperance, health, and rational healing led to the establishment of the Western Health Reform Institute in 1866, in Battle Creek, Michigan, which already in 1855 had become the headquarters of Seventh-day Adventist publishing and eventually of the organization. The Institute grew into the famous Battle Creek Sanitarium under the vigorous leadership of Dr. J. H. Kellogg, inventor of breakfast foods and meat substitutes.

1874 saw the founding of the first denominational college in Battle Creek, and the sending out of the first overseas missionary (to Switzerland), J. N. Andrews, who was also the most able scholar in the early days of the denomination. By that time the number of members had grown from less than a hundred in 1848 to over six thousand.

Since that time the membership has grown to more than four million worldwide. What began with a small band of New Englanders has become an international church with four-fifths of its members outside North America, its greatest numerical strength being in the developing nations of Latin America, Africa, and Asia. Seventh-day Adventists belong to 24,182 organized congregations, served by over ten-thousand ordained ministers. They operate a school system, which in 1983 enrolled 657,035 students and which included ninety colleges and three universities. They also operate 155 sanitariums and hospitals and 276 clinics, in 1983 employed 2,499 physicians and dentists, and 12,499 nurses. They have fifty publishing houses turning out literature in 177 languages. In 1983 the members of the church contributed to its work a total of $671,500,181 in tithes and offerings, reflecting in part the fact that they have had for years the record of the highest per capita giving of any religious body in the United States.[4] World headquarters are located in Washington, D.C.

Beliefs

While Seventh-day Adventists, in order to sustain a recognizably continued existence, were unable to avoid becoming a denomination, they have resisted the tendency to credalism. They have some definite doctrines and feel that they are important, but they reserve the right to revise them in the light of increasing insight. The first formal list of "Fundamental Principles" was promulgated in 1872.[5] It was prefaced with a substantial preamble which began as follows:

> In presenting to the public this synopsis of our faith, we wish to have it distinctly understood that we have no articles of faith, creed, or discipline, aside from the Bible. We do not put forth this as having any authority with our people, nor is it designed to secure uniformity among them, as a system of faith, but is a brief statement of what is, and has been, with great unanimity, held by them....

The most recent formulation, voted at the General Conference session of 1980,[6] begins with this preamble:

> Seventh-day Adventists accept the Bible as their only creed and hold certain fundamental beliefs to be the teaching of the Holy Scriptures. These beliefs, as set forth here, constitute the church's understanding and expression of the teaching of Scripture. Revision of these statements may be expected at a General Conference session when the church is led by the Holy Spirit to a fuller understanding of Bible truth or finds better language in which to express the teachings of God's Holy Word.

Changes have demonstrably occurred, but certain convictions have never wavered.

Seventh-day Adventists believe that the final authority in religious matters is the Bible, meaning sixty-six canonical books in the Old and New Testaments. They further hold, in common with most conservative Christians, belief in the Trinity, Jesus Christ as the incarnate Son of God, and many

other central doctrines of Christian consensus. They practice believers' baptism by immersion and the ordinance of
the Lord's Supper, preceded by pedilavium.[7]

Other doctrines are more distinctive, being shared with
only a few other groups; some may be unique, or may receive
a distinctive emphasis. Adventists see themselves, and
indeed all humanity, caught up in a "great controversy"
between Christ and Satan regarding the character of God,
His law, and His sovereignty over the universe—a controversy in which God will be finally vindicated. Everyone must
serve one side or the other. One's salvation depends on his
relationship with God in Christ, through whom "we are
justified, adopted as God's sons and daughters, and delivered from the lordship of sin."[8] This relationship is jeopard-
ized by all deliberate disobedience to truth, which constitutes a denial of faith and an affront to the Holy Spirit,
placing the soul in mortal peril. Seventh-day Adventists see
themselves as being called to restore a number of biblical
truths that have been neglected or subverted, and which
constitute their special message.

Their denominational name points to two of these doctrines. "Seventh-day" signifies that they keep the seventh
day of the week as the Sabbath, in obedience to a literal
reading of the Ten Commandments. For them the Sabbath
begins at sundown on Friday and lasts until sundown Saturday. "The Sabbath is a day of delightful communion with
God and one another. It is a symbol of our redemption in
Christ, a sign of our sanctification, a token of our allegiance,
and a foretaste of our eternal future in God's kingdom."[9]

"Adventist" refers to the hope and expectation of the
imminent second coming of Jesus Christ, according to His
promise and the faith of the apostolic church. His advent
will be literal, personal, visible, and worldwide.[10] When
Jesus returns, the righteous dead will be resurrected, and
together with the righteous living will be glorified and taken
to heaven, but the unrighteous will die.[11]

According to Revelation 20, the unrighteous will remain
dead for one thousand years while the righteous reign with

Christ in heaven. At the end of this millennium the unrighteous will rise in the "second resurrection" only to be judged and then destroyed in the "lake of fire," along with Satan and his angels. This fiery destruction, referred to in the gospels as Gehenna, also serves to purify the earth, upon which the Holy City descends. Forever afterward this earth, made new, becomes the eternal abode of the righteous, and indeed (according to Revelation 21) the capital of the universe.

This leads to consideration of the nature of man and of death, about which Seventh-day Adventists hold views which were long castigated as peculiar or perverse, but which are now obtaining increasing respect among biblical scholars of many denominations.[12]

The Nature of Man

Seventh-day Adventists agree with the famous dictum of H. Wheeler Robinson, "The Hebrew idea of personality is an animated body, and not an incarnated soul." This conception stands in contrast with the dualistic Platonic view that the body is the prison house of the soul. Though the latter view has been extremely influential, penetrating both Judaism and Christianity, the normative view of the Bible is that which Robinson describes as the Hebraic one. A paradigmatic passage is Genesis 2:7, "The Lord God formed man of dust from the ground, and breathed into his nostrils the breath of life; and man became a living soul (*nephesh chayyah*)." Adventists are therefore fond of saying, "You don't *have* a soul; you *are* a soul." The soul is a composite of the physical body and the mysterious life force breathed into it by God. Man is thus psychosomatic unity, and when God withdraws the life force from the body, the man is no more,[13] except as he remains in the eternal memory of his Creator. Man's spirit is not a conscious individual entity that continues in another mode of life apart from the body. Rather, man is unconscious in death, as described in Ecclesiastes

9:5, "For the living know that they will die, but the dead know nothing, and they have no more reward; for the memory of them is lost." For this reason, and also doubtless because of the appearance of the corpse, both Testaments frequently refer to death as a sleep. The life to come depends on the resurrection of the body.

Viewed as a life-force, the spirit that animates the body and makes man a living soul must be regarded as an impersonal energy, though its source is the Spirit of God. The locus of a man's individuality and personality is nothing less than his total being. In the terminology of Genesis, spirit infused into the body of dust produces the living soul. In more modern language, life joined to body produces the self, the conscious ego. A crude analogy is the electric current (also something of a mystery) passing through an incandescent bulb producing a shining light. If the spirit, which at death returns to God, were a conscious entity, then the breath of life, which God breathed into the first man, must have had the same nature, implying some sort of conscious preexistence—something taught nowhere in Scripture. It should be noted that the biblical terms for spirit, *ruach* and *pneuma*, have the primitive meaning of wind or breath, and while they take on a wide spectrum of secondary meanings, none of them contradicts this basic starting point.

It follows from this theological perception that for Adventists, the body is important, and no mere prison house of the soul. Spiritual welfare is bound to bodily condition, and both injurious indulgence and injurious mortification of the flesh can be religiously detrimental. Conversely, both care and discipline of the body are necessary to true spirituality. Deprivation of sleep, drunkenness, extreme hunger, malnutrition, drug abuse, and overwork unmistakably illustrate the truth of this perception. The doctrine of man's psychosomatic oneness provides a theoretical reinforcement for the Adventist emphasis on temperance, health reform, and healing ministries. In addition to obedience to Christ's example and command to heal,[14] the Adventist doctrine of man provides a motive for making attention to the body a facet of the work of redemption.

Life After Death

It should be clear from what has been said that for Adventists death is not ultimately a liberating friend—though it brings an end of pain to the sufferer—but rather a denuding enemy.[15] It was to defeat this enemy that Christ died, was buried, and rose from the dead.[16] The life to come is not the result of death but of the resurrection from death, which will occur at Christ's second coming. If the real self can live on without a body, Adventists ask, what use is resurrection?

Accordingly, death is a sleep of total unconsciousness. The dead therefore have no awareness of the passing of time. The next thing an individual knows after brain death occurs is the moment of resurrection when "the trumpet shall sound" and he hears the summons of his Lord, the Life-giver. Whether the intervening time is a few moments or thousands of years, it is all the same as it is experienced. This is the Adventist view of the so-called "intermediate state," as vigorously set forth by such writers as C. B. Haynes:

> Since Seventh-day Adventists reject the teaching of the natural immortality of all men, their belief regarding man's condition in death does not conform to certain popular views.
>
> They believe that death is not a modification of life, in changed conditions. Death is not a release into a fuller life. Death is not life in misery. Death is not life in happiness. Death is not life at all, in any condition, good or bad. To die is not to live. To die is to stop living. Death is a complete cessation of life.
>
> Death does not mean to go to heaven. Death does not mean to go to hell. Death does not mean to go to purgatory. Death does not mean to go anywhere. Death means the end of life.
>
> When a person dies, he does not live somewhere else, in heaven, hell, or purgatory. He does not live at all, in any condition whatsoever. He is dead. And when a person is dead, he is not alive.[17]

The *Sheol* or *Hades* spoken of in Scripture simply signifies the grave.

But there will be a resurrection of the dead, or to be precise, two resurrections—one to life and one to judgment,[18] immediately preceding and immediately following the millennium of the Apocalypse.[19] Immortality is therefore not something innate in man, nor does he have a naturally immortal soul. Rather, immortality is the gracious gift of God through Jesus Christ.[20] Only God is naturally immortal.[21] For this reason Adventists are rightly called Conditionalists, for they believe that man is only conditionally immortal: eternal life is granted on condition of obedient faith.

The resurrection of the righteous will occur on the model of Christ's resurrection. His resurrection body was glorified but not unphysical, a fact vividly portrayed by Luke:

> As they were saying this, Jesus himself stood among them. But they were startled and frightened, and supposed that they saw a spirit. And he said to them, "Why are you troubled, and why do questionings rise in your hearts? See my hands and my feet, that it is I myself; handle me, and see; for a spirit has not flesh and bones as you see that I have." And while they still disbelieved for joy, and wondered, he said to them, "Have you anything here to eat?" They gave him a piece of broiled fish, and he took it and ate before them.[22]

The ultimate destiny of the resurrected righteous, after passing the millennium in heaven while the earth lies desolate and sabbatically fallow, will be to dwell forever with their Lord in the purified and renewed earth, free from all weakness, disfigurement, sorrow, grief, and pain, and to enjoy such satisfaction as this life shall have prepared them for, without sin.

The ultimate destiny of the impenitent wicked is to be judged, to suffer punishment, and finally to perish utterly, so that their existence will eternally cease and they shall be as though they had not been. "God so loved the world that He gave His only Son, that whosoever believeth in Him should not *perish*, but have everlasting life."[23]

It should be clear that Adventists do not believe in the preexistence of ordinary man's spirit, or in reincarnation or transmigration of souls. We are given one life now, a time of probation that ends with death, followed by no second chance.

> And just as it is appointed for men to die once, and after that comes the judgment, so Christ, having been offered once to bear the sins of many, will appear a second time, not to deal with sin but to save those who are eagerly waiting for him.[24]

It will be equally clear that Adventists do not pray to the dead or for them. Probation ends at death, and there is no purgatory. Adventists pray only for the living.

The resurrection body of the righteous will be a glorified body like that of Christ,[25] delivered from defects, disfigurements, and onerous limitations. It will nevertheless possess a certain continuity with the present body, else the resurrection self would be a totally other self. Paul compares the relationship between the present body and the resurrection body to the relationship between the seed and the plant that springs from it.[26] In the resurrection we will recognize loved ones and friends. As Ellen White envisioned that time, "Little children are borne by holy angels to their mothers' arms. Friends long separated by death are united, nevermore to part, and with songs of gladness ascend together to the city of God."[27]

Post Mortem Practices

Death brings separation, loss, and grief to the survivors, even though by faith they believe the separation is only temporary for believers. Ministers and fellow church members will make their sympathy tangibly felt by their words, presence, and loving acts of assistance to the mourners. But it is an observable fact that consolation comes easy to Adventists, for they have been taught that death is but an episode. They have often heard and read the words of Paul: "But we would not have you ignorant, brethren, concerning those who are asleep, that you may not grieve as others do who have no hope."[28]

Typically a dying Adventist will admonish children and spouse to be faithful, so that all will be reunited in the world to come. The remembrance of such words has often been a strong motivation for perseverance in the faith. Similar exhortations are often included in the funeral service.

Funeral customs do not differ radically from those of the cultures in which the Adventists live, except for modifications when those customs clash with Adventist theology. No candles are burnt for the dead, and no offerings are presented to them. But contributions to various good works and causes of the church are commonly made as memorials. In the United States the funeral service does not greatly differ from that of other Protestant churches, and they are quite commonly conducted in the existing mortuary establishments. There is a tendency to frown upon ostentatious or extravagant funeral arrangements, expensive caskets and monuments; it is that simplicity is more in keeping with the faith and hope of Adventism, not a deficiency of love. But anything that will both console and edify the mourners is appropriate.

It is understandably an awkward situation when the deceased is known to have lived an impenitently sinful life to the end or to have committed suicide. There is a temptation in such cases to seize upon the occasion to make an object lesson of him as a warning to the living, but most Adventist ministers have the good taste to avoid such crudeness and make the theological point that judgment must be left to the hands of a loving God, who can be trusted to do what is best for all. No human being really knows the heart of another at the end of life. Moreover, Adventists do not believe that a momentary aberration just before death is enough to forfeit eternal life. Ellen White wrote: "The character is revealed, not by occasional good deeds and occasional misdeeds, but by the tendency of the habitual words and acts."[29]

In most cultures the funeral service is normally conducted by a minister. In the absence of an ordained minister, a licensed minister—that is, a ministerial intern who has not yet received ordination—may officiate at a funeral. An Adventist minister may conduct a funeral for a nonmember, and requests for him to do so are not uncommon. Adventists do not believe that persons who do not belong to their denomination have no chance of salvation; indeed, even persons who seem to be heathen who have never heard the gospel cannot with certainty be excluded. Ultimately God will be the judge of such matters, a prerogative no man can usurp.

The dead body is usually buried, but Adventists have no objection to cremation or to the donation of the body to a medical or scientific institution. While they base their belief in a future life on their hope of the resurrection of the body, they do not think the resurrection is dependent upon preservation of the cadaver. Ellen White wrote:

> Our personal identity is preserved in the resurrection, though not the same particles of matter or material substance as went into the grave. The wondrous works of God are a mystery to man. The spirit, the character of man, is returned to God, there to be preserved. In the resurrection every man will have his own character. God in His own time will call forth the dead, giving again the breath of life, and bidding the dry bones live. The same form will come forth, but it will be free from disease and every defect. It lives again bearing the same individuality of features, so that friend will recognize friend. There is no law of God in nature which shows that God gives back the same identical particles of matter which composed the body before death. God shall give the righteous dead a body that will please Him.[30]

The Adventist view is not unlike the metaphor used by Benjamin Franklin in the epitaph which he composed for himself:

> The body of B. Franklin, Printer.
> Like the Cover of an old Book,
> Its Contents torn out,
> And stript of its Lettering & Gilding,
> Lies here, Food for Worms.
> But the Work shall not be lost;
> For it will, as he believ'd, appear once more
> In a new and more elegant Edition
> Corrected and Improved
> By the Author.

Notes

[1]   This general social and religious background is vividly described in the volume edited by Edwin S. Gaustad, *The Rise of Adventism: Religion and Society in Mid-Nineteenth Century America* (New York: Harper and Row, 1974).

[2]   This and the following matters can be studied in greater detail in the numerous books on Seventh-day Adventist denominational history. Among the more reliable is R. W. Schwarz, *Light Bearers to the Remnant* (Mountain View: Pacific Press, 1979). For the earliest period see especially P. Gerard Damsteegt, *Foundations of the Seventh-day Adventist Message and Mission* (Grand Rapids: Eerdmans, 1977).

[3]   Cf. Exodus 20:8-11; Deuteronomy 5:12-15; Genesis 2:1-3.

[4]   The statistics are found in the *Seventh-day Adventist Yearbook 1983* (Washington: Review and Herald, 1983).

[5]   Reprinted in Appendix II of Damsteegt, *op.cit.*, pp. 301-305.

[6]   See *Seventh-day Adventist Church Manual*, revised 1981, pp. 31-46.

[7]   They find pedilavium, or footwashing, which they refer to as "the ordinance of humility," commanded in John 13:1-17.

[8]   Article 10 of the "Fundamental Beliefs" (1981), printed in *Seventh-day Adventist Church Manual*, rev. 1981, p. 35.

[9]   Article 19, *Ibid.*

[10]   Article 24, *Ibid.*

[11]   Ibid.

[12]   For a few of many examples, see Oscar Cullmann, *Immortality of the Soul or Resurrection of the Dead? The Witness of the New Testament* (London: The Epworth Press, 1958); H. Wheeler Robinson, *The Christian Doctrine of Man* (Edinburgh: T. & T. Clark, 1958); David G. Myers, *The Human Puzzle: Psychological Research and Christian Belief* (New York: Harper and Row, 1978). The Adventist historian Leroy Froom has compiled a two-volume history of these views, *The Conditionalist Faith of Our Fathers* (Washington: Review and Herald, 1958).

[13]   Ecclesiastes 12:7 and Psalm 104:29 describe this dissolution which occurs at death.

[14]   See Matthew 10:8; cf. Luke 10:9.

[15]   Cf. 1 Corinthians 15:26; 2 Corinthians 5:3.

[16]   Cf. Revelation 1:17-18.

[17]   Carlyle B. Haynes, *Seventh-day Adventists: Their Work and Teachings* (Washington: Review and Herald, 1940), pp. 26-27. A

thorough medical and theological treatment of near-death, supposed "out-of-body" experiences is provided by Jack Provonsha, *Is Death for Real? An Examination of Reported Near-Death Experiences in the Light of the Resurrection* (Mountain View: Pacific Press, 1981); see also the same author's article "Life after Life? " *The Ministry* (July, 1977), 20-23; cf. David G. Myers, *op.cit.*, pp. 82-86.

[18]   John 5:28-29.

[19]   Revelation 20:1-10.

[20]   Romans 6:23.

[21]   1 Timothy 1:17; 6:15-16; cf. John 5:26.

[22]   Luke 24:36-43. This and most scriptural quotations are from the Revised Standard Version.

[23]   John 3:16.

[24]   Hebrews 9:27-28.

[25]   Philippians 3:20, 21; cf. 1 John 3:2.

[26]   1 Corinthians 15:34-44.

[27]   Ellen G. White, *The Great Controversy* (Mountain View: Pacific Press, 1950), p. 645.

[28]   1 Thessalonians 4:13.

[29]   Ellen G. White, *Steps to Christ* (Mountain View: Pacific Press, 1942), p. 62.

[30]   Ellen G. White, Manuscript 76, 1900; printed in *The Seventh-day Adventist Bible Commentary*, Vol. VI, p. 1093.

UNITARIAN UNIVERSALISM

George N. Marshall, Ph.D., Th.D.

Background of the Faith

In a day when most institutions shy away from using the word "liberal," Unitarian Universalists still find this word to be the most appropriate characterization of their faith. Unitarian Universalism is liberal in that it is a free faith, in the latitude of freedom allowed to its adherents, in the loose construction of its ecclesiastical machinery, and in its broad interpretation of Christian doctrine. There have been many outcroppings of liberal religion throughout history, arising for a period and disappearing, to emerge again. Unitarian Universalism is seen by its adherents to be the institutionalization of many of these attitudes.

In a poetic sense we see this liberal tradition emerging in ancient Egypt under the Pharaoh Akhenaten of the eighteenth dynasty, who rejected the many gods of Egypt for a concept of one God; we see it in the critical quest of Socrates in ancient Greece, and in the reforming movement of Confucius and Buddha on the Asiatic mainland. It existed in the efforts at reform of the Hebrew prophets. The liberal tradition in Christianity existed in the heresies of early Church Fathers, most notably Origen (185-251 A.D.) and Arius (256-336 A.D.).

Origen, an amazing scholar and prolific writer, set forth both Unitarian and Universalist concepts from his school in Alexandria, including the humanity of Jesus and the universal salvation of souls. At the council of Nicea (325 A.D.) Arius argued against the doctrine of the Trinity and was banished by Constantine as the Christian Church officially became Trinitarian rather than Unitarian.

At the pivotal era of the Renaissance/Reformation, such advanced thinkers as Erasmus, Servetus, Zwingli and Wycliffe all expressed non-Trinitarian views indicating an innate tendency toward Unitarian interpretations of Christianity. However the real emergence of Unitarianism as an historical movement began with Faustus Socinus (1539-1604) who carried Unitarian teachings from Northern Italy to Poland in 1579. In Racow he published the first Unitarian Catechism in 1585, and this "Racovian Catechism" was soon circulated throughout Europe and arrived in England, where it influenced non-conforming churchmen.

In Poland the Unitarians were known as Socinians, the first popular designation of Unitarians throughout the continent during this era. Persecution of Socinians and their followers in Poland upon restoration of a Jesuit regime led to their flight to Transylvania. Here, in this mountainous country, now divided between Romania and Hungary and for several centuries incorporated into the Austro-Hungarian Empire, Francis David, a remarkable Renaissance intellectual, was a dominant figure. He had been a Roman Catholic Bishop until he read the works of Luther and converted to his teachings. Later, the influence of Calvin led to his change to Calvinism. However, in 1566 he began to preach against the doctrine of the Trinity. At that time, he was opposed by Catholics, Lutherans and Calvinists. Upset by his antitrinitarian thinking, King John Sigismund summoned the bishops of these three churches to appear before him in a debate with Francis David at the Council of Torda in 1568. David's appeal to reason and call to toleration of differing religious views led the youthful king to declare the Unitarian the victor, after which he openly converted to these beliefs. Then, the king issued an Edict of Toleration, which became the first legislation for religious freedom in the history of Europe. The Transylvanian Unitarian Church has continued until the present day. However, after the breakup of the Austro-Hungarian Empire in the first World War, and the division of Transylvania between Romania and Hungary, it became necessary to establish two separate national churches.

In England the Racovian Catechism influenced such men as Thomas Biddle, Theophilus Lindsey, Joseph Priestley and a host of others. Theophilus Lindsey, an Anglican clergyman, was advised by his Bishop to "Stay and do good works, forgetting this nonsense over creeds," but Lindsey's conscience would not allow this. Consequently, he withdrew from Anglican orders and established the first openly proclaimed Unitarian chapel in England on Essex Street in London. In spite of hostile legislation and persecution, a Unitarian movement has continued in England from that day to this. Many of their churches are the old "Dissenting Chapels" in England and the "Non-subscribing Presbyterian Churches" of Northern Ireland (i.e., non-subscribers to the Westminster Confession of Faith).[1]

This faith was brought to American shores by nonconformists and non-subscribers among the early settlers, including the Pilgrim founders of Plymouth and some among the Puritans of Boston. Later, after Joseph Priestley's home, library, laboratory, and church were burned in Liverpool, during the frenzy of the reaction against the French Revolution, Benjamin Franklin urged him to come to Philadelphia, where Priestley established the first church in America using the name "Unitarian."

In a reaction against "the gloomy theology of Calvin" John Murray (1741-1815) became a follower of the English Universalist leader James Relly. Following the death of Murray's wife and child, depression set in and he came to America convinced he could never preach again. However, in 1770 he began preaching on these shores, and soon many Universalist churches were organized. Whereas Unitarians were primarily concerned with the quality of life in this world and stressed ethical values and rational thinking, Universalists began with a concern over the nature of life after death, which they believed should be a rational extension of this life, based on ethical considerations binding both God and humanity. This led to the famous quip by Thomas Starr King in the last century: "The Universalist thinks God is too good to damn him, while the Unitarian thinks he is too good for God to damn."[2]

Thus, these two denominations had long histories going back into colonial days and earlier European history. Through the passing decades they came to work more closely together, and in 1961 the American Unitarian Association and the Universalist Church of America merged into the Unitarian Universalists Association. Whether our local churches call themselves Unitarian or Universalist, they are in fact all Unitarian Universalist societies.[3]

Congregational in polity, stressing individual freedom of belief, the Unitarian Universalist Association is managed by a Board of Trustees, which is answerable to and guided by decisions of the annual General Assembly. In the General Assembly voting delegates of the local societies convene to oversee the health and activities of the movement. Officers are the President, Moderator, Secretary, and Financial Officer elected at this Assembly, which represents slightly over a thousand societies in the United States and Canada.

Geographical districts ease administrative communication, but no official of either district or continental organization can interfere in the conduct of the affairs of the local societies, which jealously guard their independent congregational status. These local societies may be called churches, parishes, fellowships, congregations, or societies according to local decision. A roster of accredited ministers able to serve local societies is maintained by the Association, and other services in education and congregational assistance are provided. Service within the realm of nearly absolute freedom is the distinguishing hallmark of this Association. This distinction differentiates it from nearly all other churches.

Principles and Purposes

Non-creedal and non-doctrinal, there is no agreed upon statement of beliefs; rather a statement of principles and purposes sum up the faith binding Unitarian Universalists together. Following several years of intense study in many of our congregations and through a study commission, a revised statement was adopted in final form at the 1984 General Assembly. It reads:

> We the member congregations of the Unitarian Universalist Association, convenant to affirm and promote:
> The inherent worth and dignity of every person;
> Justice, equity, and compassion in human relations;
> Acceptance of one another and encouragement to spiritual growth in our congregations;
> A free and responsible search for truth and meaning;
> The rights of conscience and the use of the democratic process within our congregations and in society at large;
> The goal of world community with peace, liberty and justice for all;
> Respect for the interdependent web of all existence of which we are a part.
> The living tradition we share draws from many sources:
> Direct experience of that transcending mystery and wonder,

affirmed in all cultures, which moves us to a renewal of the spirit and an openness to the forces which create and uphold life;

Words and deeds of prophetic women and men which challenge us to confront powers and structures of evil with justice, compassion, and the transforming power of love;

Wisdom from the world's religions which inspires us in our ethical and spiritual life;

Jewish and Christian teachings which call us to respond to God's love by loving our neighbors as ourselves;

Humanistic teachings which counsel us to heed the guidance of reason and the results of science, and warn us against idolatries of the mind and spirit.

Grateful for the religious pluralism which enriches and ennobles our faith, we are inspired to deepen our understanding and expand our vision.

As free congregations we enter into this covenant, promising to one another our mutual trust and support.

The Unitarian Universalist Association shall devote its resources and exercise its corporate powers for religious, educational, and humanitarian purposes.

The primary purpose of the Association is to serve the needs of its member congregations, organize new congregations, extend and strengthen Unitarian Universalist institutions, and implement its principles.[4]

The Liberal Religious Response to Death

The Unitarian Universalist believer, in keeping with all other aspects of his religious practice, is guided by his own sense of what is proper and makes sense for him or her. However, being a faith that seeks to be in harmony with science and advancing knowledge, he or she tends in most cases to prefer a memorial service to a traditional funeral. Major exceptions occur when it would seem to offer more solace to the grievers, often older family members, or others, whose suffering should be taken into account. A memorial service for the average member will seek to recall with gladness the life that was lived and shared with us. The service will seek to maintain an integrity with the life remembered, and say something to the gathered group about the meaning of his or her life, and to enfold us all in the larger community of sharing and caring for one another. When successfully carried out, such a service is an uplifting experience that brightens the gloom caused by the death itself. We prefer usually to have a closed coffin and that it not be opened following the service. On many occasions the coffin is already buried or at the crematorium, where a single bouquet may be the center of focus. Memorial services are often held in the church, a place of uplifting and challenging experiences, but they can be held in the home, the garden (weather permitting), or some place associated with the life being commemorated. Only traditional services are held in a funeral home. Memorial services can be held at a convenient time, since they are not influenced by the problem of body disposal. Thus, such a service might be scheduled on a weekend, a holiday, an evening, or any appropriate time when family and friends from distant places may attend. There are no required religious rituals, and family and spiritual leaders plan a service that seems to do justice to the life remembered. Cremation is an increasingly favored method of disposal of the body.[5]

Many of the early Memorial Societies were founded as non-sectarian societies by Unitarian Universalists, and these societies combined with the Cooperative Funeral Societies to establish the Continental Association of Funeral and Memorial Societies in Washington, D.C.[6] Many memorial societies continue to have their offices in U.U. churches. While such societies are always non-sectarian, reaching out to serve the larger community, there is a view that every U.U. church can serve as a memorial society to its own members, offering guidance to all, assisting in the prearrangement of services, and educating families to the value of memorial services.

As indicated, a growing percentage of our members prefer cremation, which is quick, easy, without complications, less costly than a traditional funeral and allows a more convenient scheduling of memorial service. It also has other advantages. It makes easier the usual desire of the religious liberal to advance the cause of science and service to humanity through an autopsy that may advance medical knowledge, and through the donation of organs and tissue that may assist the lives of others or advance research. This is very appealing to most of our members. With cremation, enbalming usually is not required.

As religious liberals we try to form a compassionate, caring community so that in sharing our deepest insights and offering our personal concern, we support and assist one another. Even our ministers, although usually trained in counseling, can do little more. We have no absolutes from On High that give definitive answers—only loving care for each other.

Unitarian Universalism is a non-proselytizing faith that offers its services to all who turn to us in need. It would be demeaning for us to deny comfort and our services at the time of mourning to any who asked help. Accordingly, our services are open to all without fear of religious pressures to join. Questions of previous religious affiliations, rites or services are not asked.

Unitarian Universalists accept a scientific view of life and see life as lived in the here and now rather than in the hereafter. Whether or not Unitarian Universalists are agnostic about the existence of God, they tend to be agnostic about the existence of an afterlife. We simply do not know. While some may argue with the position, it is common to hear said, "No one has ever returned to tell us about the afterlife." We simply do not know, and we question scriptural passages that seem to say otherwise. Since Universalism began with an emphasis on universal salvation of all souls with God, it is strange that we have moved entirely away from this concern to a total emphasis on this life. There was an intermediary step in the progression of Universalist thought: the complete denial of the existence of hell, and of course of purgatory or limbo. From this came the doubting of any afterlife, but not its denial. We simply admit we do not know whether or not there is an afterlife.

There are undoubtedly some religious liberals who believe that, if there is an afterlife, it will be found in some such mechanism as reincarnation, but there is no systematic study on the question of reincarnation to my knowledge, although I once heard a learned lecturer say, "The extent to which the nineteenth century Unitarian divines believed in reincarnation has never been fully explored." This author has never found any such evidence.

Unitarian Universalists do not associate either heaven or hell with the afterlife, or as places located either in the "heavens above" or the places beneath the earth, as these are concepts not in accord with modern astronomical, cosmological, or geological findings. Ralph Waldo Emerson, a Unitarian minister, wrote an *Essay on Compensation*, stressing that the good and evil people do is compensated for in this life. This is the Unitarian Universalist view—to the extent there is an agreed upon position. Reward and punishment are in this life, in the here and now. We have no doctrine distinguishing our members from the rest of humanity.

We accept the view of creation offered by the scientists, astronomers, and astro-physicists who depict an evolutionary view of the universe created in the "Big Bang Theory" and expanding until the end of time. We have no special doctrines or theories that differ from what we have learned from the scientists.

Our religion relies upon the scientific disciplines of all other learned professions. Thus we hold no special views of history or medicine other than those offered by historians and the medical profession.

We agree with biologists that the body is composed of material organized in living cellular fashion—material that will rapidly decay following death so that bodily resurrection is not possible. According to our understanding, the scientific world rejects bodily resurrection as not feasible, and it makes such places as purgatory, limbo, heaven, and hell improbable.

In the last century James Freeman Clarke, in a famous statement of Unitarian views, stated that we believe in "salvation by character," and this statement has often been quoted as summing up the view of salvation as something molded by our own character. This does not project salvation to a future life. Unitarian Universalism is not a salvation religion. Rather it is an ethical religion concerned with how we live. Nevertheless we are concerned with human destiny, which we see as summed up in a poem by the American poet, Edwin Markham, who, though he grew up in a church of a different denomination and was a member of it, chose in the final years of his life to attend a Universalist church in Brooklyn and was buried there. He wrote:

We men of earth have here the stuff of paradise.
We have enough.
We need no other stones to build the stairs on to the Unfulfilled,
No other ivory for the doors, no other marble for the floors,
No other cedar for the beam and dome of man's immortal dream.
Here on the common human way is all the stuff to build a heaven.
Ours the stuff to build eternity in time.

To us such a view of the place of humanity in the universe is one calling for courage, challenging us to do and dare and to achieve. Just as there is no pot of gold waiting for us at the end of the rainbow, so there is no reward awaiting us after death except that seen by Socrates as he was about to drink the hemlock:

If we reflect upon it we may well hope that death is a good. For the state of death is one of two things: either the dead wholly cease to be, and lose all sensation; or, according to the common belief, it is a change and a migration of the soul to another place. And if death is the absence of all sensation, and like the sleep of one whose slumbers are unbroken by any dreams, it will be a wonderful gain. . . . For then it appears that eternity is nothing more than a single night.

But if death is a journey to another place, and the common belief is true, that there are all who have died, what good could be greater than this, my judges? What would you not give to converse with Orpheus and Hesiod and Homer? I am willing to die many times if this be true.[7]

The religious liberal is like Socrates, not rejecting life after death, but skeptical, and able to relish the final rest as an unspeakable gain. The important point is to make death a passage beautiful and fraught with meaning, recalling a life we were privileged to have known, and to share our common humanity with one another in a period of deep crisis, when for a moment, the veil between life and death is wrent as we behold reality. When we pray, it is for ourselves and for those who mourn with us. It is part of the therapy of consoling one another. In comforting each other we truly minister. It is the mystic bond of Schweitzer's "fellowship of those who bear the mark of pain" which creates the living church.

Notes

[1] Earl Morse Wilbur, *History of Unitarianism*: Vol. 1, European Backgrounds; 1952, Vol. II, English and American Backgrounds; Cambridge, MA: Harvard University Press; re-issued by the Meadville/Lombard Theological School, University of Chicago, IL, and available through the Distribution Center, Unitarian Universalist Association, 25 Beacon Street, Boston, MA 02108.

[2] George N. Marshall, *Challenge of a Liberal Faith*, 1980 revised edition; New Canaan, CT: Chapters 5 and 6 for historical backgrounds; Chapters 7 and 8 for review of beliefs in Unitarian Universalism; also available through Distribution Center, UUA. *op.cit.*

[3] *Unitarian Universalist Association Yearbook*, an annual directory listing all organizations, societies, religious leaders, by-laws and minutes of last General Assembly: Boston, Unitarian Universalist Association, 25 Beacon St., Boston, MA 02108.

[4] *Unitarian Universalist World* (The Journal of the Unitarian Universalist Association) 25 Beacon St., Boston, MA 02108: see issue of July 15, 1984 for report of the General Assembly with text of the By-law Revision on Principles and Purposes, p. 10.

[5] George N. Marshall, *Facing Death and Grief*, 1981, Buffalo: Prometheus Books; Chapter 6: "The Church and the Clergy"; Chapter 7: "The Service—How Traditional?"

[6]   Publications of the Continental Association of Funeral and Memorial Societies, 1828 L Street, N.W., Washington, D.C. 20036.

[7]   Plato, *Apology*.

See also: David B. Parke, Epic of Unitarianism, New Edition, 1981, Unitarian Universalist Association. A collection of primary source material from historical documents throughout the ages for the student of this history.

Ernest Cassera, ed. *Universalism in America*, New Edition 1984, Unitarian Universalist Association. A collection of primary source materials on American Universalism. Order these two books through the Distribution Center, UUA, address above.

UNITED METHODIST CHURCH

James Ivey Warren, Jr., Ph.D.

Background of the Faith

Theodore Roosevelt was reported to have said, "I would rather address a Methodist Church in America. . . . The Methodists represent the great middle class and in consequence are the most representative church in America."[1]

Indeed, the United Methodist Church has shared the history of the United States of America. Its growth periods reflect national growth. Its character reflects a democratic spirit. Its social involvements parallel national issues and crises. Its activist nature agrees with the national taste for adventure, opportunity, and accomplishment. In 1980 the United Methodist Church reported membership of 9,561,028 and local churches (congregations or charges) numbering 38,795. Its church property is valued at $8,400,000,000 not including 145 institutions for church care and education. The United Methodist Church is at work in 48 foreign countries, and its publishing house is the oldest and probably the largest religious publishing concern in the world.[2]

The Methodist movement began in the eighteenth century in England under the influence of John and Charles Wesley. English social, moral, and religious conditions during the first half of the eighteenth century were deplorable. Generally, the wealthy upper class were callous and immoral, the middle class self-satisfied, and the lower class neglected and brutalized. For example, penal conditions were shameful— beyond our imagination, and punishments were so severe that even children could be legally hanged for 160 different offenses including poaching a rabbit on a gentleman's estate. The child death rate was alarming, with three out of four children of all classes in London dying before the age of five. Harlotry and alcoholism were rampant. Hogarth's famous picture of this period, "Gin Lane," depicts a gin shop with the inscription, "Drunk for a penny. Dead drunk for two pence. Clean straw for nothing."[3]

The religious life of eighteenth-century England was also at low ebb. Some ecclesiastic appointments paid handsomely (the Bishop of Durham received the equivalent in today's purchasing power of $500,000 per year), while others barely allowed their parsons to eat and be clothed adequately. Generally, the "established church" neglected the hordes of poor persons being produced by the industrial revolution, and the "dissenting" churches, made up of thrifty, middle-class citizens, saw little need to advocate reform. Theologically, deism and predestination pervaded English thought. God was understood in terms of transcendence and viewed as "an intelligence" who, having created the universe with certain natural laws, refrained from interfering in the world's affairs. Predestination, with its accompanying notion of "the elect," resulted in little effort to reach the multitudes outside the care and edification of the church.

Within such conditions the Methodist Church was born. A few students at Oxford University, including John Wesley, his brother Charles, and George Whitefield, founded an association that contrasted markedly with the times. This group had fixed times and practices for Bible study, prayer, corporate worship, and acts of love such as visiting those in prison, teaching the poor, and caring for the ill. Their fellow students derisively referred to them as "Bible moths," "enthusiasts," and "methodists." They were called Bible moths because of their study of scripture, enthusiasts because of their zeal for worship and service, and methodists because of their methodical and disciplined practices. John Wesley, the leader of the group, accepted the term "methodist" and referred to himself and his colleagues as "the people called methodists."

The two Wesleys, Whitefield, and others began to preach to the masses of the unchurched people of England. Albert Bailey said of John Wesley:

> Until the days of the airplane he traveled more miles, a quarter of a million, mostly on horseback; he preached more sermons—upward of forty thousand; he converted more people —at least one hundred thousand—than any person who ever lived.[4]

As people responded to these "methodist" ministries, they were organized into bands, classes, and societies for study, mutual encouragement and admonition. Wesley did not intend to form a new church, but historical circumstances and needs of the populace led to the organization of the Methodist Church in England.

From England, the Methodist Church spread to Ireland and to the United States, which was then an English colony.

Methodism was especially adapted to American life. . .itiner-

ent preachers served the people under conditions where a
settled ministry was not feasible. They sought out the scattered homes, followed the tide of migration as it moved West,
preached the Gospel, organized societies, established "preaching places," and formed these into "circuits." Thus by the
close of the American Revolution the Methodists numbered
some 15,000 members and 80 preachers.[5]

Among the German speaking colonists in America there
were two churches whose theology, zeal, and ecclesiology
were very much akin to those of the Methodists. One group
was led by William Otterbein and Martin Boehm, and in
1800 formed the United Brethren Church. The second group
was led by Jacob Albright, and in 1816 became the Evangelical Association. After a division and a subsequent reunion
in 1922 this group became known as the Evangelical Church.
In 1946 the two German speaking bodies merged to become
the Church of the United Brethren in Christ. In 1968 the
German speaking Evangelical United Brethren merged
with the English speaking Methodist Church to form the
United Methodist Church.[6]

General Beliefs and Practices

Two words may be used to characterize United Methodists' beliefs and practices—mainstream and pluralistic.
Their theology traces back to the historic confessions of
faith, and the United Methodist Church is one of the few
major denominations that did not develop a creed of its own.
It is probable that most United Methodist congregations use
the Apostles' Creed either every Sunday or more times than
any other confession of faith. This being true, United Methodists affirm the historic, orthodox elements of belief—God
as creator, Christ as Savior and example, (true God and true
man) the Holy Spirit as guide and source of power, the
church as God's agency and as the communion of saints, the
resurrection of the body, and the life everlasting. Indeed the

Methodist movement began not to establish a new doctrine, but to recover and recall the church to its historic understanding of God as transcendent and imminent, of human beings as free and responsible persons, and of the necessity for Christians to pursue lives of holiness.

Within this comprehensive understanding of Christian belief, however, Methodists emphasized certain elements. Arminianism, the belief that persons possess free will which allows them to respond to God's grace, was a major Methodist stance. This stance arose largely in opposition to the "horrible decrees" of Calvinistic thought which contended that God preordained some persons to be elect, to be chosen for heaven, and other persons to be consigned to hell. This emphasis of Methodist evangelicalism is most apparent in John Wesley's sermons and in Charles Wesley's hymns. Hymn after hymn concludes with the call and/or a plea for the sinner to respond. For example, note these lines in Charles Wesley's hymn, "Where Shall My Wandering Soul Begin?"

> Come, my guilty brethren, come,
> Groaning beneath your load of sin!
> His bleeding heart shall make you room;
> His open side shall take you in.
> He calls you now, invites you home:
> Come, O my guilty brethren, come.[7]

A second emphasis of Wesleyan theology is experiential faith. One *knows* one's sins forgiven. One "feels" Christ's blood applied for one's self. Again Charles Wesley gives this emphasis poetic expression:

How can a sinner know his sins on earth forgiven?
How can my precious Savior show my name inscribed in heaven?
What we have felt and seen with confidence we tell;
And publish to the sons of men the signs infallible.[8]

Not only is this assurance, but it is personal to the point of being overwhelming and mysterious.

And can it be that I should gain
An interest in the Savior's blood?
Died He for me who caused His pain?
For me who Him to death pursued?
Amazing love! How can it be
That Thou, my Lord shouldst die for me?

'Tis mystery all! Immortal dies
Who can explore His strange design?
In vain the first-born seraph tries
To sound the depths of love divine.
'Tis mercy all! Let earth adore.
Let angel minds inquire no more.[9]

A third Methodist emphasis relates to the "saved" life. In Wesleyan thought salvation is being saved from *sin* and from the *power of sin*. Another way of saying this is to speak of the Christian life as the holy or sanctified life. Methodists believe not only in forgiveness of sin but in God's gift to us of power over sin.

Charles Wesley's poem stating that Jesus ". . .breaks the power of cancelled sin. . ." refers to Christ's victory over *ingrained*, (as the watermark on writing paper or the impressed cancellation of a stamp on a letter) sin. So Methodist belief takes seriously the admonition to "go on to perfection."

Finally, United Methodists emphasize the social dimension of the Christian life. From the Holy Club's involvement with the poor, uneducated and imprisoned to the development of the United Methodist Church's statement of the Social Creed, United Methodists have seen their charge as, "to serve the present age, my calling to fulfill; O may it all my powers engage to do my Master's will."[10]

The basic beliefs and emphases of United Methodists are contained in two historical documents—"The Articles of Religion of the Methodist Church" and "The Confession of Faith of the Evangelical United Brethren Church." "The Articles of Religion" number 25 and are an abridgement made by John Wesley of the 39 Articles of Faith of the Anglican Church. "The Confession of Faith" is a similar statement, consisting of 26 articles, and is taken from the Discipline of the Evangelical United Brethren Church.

Pluralism is the second major characteristic of United Methodist belief and practice. Within the broad mainstream of faith and life there is ample allowance for diversity, and there is wide acceptance of the dictum: "As to all opinions which do not strike at the root of Chistianity, we think and let think" (Discipline, Paragraph 67, p. 40). Moreover this "root of Christianity" is determined by a broadly based process that uses four sources—scripture, tradition, experience, and reason. "This living core. . .stands revealed in scripture, illumined by tradition, vivified in personal experience and confirmed by reason."[11]

In regard to ecclesiastical practices. United Methodists form a bridge between "high" church rituals and liturgies and "low" church emphasis upon spontaneous, less formal worship services. John Wesley clearly favored "order" and thought highly of the historic forms of worship. He desired that the people called Methodists partake of the sacrament of Holy Communion at least weekly. He stated that when he first began outdoor preaching, he found it abhorrent. However, Wesley's pragmatic nature led him to see the value of departing from and adapting orderly, traditional forms in order to reach unchurched persons. The United Methodist Church today continues this breadth of practice. It not only allows one to think and let think; it allows different local churches to "practice and let practice." Article XXII, on "Rites and Ceremonies of Churches," states:

> It is not necessary that rites and ceremonies should in all places be the same, or exactly alike; for they have been always different, and may be changed according to the diversity of countries, times, and men's manners, so that nothing be ordained against God's word.[12]

Death and Life After Death

Most of the creedal statements used by United Methodists affirm the reality of death and eternal life. The Apostles'

Creed states, "I believe in...the resurrection of the body, and the life everlasting." The Nicene Creed concludes with, "and I look for the resurrection of the dead, and the life of the world to come." The Korean Creed asserts "we believe in the final triumph of righteousness, and in the life everlasting." A Modern Statement speaks of "...our deliverance from sin and death," and of "the Kingdom of God coming upon earth." All of these affirmations attest to the reality of life after death but do not describe it in fine detail.[13]

Two points stand out and call for notice. First the "resurrection" is the resurrection of the *dead*. Christian faith does not deny, avoid, or prevent death. Death remains real and inescapable. Rather, the Christian faith proclaims triumph over death. Resurrection is not to be confused with "immortality" (which asserts that we possess some part of us that never dies) or with a "dualism" (that exalts "soul" and denigrates "body"). Instead, resurrection of the dead presupposes the reality of death.

The section on worship that the Board of Discipleship of the United Methodist Church has printed a suggested "service of death and resurrection" with an accompanying theological rationale and commentary. In its commentary it urges its readers to confront bereaved persons with the reality of the body of the deceased, arguing that a "genuinely felt admission of the reality of death, in so far as a bereaved person is capable, best fosters spiritual and emotional health." It points out that the use of euphemisms for death such as "asleep" or "resting" may reflect a tendency to deny the reality of death.[14]

It is even more important, however, to affirm the reality of resurrection. Resurrection is God's action, not ours. It refers to new life and the reorientation of the quality of life. In a sense, the new quality of life begins before death with a spiritual birth, but life after death is "marked by disjunction, renewal, and reorientation of life of a quality incommensurate with what we may know or are able to imagine."[15]

A question frequently asked is, "Will we know each other in the life after death?" The answer most United Methodists give is yes. This is, in part, what is meant by "the resurrection of the body." Consider two expressions. First, the Section of Worship's report contends that "body" refers to "the total matrix of personality." The second expression comes from the pen of Costen J. Harrel, late bishop of the United Methodist Church.

> ...Of some things we may be confident. We know that because God loves us as individuals, our personal identity will not be lost in the spirit world. We shall know and be known, we shall love and be loved; we are integral persons whom on earth he called to be his sons and daughters. The New Testament knows no other kind of immortality. And since those with whom we walked on earth shall, like ourselves, continue their personal existence, we know that they will be known by us, and we shall see again "...those angel faces smile which we have loved long since and lost a while."[16]

A third expression comes from Bishop Mack B. Stokes, who asserts even more strongly:

> . . .Eternal life is one of peace and joy because it brings together the redeemed souls into a perfect fellowship. Many people ask will we recognize our friends in heaven? The answer is that we shall not only recognize them, we shall see how truly wonderful they are and we shall more perfectly love them.[17]

This position regarding death and life after death is very much in the mainstream of orthodox Christian belief. However there are three important ideas that should be noted. 1) It is *resurrection, new* life that is offered. "Immortality is a negative assertion that merely claims the soul does not die. Resurrection is a positive assertion: the person is raised to life."[18] 2) It is resurrection of the *person*—body and spirit, the recognizable and lovable person. 3) Resurrection is a present reality (a new life of grace conquering the enemy, sin) *and* a future reality (eternal life conquering the enemy death).

The genius of United Methodism, as we have noted, is not distinctive faith assertions but the enthusiastic attempt to express its belief in Christian life and worship. Therefore, it is appropriate and important for one to examine the ministries of the United Methodist Church at the time of death and to note how beliefs are expressed in the services of worship of the church.

Four terms can help us understand the ministries of the church at the time of death—death, bereavement, grief, and mourning. Death refers to the physical event in someone's personal history. Bereavement is loss experienced by friends of the deceased, and grief is the emotion caused by death. "Mourning is the spiritual, psychological, even moral process of coping with and working through grief, of regaining inner wholeness and balance."[19]

Persons' attitudes toward and responses to death vary and call for different kinds of ministries. Different people respond differently to the inevitability of their own death—responding with denial, avoidance, fear and/or superstition. So it is that the church in its ministries must teach the reality of death, refute unchristian notions such as reincarnation, and make clear the Christian hope and its basis.

Similarly, bereavement expresses itself in varying responses. Some bereaved persons feel anger, questioning, bewilderment, guilt, and/or relief. For example, in cases of untimely death as might occur in an accident or to a child, bereaved persons may become angry with God or may question God's goodness. A close relative may feel guilt, blaming himself or herself for not spending more time with or giving more help to the deceased while he or she was alive.

Even when responses are not so pronounced, bereaved persons express some degree of grief. Grief may express itself as a sense of loss, in a feeling of emptiness, or, as C. S. Lewis observed, in a persistent physical and mental fatigue. In dealing with bereavement and guilt, Christian ministries require sensitivities to human need, awareness of cultural practices, and insights of psychology. Help needs to come not only from the pastoral leadership but from church members and neighbors. Since one's bereavement and grief is occasioned by the loss of a friend and since the felt absence or questioning of God is occasioned by the death of a loved one, it is likely that comfort and renewed faith must be mediated also by a close friend or relative.

Mourning is a necessary process of working through one's grief and may take from six weeks to several months. This process should have several results: 1) a letting go of the dependence that one had on the deceased 2) an ability to distinguish those concerns that are permanent from those that are transient 3) an awareness of one's sins of omission and commission 4) an awareness of one's love for the deceased and the love of one's friends.[20]

However, Christian mourning is more than simply discovering one's inner strengths and the support of friends. Christian mourning is "an experience of divine grace" and "locates the source of comfort in God." We do not simply comfort ourselves. Nor are we simply comforted by others. We find God's comfort through the efforts of our friends and ourselves. Leslie Weatherhead tells of an occasion when he visited a home where a young person had died. A neighbor was present comforting the mother of the child who was her friend, but the bereaved mother addressed Dr. Weatherhead with anger and questioning. "Padre," she said, "you've often preached about the everlasting arms. Where are those arms now?" Weatherhead pointed to the neighbor whose presence and faith were strengthening the mother and replied, "God's arms are working through her arms."

To summarize, there are several Christian ministries at the occasion of death in which all Christians can participate. 1) We can confront the bereaved persons with the reality of death by refusing to use euphemisms that deny it— words like "asleep" or "resting." "A genuinely felt admission of the reality of death, insofar as a bereaved person is capable, best fosters spiritual and emotional health."[21] 2) We can offer supportive presence and action. In many cultural settings persons bring food, send flowers, write messages of sympathy, and visit in the homes where death has occurred. These acts are "Christian graces of faith, hope and love. . . visibly acted out."[22] 3) Christians can affirm their faith and use the occasion of death "to reexamine their life in Christ, to repent, to renew their faith, and to rededicate themselves to service in Christ's name."[23]

The Funeral Service

The funeral service is: 1) a corporate act of Christian worship that is 2) comforting and confrontational 3) which focuses on Christ's victory over sin and death and 4) which emphasizes committal. As an act of Christian worship, the service should center around Christian themes, use Christian symbols, and be a corporate act. Where possible the service should be held in the church building where the deceased worshipped. This setting, itself, expresses Christian themes and points to the continuity between one's participation in Christ's victory over sin and one's participation in Christ's victory over death. It is an ideal setting to recall God's goodness in creation and redemption and to remember the deceased's participation in the Christian faith. If the service takes place in a home or a funeral home, then appropriate Christian symbols should be present—the cross to point to God's light and guidance. The funeral service is not a private affair. It is a corporate act of the people of God, where God is affirmed as worthy of praise and where God is thanked for the life and the witness of the deceased.

The proclamation during the service speaks to the persons assembled in terms of confrontation and comfort. The people are confronted with the reality of their own death, sin and dependence on God. They are challenged to examine their own faith and hope. The people are also comforted, made strong. Christian comfort goes beyond a sentimentally transient level and emphasizes the mercy and power of God's act in Christ as the basis for one's hope and peace. So it is that worshippers are comforted in their grief over the death of a loved one, and confronted with their own hope in Christ.

It is appropriate to name the deceased and to praise God for God's love and goodness to him or her, and to thank God for his or her life, service, and witness. But, the central thrust of the proclamation should not be a eulogy to the deceased.

Rather, thoughts of and prayers for the deceased should be in the context of Christian worship and his or her death should be viewed as the occasion to affirm one's faith, to recall God's goodness, and to express one's gratitude to God for the life and witness of the deceased. "Understood as 'tribute' or 'appreciation', eulogy is essentially thankfulness, and surely thankfulness to God—even when verbally addressed to people—is not out of place in proclamation."[24]

Finally, the Christian funeral service deals with committal of the physical remains. United Methodists see the importance of committing the deceased's body (or ashes in the case of cremation) to the earth or sea. This part of the service usually takes place at the burial site and recognizes that "...the body has been the temple of the Spirit of God. It has been valued and loved. When it no longer serves its purpose in its old form, it is returned to the elements from which it came, with thanksgiving to God for the gift of its wonder."[25]

Secondly, the service commits the deceased person to God's keeping. Building upon the words of Jesus on the cross when he committed His spirit to the Father, United Methodists commit the deceased person to God. Such committal also points to belief in the resurrection of the person. As Bishop Stokes reminded us, eternal life brings the redeemed together in perfect fellowship where we know and love each other even more perfectly. So the funeral service commits the deceased to God and to the "church triumphant."

Further the committal service attests to the truth that "...God's love does not cease being the same love after death as it was before."[26] A third sense of committal is present in this service since the service of committal gives one the opportunity to commit oneself to God, to recall that our hope is in God.

Some Specific Questions
Related to Belief and Practice

Such then are the United Methodist's general beliefs and practices relating to death and life after death, but there remain some specific questions that deserve to be addressed. Some of these questions concern belief about life after death, while others relate to acceptable practices and ethical stances.

First let us look at some frequently asked questions concerning United Methodist beliefs. Do United Methodists believe in heaven and hell? The pluralism that one finds generally in the United Methodist Church is found specifically in the belief about heaven and hell. The vast majority of United Methodists believe in life after death, that "heaven" is being in the presence of God, and that "hell" is separation from God. Within this broad affirmation, beliefs vary among individuals and groups. Some United Methodists interpret some parts of scripture literally and describe heaven as a place where streets are paved with gold, and where prosperity abounds as milk and honey. They also view hell in specific, concrete images as a place where torment is present in the form of fire and worms. Other United Methodists understand such language as pictorial and suggestive. They interpret heaven as a place or state of being where fulfillment of persons and communion with God and others are realized. Hell is frequently seen as the absence of such fulfillment and communion. This latter group, while believing in heaven and hell, are not greatly concerned about the specifics, about the "temperature of hell or the furniture of heaven."

Most United Methodists affirm the doctrine of salvation by grace through faith. Persons are "saved" by God's grace through Jesus Christ from sin to holiness and from eternal death to eternal life. This salvation has three tenses. We *have been saved* by God's act in Christ. We *are being saved* by God's continuing grace and our response. We *shall be saved* in the consummation of God's love in the fuller realization of God's kingdom after death. United Methodists affirm quite readily that all who respond in faith and obedience to God's act in love in Jesus Christ are saved, but they are less ready to assert that those who do not respond positively go to hell. Some see this position as a natural corollary to the first position, but others are content to leave the ultimate decision about the unresponsive to God's judgment. However, the missionary and evangelistic fervor typical of United Methodists at least points to the "fear" that the unresponsive may not be saved. What happens to those who have never been confronted with God's grace in Jesus Christ is even less seen from a judgmental position. Generally, United Methodists profess to "know" that God saves through faith in Christ, and therefore, they seek to share this good news. This is the practical result of this belief. The ultimate place of those of other faiths is seen as somewhat speculative and consigned to the area of God's judgment.

Is the body or spirit resurrected after death, and will the resurrected know each other? We have already seen that the basic belief in the "resurrection of the body" points to the resurrection of the person in a way that has continuity with earthly life. Moreover, United Methodists believe that we shall not only recognize each other in that fulfillment, but that the communion we partake of on earth shall be complete and full in the "Church triumphant."

All praise to our redeeming Lord who joins us by his grace,
And bids us, each to each restored, together seek his face.

And if our fellowship below in Jesus be so sweet,
What height of rapture shall we know when round his throne
we meet?[27]

One further doctrinal area deserves attention. What about the second coming, a final judgment and purgatory? United Methodists strongly affirm the notion of judgment and call (even plead) for persons to respond to God's grace. For some persons, this judgment is coincidental with response, i.e., heaven begins with one's saying yes to God's grace in Jesus Christ and continues after death; hell is separation from God, both presently and eternally. Other persons believe that there will be one specific "day" when Christ will come again, judge all peoples, welcoming some to heaven and assigning others to hell. Generally, United Methodists do not believe in purgatory, because they fear it smacks of "salvation by works" and blunts the importance of decision and response to God's grace in this life. Indeed, Article 13 of "The Articles of Religion of the United Methodist Church" (which have been seen as theologically binding since 1784) states:

> The. . .doctrine concerning purgatory. . .is a fond thing, vainly invented, and grounded upon no warrant of Scripture, but repugnant to the Word of God.[28]

There are also several other matters of United Methodist practice that merit specific attention. Here we shall discuss four: euthanasia, participation in funeral services of non-Christians or unchurched persons, local/cultural practices regarding death and funerals, and the participation of children in funeral services and related questioning.

1) United Methodists view life positively. Persons are seen not as a duality of body and spirit, but as a unity. Therefore, Christian responsibility includes care for and service to bodily as well as spiritual aspects of human life. We believe that persons should have all possible opportunity to maximize life, and that physical death is a part of life that calls for ministry to persons approaching death and to friends of those who are dying or have died. Euthanasia means "good death" and United Methodists are committed to helping persons have good, positive lives and good, positive deaths. The 1980 United Methodist Discipline addresses the issue of death with dignity and concludes:

> We applaud medical science for efforts to prevent disease and illness and for advances in treatment that extend the meaningful life of human beings. At the same time, in the varying stages of death and life that medical science have occasioned, we recognize the agonizing personal and moral decisions faced by the dying, their physicians, their families, and their friends. Therefore, we assert the right of every person to die in dignity, with loving personal care and without efforts to prolong terminal illnesses merely because the technology is available to do so.[29]

2) What shall be the United Methodist's participation in the funeral of someone who was unchurched or was a non-Christian? The task force on worship of the United Methodist Board of Discipleship judges that the Christian position is that one is "free to minister as may be judged appropriate according to circumstances."[30] The task force suggests that such services should be rendered *as a Christian* and that the Gospel should be spoken in ways that respect the integrity of the hearers. Moreover, it is appropriate to share leadership at funeral services with persons of other religious communities so long as each can witness with integrity and so long as each can respect the faith of the others.[31]

3) How important are local practices in the ministries and worship associated with death and resurrection? Generally, the pluralistic nature and open stance of the United Methodist Church allows and encourages meaningful local practices *when such practices are not incompatible with Christian orthodox beliefs*. Take the example of the viewing of the body before the worship service or before interment. This custom is not prohibited and, indeed, may help persons confront the reality of death. However, neither the body nor the coffin should be the center of the funeral service.

4) Should the Christian faith concerning death and resurrection be communicated to children and should children be encouraged or permitted to attend Christian funerals? Generally, United Methodists answer these questions affirmatively. Children are greatly affected by the death of a loved one, but they are more likely to be affected negatively by not being allowed to attend funeral services than by being allowed to attend them and to ask questions concerning death and resurrection. Children should be allowed to participate at their own level of understanding and should not be deceived about the reality of death. More important, children should be exposed to the Christian understanding of eternal life. "From the funeral experience, children can learn that their own life is valued and valuable and that it is in the hands of a loving God."[32] May all of us so learn!

Notes

1   J. Paul Williams, *What Americans Believe and How They Worship* (New York: Harper and Brothers, 1952), p. 274.

2   Frank S. Mead, *Handbook of Denominations* (Nashville: Abingdon Press, 1980), pp. 177-180.

3   Albert Edmond Bailey, *The Gospel in Hymns: Background and Interpretations* (New York: Charles Scribner's Sons, 1950), pp. 74-76.

4   Ibid., p. 77.

5   *The Book of Discipline of the United Methodist Church* (Nashville: The United Methodist Publishing House, 1980), p. 9.

6   Ibid., pp. 7-18.

7   *The Book of Hymns* (Nashville: The Methodist Publishing House, 1966), Hymn 528.

8   Ibid., Hymn 114.

9   Ibid., Hymn 527.

10   Ibid., Hymn 150.

11   *The Book of Discipline*, Par. 67, p. 41.

12   Ibid., Par. 68, p. 61.

13   *The Book of Hymns*, Number 738-741.

14   *A Service of Death and Resurrection* (Nashville: Abingdon Press, 1979), p. 22.

15   Ibid., p. 15.

16   Costen J. Harrell, *Christian Affirmations* (Nashville: Abingdon Press, 1961), p. 115.

17   Mack B. Stokes, *Major Methodist Beliefs* (Nashville: Abingdon Press, 1956), p. 86.

18   *A Service of Death and Resurrection*, p. 15.

19   Ibid., p. 17.

20   Ibid., pp. 20f.

21   Ibid., p. 22.

22   Ibid., p. 23.

23   Ibid.

24   Ibid., p. 60.

25   Ibid., pp. 27f.

26   Ibid., p. 29.

27   *The Book of Hymns*, Hymn 301.

28   *The Book of Discipline*, Par. 68, p. 58.

29   Ibid., Par. 71, p. 91.

30   *A Service of Death and Resurrection*, p. 37.

31   Ibid., pp. 37f.

32   Ibid., p. 42.

CONCLUSION

The Gospel gives expression to Jesus Christ's beliefs about death and life after death, and missionaries have spread Christian teachings throughout the world during the last 2,000 years. In like manner, twelve hundred years ago, a Buddhist monk prophesied, "When the iron bird flies (airplane) and horses run on wheels (car), and when Tibetans are scattered like ants across the face of the earth, then the dharma (the universal laws concerning death and life after death or "rebirth" taught by Buddha) will come to the land of the red man" (the United States). Today we see that prophecy fulfilled. Within a predominately Christian America, we see Buddhists, Hindus, Moslems, Jews, and people of various other faiths worshipping according to their beliefs. Although most Americans who are interested in religion have chosen a particular Christian group for their own affiliation, it is evident in this book that the faiths covered have some important views in common.

Whether it be the Christian Gospel, the Law of Karma, the Book of Mormon, or the Baha'i Sacred Writings, the different faiths maintain that human thought or good behavior leads to happiness and/or heaven. On the other hand, evil thought or evil behavior leads to pain, torment, and/or hell. One attains salvation, or a place in heaven, or individual happiness through following religious teachings, engaging in good works done selflessly for the benefit of others, and/or having faith in prophets' teachings as sources to the door to eternal union with the Creator. Hell, whether it be the literal, fiery state believed in by some branches of Islam or Christianity or the eight hot and cold hells of Buddhism, or the spiritual torment of being alienated from the Creator either in this lifetime or after, involves the tragic suffering of separation from God. Heaven, no matter what its description, time of occurrence, or location exists when humans and Creator come together in a celebration of love and harmony.

APPENDIX

Questions and Answers

Is there a heaven, and if so, what is it like?

Assemblies of God Heaven is a real place, a pleasant place. Jesus Christ is present there. God manifests His throne and rules in a special way there.

Baha'i Faith Though beyond any complete comprehension to anyone in the temporal world, heaven designates spiritual proximity to God, not a physical place. Since spiritual development continues after physical life, heaven is not a fixed point of achievement, but part of an eternal spiritual evolution of the soul.

Baptist Heaven is a place where the redeemed go to receive the reward of eternal companionship with God. It is depicted as being filled with mansions and golden streets. A new heaven and new earth will be formed after the final judgment.

Buddhism	There are numerous heavens, hierarchically arranged and inhabited by joyous, long-lived, but ultimately mortal beings known as "gods" and "demi-gods." There are also heaven-like realms, usually called Pure Lands, where the Enjoyment Body—an exalted body composed of light—of an enlightened being resides. This heaven is itself made of light that arises from that being's enlightened wisdom: it has no independent existence without his or her presence there.
Churches of Christ	Heaven is the dwelling place of God and the future residence of the righteous. It is a realm of peace and love. Much of the Biblical description of heaven is metaphorical, and therefore its features are not now known by humans.
Church of Jesus Christ of Latter-day Saints	There are three "degrees of glory" (1 Cor. 15). All are places of continuing growth and progress. The highest of these is the "Celestial Kingdom." Those who attain this level will live with God and Christ and with their own families. (Mormon Temple marriages are "for time and all eternity" rather than "til death do us part.")
Hinduism	According to Hinduism, heaven is merely a relative plane of existence to which souls after death depart in order to reap the results of their virtuous actions on earth. According to the Vedas, the dwellers in heaven enjoy long life and are free from old age, thirst, hunger, sorrow, and fear, and the many limitations of earthly life. However, after the exhaustion of the results of their virtuous deeds on earth through enjoyment in heaven, they again are reborn as human beings on earth. Hindu scriptures speak of the seven planes of heaven and of these, the three upper ones, taken together, constitute the highest heaven known as *Brahmaloka*. This realm is attained by those fortunate souls

who led an intense spiritual life on earth and sought the reality of God, but who for some reason failed to attain supreme liberation. Some of the dwellers in *Brahmaloka* attain to liberation at the end of the cycle and some return to earth for the fulfillment of their still lingering desires.

Islam	Heaven is described as a "Garden" having several layers (usually seven) with the highest being directly under God's throne. Souls are content; they eat, drink, and are able to gaze into the face of God.
Judaism	Heaven is a place where anxiety and travail are ended. Some sages have said that quiet, peaceful intellectual activity takes place, and the mysteries of life are solved there. A praiseworthy life is of greater importance to the Jew than is seeking Heaven.
Lutherans	Lutherans generally believe that there is a heaven but are not given to speculative theology as to what the nature of heaven might be like.
Presbyterianism	Heaven is dwelling in perfect holiness and joy with God; little is said about the nature of the next world because both heaven and hell are indescribable.
Roman Catholicism	"Heaven" designates a condition rather than place: eternal fullness of life, supreme happiness flowing from intimacy with God.
Seventh-day Adventist	Heaven is being in the presence of God. It is the dwelling place of God and will ultimately be located in the renewed earth.
Unitarian Universalism	This faith accepts a scientific view of life and sees life as lived in the here and now rather than in the hereafter. It is not known whether or not there is an afterlife.

United Methodist   Most believe heaven exists and is characterized by being in the presence of God. (As with
most of the other groups, among the United
Methodists there are those who literally
expect streets of gold and those who interpret heaven and hell more symbolically.)

Who will be saved?

Assemblies of God   All will be saved who place active faith in
Jesus Christ, accepting Him as their Lord
and Savior, their assurance of future resurrection.

Baha'i Faith   Salvation is not a single experience, but a
process of becoming secure in one's efforts to
recognize the reality of God and to follow His
guidance. Whoever turns towards the light
of truth and sincerely strives for this truth
will achieve salvation. More specifically,
Baha'is believe that two things are incumbent on every person—to recognize the Divine
Manifestations when they appear and to
obey their law and guidance for our lives.
Baha'is believe that since Baha'u'llah is the
most recent of these Manifestations, it is
especially important for mankind to recognize Baha'u'llah and to follow His teachings.

Baptist   Those will be saved who believe in Jesus
Christ. Baptism is not required for salvation, but it is the visible sign of the
emergence from spiritual death.

Buddhism   "Saved" is not an entirely appropriate word
for Buddhism because the emphasis there is
on achieving liberation or enlightenment by
one's own efforts. However, Mahayana does
speak of receiving significant help to this
end through the blessings of those already
enlightened. According to Hinayana, anyone
who, motivated by a wish to leave cyclic

existence (*saṃsāra*), gains insight into impermanence and selflessness, will be free. Mahayana maintains that anyone, male or female, lay or clergy, who aspires to enlightenment out of a loving and compassionate wish to be of maximal help to others, and who achieves wisdom realizing the selflessness taught in their philosophies, will be enlightened as a Buddha.

Churches of Christ The saved are those who hear the proclamation of the gospel, believe and confess that Jesus is the Christ the son of God, repent of their sins, and are baptized (immersed) for the forgiveness of sins.

Church of Jesus Christ of Latter-day Saints Salvation, in the sense of being resurrected, comes as a gift to all men through the atonement of Christ. However, *exaltation* (or the privilege of living in the Celestial Kingdom with God) comes through our works and our obedience to the laws and ordinances of the Gospel.

Hinduism According to Hinduism, a soul is saved only through Self-Knowledge, which is the realization of its identity with the all-prevading supreme Self. The individual soul, even though divine and immortal by nature, becomes lost in the world of time, space, and causation because of its ignorance, desire, and delusion. Identifying itself with the body, it wanders around assuming many births—human, subhuman, and superhuman. At last, it develops dispassion for all worldly enjoyments, here and hereafter, and practices moral and spiritual disciplines, attains Self-Knowledge and becomes liberated. From the ultimate point of view of Hinduism, the embodiment of the individual soul is apparent and not real, and so also its sojourn in heaven or hell or on earth. Self-Knowledge alone can put an end to all sense of embodiedness and therefore overcome death. Immortality is neither a new production nor an attainment; it is the realization of one's real nature. So Sankaracharya says in his *Vivekachudamani* (verse 6): "Let people quote the scriptures and sacrifice to the gods, let them perform rituals and worship the deities, but there is no liberation without the realization of one's identity with the Atman (supreme Self), no, not even in the lifetime of a hundred Brahmas put together (that is, an indefinite length of time)."

Islam
Those who live ethically and have faith in God's "oneness" will be saved. There are five clearly stated responsibilities required to be judged worthy of heaven. These include: verbal testimony of belief in God and Mohammad, praying, fasting, paying alms-tax, and at least one pilgrimage to the holy city.

Judaism
Entrance to Heaven is gained by righteous deeds and an ethical living pattern. Even so, anyone can repent until the end of life and be saved.

Lutherans
Those will be saved to whom God extends the gift of salvation.

Presbyterianism
Those who have loved God, purity, and other people will be saved. Salvation comes through faith in Christ. Believers must witness to others and engage in good works. Faith without works is not saving.

Roman Catholicism
No person, however holy, earns salvation, which can only be received as a pure gift bestowed upon the undeserving. Salvation comes only through Jesus, normally mediated through baptism and active membership in his church. Non-believers can also be saved through Jesus. They too can serve him, hidden and intimately identified with needy persons. To be a Christian means set apart for service, commissioned to share God's Good News with the whole world.

Seventh-day Adventist	God in Christ saves from sin now, and those who are obediently faithful will be saved. Care and discipline of the body are helpful on the path to salvation. The resurrected righteous pass a millennium in heaven and then dwell forever with the Lord in the purified and renewed earth, free from all sorrow, pain, and sin.
Unitarian Universalism	"Universal salvation of all souls" was the original concept on which Universalism was founded. Modern Unitarian Universalism has not altered this assumption.
United Methodist	The United Methodist understanding speaks of salvation both now and hereafter. In this life one may be saved from a life of sin to a life of holiness. Life everlasting is the gift of salvation that continues after death. Such salvation is available to all, and whoever responds to God's grace through Jesus Christ may be saved.

Is there a hell, and if so, what is it like?

Assemblies of God	Hell is a place of fire and darkness. Its inhabitants are full of remorse and frustrations cut off from faith, hope, and love. But this is not the final state. After the final judgment the unsaved will be placed in the lake of fire for eternity.
Baha'i Faith	Just as "heaven" designates turning towards God or proximity to God, "hell" designates the spiritual condition of those who willfully reject this divine reality, whether in this life or in the next. Hell is thus not a place but a spiritual condition of remoteness.
Baptist	Most Southern Baptists literally believe in a place of punishment as it is described in the Bible, characterized by outer darkness, fire, torment, and isolation.

Buddhism	There are eight hot and cold hells, each associated with a particular type of suffering. These tortures are described in detail in order to develop compassion for the beings there as well as to create an incentive not to engage in the types of non-virtuous behavior that will cause one to end up there. As with the heavens, one remains here for a very long period, but is eventually reborn elsewhere.
Churches of Christ	There is a literal hell. The characteristics of hell set forth in the scriptures are to some extent metaphorical and its features are not known except for eternal fire.
Church of Jesus Christ of Latter-day Saints	Persons who obtain a lower degree of glory may experience a form of hell in their regret or in the knowledge of what they could have achieved. Outer darkness, or the absence of any glory, will occur only in the rare instances of those who knowingly deny the Holy Ghost.
Hinduism	Like heaven, hell too is a relative plane of existence, and souls sojourn here to expiate, through suffering, the results of their unrighteous action on earth. In due couse these souls are born once again on earth as human beings to take up the thread of their spiritual evolution. Hindu scriptures mention seven nether worlds, or hells, of which *patala* is considered the lowest. Heavens and hells are only visions that arise in succession before the soul, which itself being a portion of absolute and all-pervading pure Consciousness neither comes nor goes. Our sense-perceived world is also a similar vision.
Islam	Hell is described as a fire having seven levels. The lowest crackles and roars with fierce boiling water, scorching wind, and wailing, wretched souls.

Judaism — The assumption is that God's caring nature rules out a sadistic punishment. The nature of hell is a mystery left alone by the Jew.

Lutherans — Traditional Lutheran belief suggests that there is a hell. As with heaven, Lutherans have not been inclined to speculate as to what the nature of hell might be like.

Presbyterianism — Hell is a place apart from God, filled with everlasting suffering and misery.

Roman Catholicism — "Hell" designates a condition of self-chosen, permanent alienation from God who bestows all blessings.

Seventh-day Adventist — It is the punishment and destruction of the finally impenetent wicked at the end of history.

Unitarian Universalism — As with the good, what evil people do is compensated for in this life. "Compensation" is the U.U. position.

United Methodist — Hell is separation from God, the absence of fulfillment and communion with God and others.

Who goes to hell?

Assemblies of God — All who do not change their attitudes toward Jesus Christ and accept Him as their personal savior and Lord will go to hell.

Baha'i Faith — In the sense that hell is not a physical place, one does not "go to it," and because it is a spiritual condition resulting from willful rejection of God's guidance, it can occur during the physical experience as well as in the afterlife experience. Thus, those who experience the pain of this remoteness are those who willfully reject the truth and continue doing so, though forgiveness and reformation are never beyond attainment, whether in this life or the next.

Baptist	The wicked who have not been "born again" are consigned to hell.
Buddhism	Any type of non-virtuous action, if powerful enough, can result in birth in a hell. Words, thoughts, or deeds motivated by strong hatred are particularly likely to have this result.
Churches of Christ	The unrighteous will be punished there forever. Everyone who does not accept the salvation offered by God and live according to his rules will be cast into hell.
Church of Jesus Christ of Latter-day Saints	Outer darkness, or the absence of any glory, will occur only in the rare instances of those who knowingly deny the Holy Ghost.
Hinduism	Those who have led a life of extreme wickedness and performed actions forbidden by the scriptures assume after death various sub-human bodies and sojourn in one or another of the nether worlds, depending upon the degrees of their wickedness.
Islam	Sinners who do not follow basic responsibilities of ethical living go to Hell. Denying the one God leads to sure damnation. Many believe sinners will eventually be pardoned, and the fire will be extinguished forever.
Judaism	The unrepentant sinner will be punished. All humans are accountable before God for their misdeeds. The nature of the punishment should reflect divine justice, compassion, and wisdom.
Lutherans	According to traditional belief, the devil and all who do not receive the gift of salvation go to hell.

Presbyterianism   Hell receives those who have loved self, sin, and evil.

Roman Catholicism   God intends and works for the salvation of everyone. Unbelievers unknowingly accept or reject Jesus as their Savior by caring or refusing to care for the needy.

Seventh-day   The impenitent wicked are judged, punished, and will finally perish utterly; and it will be as though they had never been.
Adventist

Unitarian   No one "goes" to hell; people create their own hells here on earth.
Universalism

United Methodist   There is fear but not assurance that those who do not respond positively to God's act of love in Jesus Christ go to hell. God will be the judge.

What happens at the end of time and/or at a Judgment Day?

Assemblies of God   At the end of time, following a millennium of a thousand years of peace under Christ's rule, Satan will be released for a time. Then the wicked will be judged, cast into the lake of fire, and God will bring into being a new heaven and a new earth where there will be no more death.

Baha'i Faith   As this term is usually discussed, it designates the period immediately after the coming of a new Revelator, a new Manifestation, when the followers of the previous religions are tested ("judged"), as were the Jews at the time of Christ, then Christians at the coming of Muhammad, and the Moslems with the coming of Baha'u'llah. The particular judgment alluded to in the New Testament refers to this present time in history when all peo-

	ple are challenged to recognize the essential unity of God's prophets and the oneness of humankind.
Baptist	Judgment is inevitable and occurs at death, but the *final* judgment occurs at the second coming of Christ at the end of the age, at which time the saved will go to be with Christ eternally, and the wicked will be cast into Hell for eternity.
Buddhism	There is no end of time, there is only a cyclical process of world systems arising, abiding, and ceasing. The beings in those systems do not cease to exist when their world disappears, they are simply reborn in another world system. There is no time foreseen when all the 100 billion world systems, each containing 100 billion worlds, will disappear.
Churches of Christ	When Christ returns it will not be to set up a kingdom on earth, but to collect all those raised for the great judgment. Each person will appear before the judgment bar of God and his fate will be sealed. Those who have responded to the gospel and lived consonant with the commands of God will enter heaven. The unrighteous will be cast into the fires of hell.
Church of Jesus Christ of Latter-day Saints	The resurrection is followed by continued progression in one of the three degrees of glory. We lived, as spirits, *before* this life with our Heavenly Father. The growth we experience in mortality and our resurrection into perfected bodies are part of our preparation to return to His presence and continue our eternal progress.
Hinduism	According to the Hindu view, creation is beginningless and therefore endless. But

Hinduism does speak of the manifestation of the universe as the beginning of a cycle of creation, and its non-manifestation as the termination of the cycle. This manifestation and non-manifestation are also known as the outbreathing and inbreathing of Brahman, the Supreme Being. At the beginning of each cycle all the beings of the previous cycle who had not attained liberation come into existence once again along with their desires and tendencies. The names and forms repeat themselves in every cycle. Individual souls attain liberation, while the universe continues in its movement of manifestation and non-manifestation.

Islam — Moral chaos occurs. Cosmic events signify the coming of the Judgment Day. Nothing but God will remain. The Day of Judgment is terrifying even for the good.

Judaism — God will never again destroy the world. The coming of the Messiah will herald a peaceful age the likes of which the world has never known.

Lutherans — Traditional Lutheran belief holds that Jesus will return, the dead will be raised, and a day of judgment will be held, with the just (i.e., the recipients of the gift of salvation) going to heaven and the unjust to hell for eternity.

Presbyterianism — Doctrinal statements have seldom dealt with this question. Most say they do not know what will happen, but there will be a Day of Judgment.

Roman Catholicism — Immediately at death, God solemnly ratifies definitive acceptance or rejection of the salvation offered everyone. The Kingdom comes to individuals at the particular judgment, but God's grand salvific purpose of total renewal for all creation will be realized only at final or general judgment.

Seventh-day Adventist
The righteous dead will be resurrected and together with the righteous living will be glorified and taken to Heaven, but the unrighteous will die. After remaining dead for 1,000 years, they will rise, be judged and destroyed in Hell. Afterwards the earth, made new, will become the eternal home of the righteous.

Unitarian Universalism
No one knows, but a loving God would not condemn any person to eternal damnation.

United Methodist
Some believe in a specific day Christ will come again, judge, and assign some to heaven and some to hell. Others believe judgment coincides with response to God's grace and continues from this life to the next.

Does your faith believe in resurrection, and if so, will the body or spirit rise?

Assemblies of God
The resurrection of the body occurs.

Baha'i Faith
Resurrection is spiritual, not physical. As it is alluded to in the scriptures, "resurrection" refers to the spiritual transformation of the planet.

Baptist
The body is resurrected in a glorified and perfected state to dwell with the Lord. The final judgment is preceded by this resurrection.

Buddhism
No future time of resurrection is foreseen; each person's consciousness leaves his or her body at death and takes rebirth soon thereafter, unless and until Enlightenment (Buddhahood) is achieved.

Churches of Christ — When Jesus Christ returns to earth there will be a resurrection of the dead both righteous and wicked. The resurrection will be of a spiritual body, not the body of flesh and blood.

Church of Jesus Christ of Latter-day Saints — Yes. The spirit, which has awaited the resurrection in a Spirit World, reunites with a perfected physical body.

Hinduism — Hinduism does not speak of resurrection but of the liberation of the soul through Self-Knowledge. Liberation is the supreme awakening of the soul to the reality of the oneness of existence. Through liberation the individual soul is merged in Brahman, the supreme Soul. Liberation is the eventual destiny of all souls.

Islam — Descriptions of afterlife are of highly physical pains and pleasures.

Judaism — Yes. Reform Jews believe only in resurrection of the soul. Other Jews believe in the resurrection of both body and soul.

Lutherans — The traditional Lutheran view is that of the resurrection of the body.

Presbyterianism — Although disagreement exists, most Presbyterians believe in the resurrection of a new body. Beliefs differ widely about the nature and timing of this event.

Roman Catholicism — Bodily resurrection means eternal life as full and integral persons, sharing the perfected existence already enjoyed by the risen Jesus. Christian theology distinguishes between full resurrection at End Times, and perfected life with God immediately upon death.

Seventh-day Adventist — The glorified body will be resurrected for the life to come. This occurs at Christ's second coming. The glorified body has no defects or disfigurements but possesses continuity with the present body.

Unitarian
Universalism
Because bodily decay occurs rapidly following death, from the scientific point of view, bodily resurrection is not possible. The spirit may continue somehow or in some form.

United Methodist
Resurrection of the dead is of the body and spirit, the recognizable and lovable person.

What happens to other Christians and people of other faiths after death?

Assemblies of God
Other Christians after death are immediately in paradise in heaven with Christ. People of other faiths awake in Hades (hell).

Baha'i Faith
God does not judge people according to what they call themselves, but rather according to the lives they have lived, how sincerely they have strived to follow God's plan for their lives.

Baptist
Those who have consciously rejected Christ are thought to be damned, but God only is the judge. The incompetent, unenlightened, etc., are left in God's hands.

Buddhism
All people are the same in this regard: depending on their own actions of that or former lifetimes, one takes rebirth in a good or bad situation. Except for persons highly developed spiritually, this is not a matter over which one has any control.

Churches of Christ
There is one faith according to the Scriptures. God will determine who belongs to that one faith.

Church of Jesus Christ of Latter-day Saints	All people go to the Spirit World (spoken of in II Peter chapters 3 and 4) where they await the resurrection. Those who have not had the chance to learn of Christ and of His Gospel while on this earth will have that opportunity in the Spirit World.
Hinduism	Hinduism maintains that its teachings are universal and applicable to all, irrespective of anyone's religious views and affiliations. They are more than theological beliefs or philosophical speculations; they are direct experiences of the saints and sages. God-consciousness is the destiny of the soul, through life and death. According to Hinduism, different faiths are only so many paths to reach one and the same goal—union with God as ultimate Reality.
Islam	Most Sunnis believe non-Muslims can achieve salvation and reach the Garden, but only after a period of purgation.
Judaism	There is tolerance for other religions. Anyone who fulfills the basic commandments of proper relationships with others has nothing to fear after death.
Lutherans	The determining factor is whether people have received the gift of salvation from God. Not all who profess to be Christians, according to traditional Lutheran theology, are recipients of this gift. Nor is it restricted to those who claim to be Christians. There has been considerable softening of this doctrine in the course of the centuries.
Presbyterianism	All who believe in Christ have a heavenly home. Presbyterians disagree about the fate of non-believers. Most leave non-Christians in the hands of a loving God.

Roman Catholicism "Afterlife" doesn't mean just a continuation of present earthly existence. Eternal happiness doesn't come as reward earned by an elite few who did and said the right things to cajole blessings from a reluctant deity. Nor is it a gift limited to members of one particularly religious group. Life in God's Kingdom comes as a purest gift needing only grateful acceptance. It corresponds to creation's deepest longings and reflects divine selfless love. Humans will share his being so completely that they become as much like him as possible, while remaining themselves.

Seventh-day Adventist This is left to God's judgment. No human can judge another's heart or his or her relationship to God.

Unitarian Universalism There are no religious distinctions following death.

United Methodist The ultimate place of other faiths and of those who have not been exposed to Christianity is left to God's judgment.

Is there a purgatory or limbo after death?

Assemblies of God There is no Purgatory or Limbo after death.

Baha'i Faith Inasmuch as there is an infinite variety of spiritual conditions, there are, we can assume, an infinite variety of individual experiences after death, not just a positive or a negative one. Consequently, there may be some spiritual conditions that would comply with purgatorial or so-called "limbo" states.

Baptist No. The dead are souls waiting for the resurrection of the body, but they go either to heaven or hell immediately at death.

Buddhism

Hinayana maintains that the consciousness exits he body and immediately enters its next place of rebirth, for example, the mother's womb. Mahayana says that one may linger in an intermediate state, usually no longer than 49 days, before taking rebirth. During this period one has only a mental body, no physical form; however, one has all five senses and is able to travel as if magically through walls and instantaneously arrive where one wishes to go until finally one's passage is obstructed, in accordance with one's karma, by the next place of rebirth.

Churches of Christ

The place of the dead awaiting the great judgment is Hades. It is divided into two sections: Paradise, the abode of the faithful, and Tartarus, the realm of unbelievers and evil doers. Purgatory and Limbo are not found in scripture and for that reason are non-existent.

Church of Jesus Christ of Latter-day Saints

When this life ends, our spirits leave our bodies and go to a spirit world where they continue to progress and await the resurrection and judgment.

Hinduism

From the standpoint of Hinduism, dying may be compared to falling asleep and the after-death experiences to dreams—of heaven and hell. When the soul awakes, after this sleep, it finds itself reborn on earth as a human being. It again takes up the thread of life and continues to progress toward its goal. The after-death experiences, though of the nature of dreams, are real and vivid as long as they last. They also seem to cover ages. Some souls, however, after death, may be reborn directly as human beings without going through the experiences of heaven or hell. According to Hinduism, no soul is ever lost. Divinity is its real nature and ultimate liberation is its destiny. By its sojourn in heaven or hell, the soul only reaps the results of its past actions. In these realms it cannot perform any new action, the result of which would change the course of its future life. Such action can only be performed through a human body on earth.

Islam   There is a place where souls wait after death for the day of resurrection. Muslims speculate about what this is like. Good souls are allowed visions of God, and the wicked also are allowed to see what awaits them, then both return to the grave. Even after the Judgment Day, some remain in limbo.

Judaism   Purgatory has deep origins in Jewish literature and has been described in different ways, but this has never become an influential Jewish doctrine.

Lutherans   Most of the medieval beliefs related to purgatory were not continued by the Lutheran movement.

Presbyterianism   One of our creeds says, "The souls of believers are at their death made perfect in holiness and do immediately pass into glory." The wicked immediately enter the torments of hell. Some believe souls will sleep until resurrection. Others believe souls may come to know Christ in an intermediate state.

Roman Catholicism   Part of official Catholic doctrine, purgatory is a condition (rather than place) of transition and adaptation for those entering heavenly beatitude, a passage at once painful and joyful into purified fullness of life with God. By contrast, limbo was never part of required belief, and is now generally rejected as a well-meaning answer to a wrong question.

| Seventh-day Adventist | Death is a sleep of total unconsciousness until the second coming of Christ. Souls do not live before the Resurrection. There is no purgatory. |

Unitarian Universalism — As with heaven and hell, the scientific view sees purgatory or limbo as being improbable. They are not places.

United Methodist — Generally, there is no belief in purgatory because it alludes to salvation by works, and United Methodists believe in salvation by grace and faith.

Will we recognize friends and relatives after death?

Assemblies of God — There will be recognition of friends and relatives after death.

Baha'i Faith — Yes. We will recognize them and commune with them and other souls with whom we have been associated in life.

Baptist — Yes, we will be reunited with our loved ones.

Buddhism — In the intermediate state we can see our living friends and relatives, but they cannot see or hear us. Those who have died before us will have taken rebirth themselves; we do not meet them. However, there is some likelihood of being reborn in situations where we continue relationships with persons from the past, though neither they nor we may be aware of this previous connection.

Churches of Christ — It is now commonly believed that we will recognize friends and relatives after death.

Church of Jesus Christ of Latter-day Saints — Yes.

Hinduism	While some texts of Hinduism mention the meeting of departed ancestors after death in heaven, from the ultimate point of view these are visions appearing before the soul as if in a dream.
Islam	Some traditions believe families are reunited in the Garden. The Qur'an does not discuss this.
Judaism	Yes. It is a fervent hope of pious believers that husband and wife, parents and children all close relatives will be reunited in loving togetherness after death.
Lutherans	Yes.
Presbyterianism	Creeds do not deal with this, but most believe we will know our loved ones. Relationships will be lifted to a higher level, and family will be superseded.
Roman Catholicism	Biblical teaching indicates a radically transformed existence in afterlife that is both continuous and discontinuous with life as we know it now. Friends and relatives will recognize each other, but in a situation of changed relationships. Since the entire community of saved will know an intimacy beyond anything achieved on earth, private groupings in families and friendships have no place.
Seventh-day Adventist	Yes, we will recognize those we have known and will be reunited with them, nevermore to part (after the second coming).
Unitarian Universalism	Not in a physical sense.
United Methodist	Yes, we will know friends and relatives in the afterlife and may know and love them more perfectly than on earth.

Is cremation allowed by your faith?

Assemblies of God	Cremation is not encouraged, but God can and will bring together whatever is necessary for resurrection of the body.
Baha'i Faith	No. Since the body has been the temple of the spirit in the physical plane of existence, it should be treated with appropriate respect.
Baptist	Cremation is allowed but not encouraged.
Buddhism	Cremation is generally preferred; also, in Tibet the body is often left on a charnel ground to feed wild animals.
Churches of Christ	Cremation is permitted, but not widely practiced. Since so few are cremated, most persons who are members of the Churches of Christ feel very uncomfortable about the prospect. The majority of members of the Churches of Christ live in regions where cremation is infrequent.
Church of Jesus Christ of Latter-day Saints	Yes, but not encouraged.
Hinduism	Cremation is the most common method of disposal of th body. Fire is sacred and is a messenger between this life and the afterlife.
Islam	Cremation is not practiced because Muslims understand that the agonies of the fire are for God alone to prepare for the sinful.
Judaism	It is not allowed by traditional Jews, because it interferes with the return of the body to its natural state. Reform Jews permit it, but not very many reform Jewish families request it.
Lutherans	Yes, but not widely practiced.

Presbyterianism	Yes, and it is neither encouraged or discouraged.
Roman Catholicism	Disposal of the body in no way affects afterlife or final-day resurrection. Anything is permitted so long as minimum reverence is observed. Donation of organs, etc., are fitting final expressions of Christian neighbor-love.
Seventh-day Adventist	There is no objection to cremation, although it is not commonly done. Resurrection is not dependent upon the cadaver.
Unitarian Universalism	Cremation is an increasingly favored method of disposal of the body. It is less costly than a traditional funeral and allows a more convenient scheduling of the preferred memorial service assisting the advancement of human science through organ donation and autopsy.
United Methodist	Yes.

What happens to people who commit suicide?

Assemblies of God	The destiny of those who commit suicide is left to God. He is merciful to those who do so because of mental illness, etc.
Baha'i Faith	Suicide is forbidden and those who commit suicide will, no doubt, regret this action in the afterlife; however, they are not beyond redemption because of this act nor should they be considered to be faithless or no longer members of the religion because of this violation of Baha'i law.
Baptist	They can go to heaven if they have established a relationship of forgiveness with God in this life and ask for forgiveness for this final sin.

Buddhism	Because the mind just prior to death is a particularly powerful determinant of how one will be reborn, anyone who dies in a distressed mental state is more likely to have an unfortunate rebirth. Thus, someone who commits suicide and dies in an anguished or depressed state is apt to be propelled to a similarly unhappy situation subsequently.
Churches of Christ	Most persons argue that one should not decide the time of death. That is the prerogative of God. Therefore it is a violation of God's desires to commit suicide. But it is generally thought that God may show mercy to suicides as to others who violate his ways.
Church of Jesus Christ of Latter-day Saints	It would depend on the circumstances. Christ, as with all men, is the Judge.
Hinduism	Suicide is a heinous sin. A person who kills himself must return again and again to this world. However, the Hindu scriptures enjoin that there is no harm in giving up one's body after attaining Self-Knowledge. Although generally condemned by the Hindu lawgivers, in some cases suicide is recommended as a penance for extremely vile actions.
Islam	The Qur'an itself contains no passages that can unequivocally be interpreted as prohibiting suicide. The theologians and authorities on tradition, however, condemn suicide as a grave sin. The person who takes his or her own life is considered to be doomed to the Fire, and according to tradition must repeat the act by which life was taken for all eternity.
Judaism	For most of Jewish history, suicide was a major offense, the punishment for which was denial of normal burial and mourning. In modern times, it has become acknowl-

edged that suicide is often the result of mental imbalance, so the stringency of the burial rule has been relaxed.

Lutherans

Lutherans generally regard most cases of suicide as the result of illness, rather than as a freely chosen act for which there is moral accountability. In cases in which suicide is viewed as a sin, it is generally believed that God's mercy is sufficient to forgive this sin, as well as all other sins. Lutheran theology holds that forgiveness is entirely a gift of grace, rather than something which is contingent upon confession and penance or anything else that the individual in question might do.

Presbyterianism

One who takes his/her own life is judged not by that act but by the overall faith that prevailed in his/her life.

Roman Catholicism

Suicide is now generally attributed to unbearable stress rather than rejection of God. Victims are accordingly not refused regular Christian burial.

Seventh-day Adventist

Judgment is left to a loving God. The life stance is more important than this one act.

Unitarian Universalism

Suicide is usually due to unbearable stress and we should offer love and compassion to suicides and their survivors.

United Methodist

United Methodists view suicide as they do other misfortunes, errors, or sins. Suicide is *not* the unforgivable sin. All wrongs, errors, and sins are viewed in the light of God's intention for life abundant in the light of God's mercy and forgiveness through Jesus Christ. Suicide victims are commended to God's love and forgiveness, and Christian ministry addresses problems that lead to suicide and seeks to aid persons who contemplate taking their lives.

Does your faith believe in reincarnation?

Assemblies of God   There is no belief in reincarnation.

Baha'i Faith   No. We believe that the human soul takes its beginning at conception and exists eternally from that point, but it has only one period during which it associates through a physical body.

Baptist   No.

Buddhism   Yes. From the belief in beginningless reincarnation it follows that we have been in every possible relationship with everyone else. Most significantly, everyone has been a great friend and even our own mother at some time in the past; hence, it is appropriate to have compassion and concern for them, no matter what their present situation is or how they now behave toward us.

Churches of Christ   In scripture each individual is provided one lifetime in which to decide for or against God. For that reason reincarnation is foreign to the explicit vision of life as a boot camp for what awaits beyond the great judgment.

Church of Jesus   No. Mormons do, however, believe in a pre-
Christ of Latter-   mortal existence during which we lived with
day Saints   our Heavenly Father. Man progresses eternally and mortality is one phase in that progression.

Hinduism   Yes. We are all reborn after death according to the deeds of our past life. The destiny of

352 HOW DIFFERENT RELIGIONS VIEW DEATH

352   HOW DIFFERENT RELIGIONS VIEW DEATH

the soul is eventual immortality through Self-realization.

Islam	No. The Qur'an clearly states that we have one life on earth.
Judaism	No! Judaism as a whole has never subscribed to this belief. Some sporadic groups and Jewish sects have sometimes subscribed to it, but reincarnation has never been a belief of the Jewish mainstream.
Lutherans	No.
Presbyterianism	No. Reincarnation is vigorously denied because it is believed to be contrary to the Christian concept of salvation and God's respect for the individuality of each person.
Roman Catholicism	Life and death are essential to Christian and therefore Catholic belief. Life comes as a gift that can't be earned but only accepted, made possible by Jesus' total act of love through his death followed by resurrection. The New Testament speaks of rebirth, of entry into a radically new and different form of existence quite beyond present comprehension. Reincarnation implicitly contradicts basic Catholic (biblical, Christian) teaching.
Seventh-day Adventist	We are given only one life, a time of probation ending at death, with no second chance.
Unitarian Universalism	Reincarnation may be believed in by some of our members since there is no creedal prohibition.
United Methodist	Most United Methodists do not believe in reincarnation. The insistence upon "the present age" in following Jesus, seeking perfection, and serving human needs is a strong emphasis of United Methodism, and a belief in repeated lives weakens the appeal to respond in this moment.